Conservation Plans in Action:
Proceedings of the Oxford Conference

Edited by Kate Clark

ENGLISH HERITAGE

1999

Copyright © English Heritage 1999

First published 1999 by
English Heritage, 23 Savile Row,
London W1X 1AB

Consultant Editor: Kate Owen (Dial House Publishing; 01285 771023)
for English Heritage

Design and layout: SJM Design Consultancy (01285 652909)

Printed by Page Bros (Norwich) Ltd

ISBN 1 85074 752 0

Product Code XH20127

Sponsors of the Oxford Conference

Conservation Plans in Action:
Proceedings of the Oxford Conference

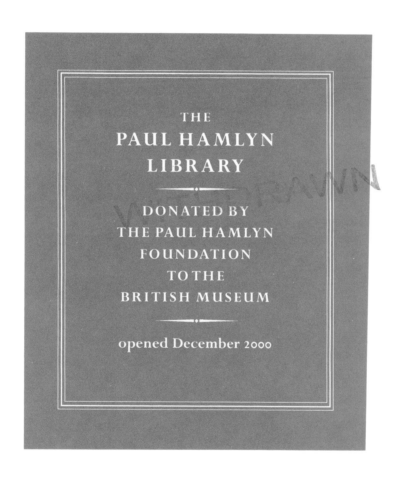

Contents

Preface   vi
Biographies of speakers and chairs   vii
List of delegates attending the conference   xvi
Acknowledgements   xx
Background to the conference *by Kate Clark*   xxi

Session One: Introduction to the Guidance on Conservation Plans   1
Introduction to the Conference *by Pam Alexander*   3
Opening Address: the Conservation Plan *by James Semple Kerr*   9
Conservation Plans and the Heritage Lottery Fund
    by Stephen Johnson   21
Introduction to the Heritage Lottery Fund Guidance
    by Kate Clark   27

Session Two: Learning From Experience   41
Benefits of Assessment — Conservation Plans and   43
    Statutory Bodies *by Paul Drury*
Conservation Plans and the Architect *by Peter Inskip*   49
Conservation Plans and the National Trust *by David Thackray*   57
Conservation Plans — an Edinburgh Perspective *by James Simpson*   65
Conservation Plans for Museums and Galleries *by Kate Clark*   69
Conservation Plans for Gardens and Landscapes *by Paul Walshe*   75
Bringing Teams Together *by Jason Wood*   83

Session Three: Conservation Plans in Practice   89
Archaeology or Architecture? *by Jane Grenville*   91
Beyond Designation — New Approaches to Value and   95
    Significance *by Martin Cherry*
Making Conservation Work in an Ecclesiastical Framework   103
    by Richard Gem
The Practicalities of Working Together *by Donald Hankey*   109
Delivered to the Tower *by Stephen Bond*   111
Conservation Plans and New Design *by Ron German*   115
One Plan Too Many? Conservation in the Planning Framework   119
    by Paul Simons

Session Four: Planning for a Sustainable Future   125
The 'S' Word — or Sustaining Conservation *by Graham Fairclough*   127
A Radical View from the Countryside *by David Russell*   133
From Conservation Plan to Management Plan *by Jeff West*   135

Closing Remarks *by James Semple Kerr*   139

Speakers' Bibliography   141

Epilogue   143
Conservation Plans since Oxford *by Kate Clark*

Appendix Model Brief for a Conservation Plan   155

Preface

There are two ways of seeing Conservation Plans. The first view sees Conservation Plans as nothing new; that this is an approach which is already well established, whether in the form of landscape restoration plans, countryside management plans, archaeological assessments, conservation area character appraisals, audits, environmental impact assessments, cultural mapping, building recording strategies, museum object documentation or as World Heritage Site management plans.

The second view sees Conservation Planning as an area where the different heritage professions have been growing both complacent and isolated from each other, an area where heritage managers, architects, countryside managers, archaeologists, museum curators, ecologists, and others have different approaches, often to the same site.

This might not matter if the heritage was robust. But it is remarkably easy to damage sites that matter to us, even with the best of intentions. Often that damage may be unconscious, and can arise more from what we do not know about a site than from any deliberate intention to cause harm.

If we are to hand on to future generations the best of what we have inherited from the past then we are bound to exercise openness, care, humility, and respect. Conservation Planning is one approach to this. That being said, it is also important to be vigilant, and for any site the first call on scarce time or resources must be basic maintenance.

This volume represents the proceedings of the first major conference on the subject in Britain, held at Oxford in March 1998. The conference brought together people from across the conservation spectrum, with a diversity of opinions on the value of Conservation Plans. We were delighted that James Semple Kerr was able to be at the conference, and tremendously grateful to all the participants — both those who took time to prepare papers or who made presentations and those who contributed to the lively debate.

The conference marked an early stage in a debate which is already moving on as we learn about the process. Like a good Conservation Plan, this volume sets out what we knew and what our philosophy was.

Kate Clark
English Heritage
March 1999

Biographies of speakers and chairs

Pam Alexander, English Heritage

Pam Alexander graduated in geography from Newnham College, Cambridge, in 1975. She joined English Heritage in July 1997 after 19 years in the Department of the Environment, followed by two years as Deputy Chief Executive of the Housing Corporation, where she was responsible for a £1.7 billion programme of new social housing across England. Pam's early career in the Department of the Environment included two years in the private office of the Minister for Housing and a spell in Brussels as the UK representative for the European Communities negotiating environmental legislation, including the first Water Protection Directive and amendments to the International Convention on Endangered Species. As Chief Executive of English Heritage, Pam is responsible for 1300 staff and manages over 400 historic properties, providing conservation grants and advising Government on England's historic buildings and monuments.

Stephen Bond, Tower Environs Scheme

Stephen Bond was educated at Whitgift Trinity School, Croydon, and Bristol University, where he gained a BA in Archaeology and Ancient History. He went on to attain an MA in Environmental and Economic Archaeology at Sheffield University and a post-graduate diploma in Building Conservation from the Architectural Association. In 1983, Stephen joined chartered building surveyors Tuffin, Ferraby & Taylor, becoming a partner in 1987. He was appointed as Surveyor of the Fabric to Historic Royal Palaces in 1991 and remained in this post until appointed the Director of the Tower Environs Scheme in April 1997. Stephen is also a course director of the RICS post-graduate diploma in Building Conservation at the College of Estate Management and a trustee of COTAC — the Conference on Training in Architectural Conservation. He has lectured and published widely on conservation and heritage issues. In 1993 he received the Association of Building Engineer's Peter Stone Award for his contribution to building surveying.

Martin Cherry, English Heritage

After a period of eight years teaching history at the Universities of Exeter, St Andrews, and Leicester, Martin moved into the field of historic buildings in the early 1980s. Working successively as a field-worker on the accelerated listing survey in Devon, an investigator for the Royal Commission on the Historical Monuments of England and Conservation Officer for Leicestershire County Council, he joined English Heritage in 1991 as an Inspector of Historic Buildings. Since then he has been promoted to the post of Head of Listing, and is now Director of Programmes, Archaeology and Survey.

Gill Chitty, Historic Conservation Consultant

Gill Chitty has worked as an independent heritage consultant for conservation projects since 1992. With training and experience in archaeology, museum studies, and building conservation, she spent several years as Archaeologist for the Greater London Council's Historic Buildings Division before joining English Heritage as an Ancient Monuments Inspector in 1986. Recent projects include work for the Monuments Protection Programme on the protection of historic industrial sites, and, for Lancashire County Council, developing an archaeological conservation service and programme for historic landscape assessment. Her principal research interests are in the early history of the preservation movement and the environmental tradition in historic conservation in Britain. She is currently writing two books on these themes.

Kate Clark, English Heritage

Kate Clark is an archaeologist specialising in buildings and landscapes of the industrial period. She was co-author of *The Landscape of Industry*, an integrated study of the buildings, archaeology, and landscape of the Ironbridge Gorge. She lectured in industrial archaeology at the Ironbridge Institute and was Monuments Manager for the Ironbridge Gorge Museum Trust. She has worked as Conservation Officer for the Council for British Archaeology and first joined English Heritage as an Inspector of Ancient Monuments, where she is now Head of the Historical Analysis and Research Team. She drafted *Conservation Plans for Historic Places* and has provided training on the Conservation Plan process to a wide range of heritage groups.

Michael Coupe, English Heritage

Michael Coupe is Head of Planning in the Conservation Department at English Heritage. He is a planner and chartered surveyor and has extensive experience of most aspects of local government, mainly at the strategic level. His interest in growth issues affecting historic towns dates from his involvement in the so-called 'Chester Study', which looked at environmental capacity and development in historic cities, culminating in the Phase 3 report published in 1995, entitled *Environmental Capacity — a methodology for historic cities*. He has also been associated with a number of guidance documents put together in collaboration with the other environmental agencies, including *Conservation Issues in Local Plans* (1996) and *Ideas into Action for Local Agenda 21* (1996). Most recently, he has been concerned with developing ideas on sustainability, and helped to steer the production of an English Heritage discussion document, *Sustaining the Historic Environment: new perspectives on the future* (1997), and a new joint research study on environmental capital, which was released for piloting in summer 1998.

Paul Drury, Conservation Consultant

Paul Drury is a chartered surveyor who, after qualifying in 1969, turned to archaeology, becoming Director of the Chelmsford Archaeological Trust in 1980. His growing interest in the archaeology of standing buildings and architectural history led to Paul's appointment to the Inspectorate of Historic Buildings within the newly founded English Heritage in 1984. He became Head of Northern Region, Historic Areas Division, in 1988. In 1990, he joined The Conservation Practice, but returned to English Heritage in 1992 and became Director, London Region, in 1993. In October 1997 Paul left English Heritage to set up his own consultancy in cultural built heritage policy and practice. Initial commissions include setting up the Townscape Heritage Initiative for the Heritage Lottery Fund and advising the States of Jersey on conservation of the built environment, as well as private sector work. He is a Fellow of the Society of Antiquaries of London.

Graham Fairclough, English Heritage

Graham Fairclough has worked as an archaeologist within English Heritage since 1978. He is currently Head of the Monuments Protection Programme, but in recent years has developed English Heritage's links with other conservation bodies such as the Countryside Commission, established English Heritage's historic landscape character policy, and spearheaded new thinking on sustainability and the historic environment.

Richard Gem, Cathedrals Fabric Commission for England

Richard Gem is Secretary of the Cathedrals Fabric Commission for England, which is the statutory body (under the Care of Cathedrals Measure 1990) at national level for the 41 Church of England cathedrals. The Commission is responsible for determining applications to carry out works to cathedrals, and for giving advice on the care and conservation of cathedrals to those responsible for them and to other national conservation bodies. The Commission works alongside the Council for the Care of Churches, which is the national body in respect of Anglican parish churches. Richard has also been a Commissioner for the Royal Commission on the Historical Monuments of England. His academic specialism is in the architectural history and archaeology of medieval buildings.

Ron German, Stanhope plc

Ron German spent the first 17 years of his career as project manager for a major contractor. He joined Stanhope plc in 1987 to manage major property developments, including Broadgate, Stockley Park, and the ITN and Mercury headquarters. Alongside its property development activities, Stanhope has also carried out a number of arts and heritage projects as either Project Manager or Clients' Adviser. These projects have included Glyndebourne, the Royal Academy, Sadler's Wells, the Royal Opera House, and the Tate Gallery of Modern Art where Ron has been involved from its inception in 1993 to the present day. Stanhope has been involved in the assessment and monitoring of Heritage Lottery Fund projects from the outset, and since 1997 Ron German has run the arts and lottery business that, to date, includes the monitoring of 35 projects with a capital value in excess of £450 million.

Jane Grenville, University of York

Jane Grenville is currently a lecturer in the archaeology of buildings at the University of York. Prior to that, she was employed on the listed buildings re-survey from 1984 to 1987. Between 1987 and 1988, she worked on the Chester Rows Research Project and held the post of Historic Buildings Officer at the Council of British Archaeology from 1988 to 1991. Her book, *Medieval Housing*, was published by Leicester University Press in 1997.

The Lord Hankey, Gilmore Hankey Kirke

Donald Hankey is Chairman of Gilmore Hankey Kirke Ltd, architects, planners, and conservation specialists, founded in 1973. Internationally, he has promoted cultural heritage conservation through the development of financial mechanisms and institutional, administrative, and legal systems. He is experienced in the protection of the heritage and its presentation and reuse. Projects include heritage analysis, repair, conservation, and reuse in Lahore, Multan, Calcutta, New Seville, Jamaica, Tunisia, Peshawar, Madeira, Ireland, and, currently, in Barbados and China. Gilmore Hankey Kirke is concerned with the conservation and reuse of major listed buildings and urban conservation areas in the United Kingdom. Donald Hankey is Chairman of the All Party Group on Architecture and Planning, a Fellow of the RSA and Royal Anthropological Institute, Vice Chairman of ICOMOS UK and Chairman of the ICOMOS Research and Recording Committee.

Peter Inskip, Inskip & Jenkins Architects

Peter Inskip is a practising architect with a particular interest in the conservation of historic buildings. His professional work includes the repair of the Albert Memorial for English Heritage and Chastleton House for the National Trust. His concern with the relationship of buildings to their setting has led to his involvement with the restoration of several historic landscapes, including that of Stowe in Buckinghamshire. He was Director of Studies in Architecture at Gonville and Caius College, Cambridge, for 10 years and subsequently External Examiner in Architecture at the University of Wales. He continues to teach at the Architectural Association where he lectures on the philosophy of the repair of historic buildings — especially stonework. His publications include a monograph on Sir Edwin Lutyens, as well as papers on various aspects of conservation and architectural history. He is a member of the Expert Panel for Historic Buildings and Land for the Heritage Lottery Fund and serves in Britain on the Architectural Panel of the World Monuments Fund.

Simon Jervis, the National Trust

Born in 1943 in Suffolk, Simon Jervis read Classics and History of Art at Cambridge. After two years at Leicester Museum and Art Gallery he joined the Department of Furniture and Woodwork at the Victoria and Albert Museum in 1966 and became Curator of the Furniture and Woodwork Collection in 1989. From 1990, Simon was Director of the Fitzwilliam Museum, Cambridge, and in 1995 became the Historic Buildings Secretary of the National Trust. He is currently President of the Society of Antiquaries of London. His interests extend beyond furniture to the history of interior decoration, architecture, design, and ornament. His books include *Victorian Furniture* (1968), *Printed Furniture Designs before 1650* (1974), *Woodwork of Winchester Cathedral* (1976), *High Victorian Design* (1983), and *The Penguin Dictionary of Design and Designers* (1984). He has published many articles in *Apollo*, the *Burlington Magazine, Connoisseur, Country Life, Furniture History*, and other magazines. He has been involved in many exhibitions, on subjects ranging from Ludwig II of Bavaria to Eileen Gray. The most memorable was perhaps 'Victorian and Edwardian Decorative Art: the Handley-Read Collection', held at the Royal Academy in 1972, the catalogue for which is still a work of reference.

Stephen Johnson, Heritage Lottery Fund

Stephen Johnson joined the Inspectorate of Ancient Monuments at the then Department of the Environment in 1973, and spent 13 years dealing with the protection of archaeological sites and properties in the care of the Department of Environment/English Heritage, primarily in the north of England. After transferring to English Heritage in 1984, he was appointed Editor of the Specialist Publications Section, before becoming Director of Conservation for the north of England in 1991. Between then and 1997, he was responsible for running the countrywide Conservation Area Partnership programme and set the framework for the production of the Hadrian's Wall World Heritage Site Management Plan, in addition to English Heritage's programmes of grant and statutory advice to a wide area of the country. He joined the Heritage Lottery Fund in August 1997, as its Director of Operations, with overall responsibility for running the grants programme of around £250 million-worth of projects a year, throughout their assessment and monitoring stages.

James Semple Kerr, Conservation Consultant

James Semple Kerr has been preparing, commissioning, and reviewing Conservation Plans for 20 years. His guide on the subject, *The Conservation Plan* (1982), now approaching its fifth edition, has been backed up by published Conservation Plans on a wide range of places in Australia, from the Sydney Opera House to Fremantle Gaol. *The Conservation Plan* has served as a model for practitioners and academics throughout Australia and in New Zealand and Canada. James was diverted into a career as a historic buildings consultant and architectural writer by attending Nikolaus Pevsner's classes at Birkbeck College, London, in the 1960s. He completed the York conservation course in its foundation year and subsequently a doctorate on penal design. This was followed by a stint as assistant and acting director of the Australian

Heritage Commission. He convened and was a member of all the Australian ICOMOS Burra Charter drafting committees from 1978 to 1988, and is an honorary life member of the National Trust (NSW).

Ingval Maxwell, Historic Scotland

Trained as an architect at the Duncan of Jordanstone College of Art, Dundee, Ingval Maxwell joined the Ancient Monuments Branch of the Ministry of Public Buildings and Works in 1969, working his way up to the position of Director of Technical Conservation, Research, and Education (TCRE) — a new division set up on 1 April 1993. He has the management responsibility for the Historic Scotland Conservation Centre and the Scottish Conservation Bureau and is head of profession for architects, other building professionals, technical, and works staff within Historic Scotland. Ingval is interested in all technical aspects of conservation and has an official involvement in conservation bodies, including the RIAS Conservation Working Group, RIAS and RICS Accreditation Panel, ICOMOS UK Executive Committee, and the Conference on Training in Architectural Conservation (COTAC). He has been External Examiner for Heriot-Watt University's post-graduate conservation course and was Chairman (1990–4) of the Scottish Vernacular Buildings Working Group. He was recently listed in the Panel of Experts by the Council of Europe and is on the European Commission Management Committee for Co-operation in the field of Scientific and Technical Research (COST) Action C5 programme on Urban Heritage — Building Maintenance.

Richard Morris, Council for British Archaeology

Richard Morris is an archaeologist whose career has included projects of field investigation, university teaching, historical research, and aspects of heritage management. His research interests include churches and religious communities of all periods, the history of settlement, and the archaeological study of buildings, upon all of which he has published extensively. Today he is Director of the Council for British Archaeology, Chairman of the Ancient Monuments Advisory Committee for England, and a Commissioner of English Heritage.

David Russell, the National Trust

David graduated in Forestry at Aberdeen University and escaped to Finland for six months in 1974. He worked for 10 years as a manager with Tilhill Forestry Ltd in Surrey and joined the National Trust as Head of Forestry in 1986. He oversees the management of 25,000 hectares of woodland. From 1992 to 1995 he managed a review of countryside policies for the National Trust and wrote and published the report *Linking People and Place* (1995), launched at the 1995 Centenary Countryside Conference at Manchester, which he also organised. David is a member of the HGTAC, the statutory advisory committee to the Forestry Commission and a member of the Steering Group of the UK Forestry Accord for which, during 1997, he chaired a workshop on Heritage and Landscape. He is currently drafting guidelines for the National Trust on the preparation of Statements of Significance.

Paul Simons, Bath Spa Project

Paul qualified as an architect in the 1970s and specialised in major conservation projects throughout the United Kingdom. He has worked in project management, fund-raising, marketing, tourism, and development. Paul was appointed to Bath City Council in 1994 to become Executive Director of the Bath Tourism Bureau where his remit included responsibility for marketing and promotion, visitor management, the Bath Conference Bureau, and the Bath Film Office. On 1 April 1996 Bath was absorbed into one of England's new unitary authorities when Economic Development, City Centre Management, and Training Services were added to Paul's portfolio. In 1997 Paul was seconded to the Bath Spa Project (funded by the Millennium Commission) as Project Director. Paul is a director of McCurdy & Co, a specialist craft-based company responsible for building the replica of Shakespeare's Globe Theatre in London; he is also a trustee of three heritage charities.

James Simpson, Simpson & Brown Architects

James Simpson (BArch (Hons), FRIAS, RIBA, FSAScot) was born in 1944, educated in Scotland, and trained as an architect at the Edinburgh College of Art, with the late Ian G Lindsay, and with Sir Bernard Feilden — with whom he worked on St Paul's and Norwich cathedrals. He established Simpson & Brown with Stewart Brown in 1977 and has been responsible for historic building projects throughout Scotland and the north east of England. He has lectured and published extensively and is the author of *The Care of Historic Buildings and Ancient Monuments by Government Departments in Scotland* (HS/DNH, 1995), and of *The British Standard Guide to the Principles of the Conservation of Historic Buildings*, BS 7913 (BSI, forthcoming). He was a member of the Ancient Monuments Board for Scotland for 12 years and was for a short time Surveyor of the Fabric of York Minster. He is presently a member of the Royal Commission on the Ancient and Historical Monuments of Scotland.

David Thackray, the National Trust

David Thackray has worked for the National Trust since 1975, and is now the Trust's Head of Archaeology. David came to the National Trust from Cambridge University where he had completed a PhD in Anglo-Saxon studies. His present role involves him in historic building conservation work, particularly recording and analysis, and he has produced guidelines for the National Trust on this subject. David is also a member of the Committee of the Institute of Field Archaeologists Buildings Special Interest Group, and is actively involved in the work of ICOMOS UK. He has long been a proponent of the Australian ICOMOS Burra Charter as a guide to the conservation of the cultural heritage. David's particular interests include castles, churches, and other medieval buildings, garden history, and landscape studies. He is a member of the Gloucester Diocesan Advisory Committee.

Paul Walshe, Countryside Commission

Paul Walshe is an architect and a landscape architect and holds a further degree in environmental conservation. He worked in private practice in Britain and France before joining the Countryside Commission where he occupies the post of National Heritage Adviser, acting for both the Countryside Commission and English Nature. He also works for the Heritage Lottery Fund as its policy adviser on Land, Countryside, and the Natural Heritage. Management Plans are an important component of his work. He steered the production of a Countryside Commission publication entitled *Site Management Plans*, published in April 1998.

Jeff West, English Heritage

Jeffrey West joined the Inspectorate of Ancient Monuments in 1974 and spent several years dealing with scheduled monuments and guardianship properties in the West Midlands and the Welsh Marches. In 1983 he was appointed as one of three Principal Inspectors of Historic Buildings and was given national responsibility for managing listed building consent casework. He moved to English Heritage on its creation in 1984, where he introduced a pilot scheme for the archaeological recording of grant-aided buildings and helped to set up the Register of Historic Parks and Gardens. In 1986 he was appointed Regional Director of Historic Properties for the Midlands and East Anglia, in which role he has overseen a number of conservation and display projects, including work at Stokesay and Clun Castles, Leigh Court Barn, Witley Court, Hill Hall, Boscobel House, and Audley End. He is now Deputy Director of Conservation for English Heritage.

Philip Whitbourn, ICOMOS UK

Philip Whitbourn is currently Secretary of ICOMOS UK, the United Kingdom's arm of the International Council on Monuments and Sites. He holds a doctorate in town planning and is both a chartered architect and a chartered town planner. He is also a Fellow of the Society of Antiquaries of London and a member of the Institute of Historic Building Conservation. After 20 years in the Historic Buildings Division of the former Greater London Council's Architects Department, Philip occupied various positions at English Heritage, including those of Chief Architect; Deputy Director of the London Group in its Conservation Department; and Director for 14 counties in the south of England. At ICOMOS UK much of his present workload is concerned with Management Plans for World Heritage Sites and he has been particularly involved in the preparation process for those at Greenwich, Hadrian's Wall, Canterbury, Ironbridge, and Avebury.

Jason Wood, Conservation Consultant

A former Head of Heritage at W S Atkins Consultants Ltd and Assistant Director of Lancaster University Archaeological Unit, Jason Wood (BA, MIFA, IHBC) now runs an independent business — Heritage Consultancy Services. He has a substantial track record of conservation work on historic buildings, ancient monuments, and archaeological sites in the United Kingdom and overseas. His experience ranges from the theoretical and academic (publications, conferences, and teaching) to a diverse portfolio of practical work in the public and private sectors, including active membership of several committees of heritage bodies such as ICOMOS UK and the Institute of Field Archaeologists. As an internationally recognised specialist in the archaeology of buildings, Jason has directed numerous projects in France and Jordan and co-ordinated business development work in Egypt and Greece. He was also seconded to Unesco to assist with training and the development of scientific documentation programmes for building conservation works to World Heritage Sites, principally in Nepal. In recent years Jason has acted as consultant to a number of Heritage Lottery-funded projects, advising on the feasibility, funding, and implementation of various schemes, and defining the significance of heritage sites in the context of developing future management initiatives and opportunities for public benefit.

Delegates attending the conference

David Adshead	National Trust
Ellis Amos	Carlisle Cathedral
Judith Anderson	National Trust for Scotland
Graham Andrews	Abbey Hanson Rowe
Ian Angus	Carden & Godfrey Architects
Tracey Avery	National Trust
Brian Ayers	Norfolk Archaeological Unit
Graham Bailey	Waterway Environment Services
David Baker	
Dr Nicola Bannister	Landscape History and Conservation
Mr A J D Barber	National Trust
Mr K Bauber	Winchester Cathedral
Paul Bedford	RIBA
Peter Bird	Caroe & Partners
Anthony Blacklay	Anthony Blacklay & Associates
Dan Bone	Civix
Sue Bowers	Heritage Lottery Fund
Dave Brady	National Trust
Paul Bramhill	Scott Wilson
Peter Burman	University of York
Neil Burton	Georgian Group
Alan Byrne	English Heritage
Krystyna Campbell	
Oran Campbell	Oran Campbell Architecture
Jane Carney	D P O Heritage
Judy Cligman	Heritage Lottery Fund
Jonathon Coad	English Heritage
Sue Cole	English Heritage
N H Cooper	
Mike Corfield	English Heritage
Lindsay Cowle	Woodhall Planning and Conservation
Dr Jo Cox	
Nick Cox	Rodney Melville & Partners
Nigel Crowe	Waterway Environment Services
Debbie Dance	Association of Preservation Trust
David Davidson	Birmingham City Council
Stuart Davies	Heritage Lottery Fund
Nicola de Quincey	
Julie Duff	National Trust for Scotland
Nic Durston	Heritage Lottery Fund
Richard Eckersley	
James Edgar	English Heritage
John Edwards	Cardiff County Council
Sally Embree	English Heritage
Nicky Evans	National Trust
Kate Felus	National Trust

Daryl Fowler	Broadway Malyan Cultural Heritage
Henry Freeland	Freeland Rees Roberts
Michael Fuller	Buttress Fuller Alsop Williams
Jane Gallagher	National Trust
Dr Honor Gay	Heritage Lottery Fund
Stephen Gee	Inskip & Jenkins Architects
Colum Giles	Royal Commission on the Historical Monuments of England
Dr Ian Goodall	Royal Commission on the Historical Monuments of England
John Goom	Architect in private practice
Frank Green	Test Valley Borough Council
Robyn Greenblatt	Heritage Lottery Fund
Alan Gilham	University of Greenwich
Bernadette Goslin	Historic Scotland
Gwyneth Guy	
Richard Halsey	English Heritage
Christopher Hargreaves	Birmingham City Council
Niki Harridge	Broadway Malyan Cultural Heritage
Sally Hart	Cardiff Castle
Tracey Hartley	National Trust
Dr Cameron Hawke-Smith	
David Heath	English Heritage
Tessa Hilder	Heritage Lottery Fund
Andrew Hill	Cardiff County Council
Gavin Hogg	National Trust
Will Holborow	English Heritage
Geoffrey Holland	Martin Stancliffe Architects
Jim Humberstone	
Rachel Hunt	National Trust
Jane Jackson	Wrekin Council
Harriet Jordan	English Heritage
Richard Keen	National Trust
Graham Keevil	Tower Environs Scheme
Francis Kelly	English Heritage
Ian Kelly	Heritage Council of New South Wales
Jane Kennedy	Ely Cathedral
Jill Kerr	English Heritage
Professor Joan Kerr	
Robert Kilgour	Michael Reardon Associates
Tim Knox	National Trust
Jeremy Lake	English Heritage
Rupert Litherland	Stowe School
Susan MacDonald	English Heritage
Ranald MacInnes	Historic Scotland
Rosemary MacQueen	Westminster City Council
Eleni Makri	Haringey Council

Marc Mallam	Blackburn Cathedral
Paula Malpelli	English Heritage
Robert Marrs	
Carol Marsden	Malvern Hills District Council
Marie-Isabelle Marshall	D P O Heritage
Paddy Matthews	Heritage Council
Alastair McGregor	Johnston & Wright
Eilish McGuinness	Heritage Lottery Fund
Jane McKenzie	Simpson & Brown
Robina McNeill	University of Manchester
Rodney Melville	Rodney Melville & Partners
Janet Miller	W S Atkins Heritage
Nick Molyneux	English Heritage
Paul Monaghan	Court Service
Canon Philip Morgan	Winchester Cathedral
John Neill	
Frans Nicholas	Frans Nicholas Architects
Tom Oliver	National Trust
Aylin Orbasli	The Conservation Practice
Henry Owen-John	English Heritage
Anthea Palmer	National Trust
Elise Percifull	Historic Landscape Management
David Pitcher	King's Lynn Borough Council
John Popham	Planning and Environment Consultant
John Preston	Cambridge City Council
Mr D M Priddle	National Trust
Carol Procter	Heritage Lottery Fund
Michael Reardon	Michael Reardon & Associates
Nicholas Renk	Buttress Fuller Alsop Williams
Peter Rhodes	Ward & Dale Smith
Helen Richards	Heritage Lottery Fund
Mr S L Rix	National Trust
Claire Roberts	Waterway Environment Services
Faith Rose	Island Development Committee
Henrietta Ryott	Heritage Lottery Fund
Philip Schreiber	National Trust for Scotland
Marilyn Scott	University of Greenwich
Mr R Sharp	Stowe School
Claire Sheppard	Bridgend County Borough Council
Ian Stainburn	Wheatley Taylor Stainburn Lines
Jane Stancliffe	Heritage Lottery Fund
Martin Stancliffe	Martin Stancliffe Architects
Tim Steene	English Heritage
John Stewart	National Trust
Barry Stow	The Conservation Practice
Nino Strachey	National Trust
Grant Suckling	W S Atkins
Marrianne Suhr	Ferguson Mann Architects

Neil Sumner	Bridgend County Borough Council
Nigel Sunter	Purcell Miller Tritton & Partners
Adam Swan	Dundee City Council
Dr June Taboroff	World Bank
Matthew Tanner	SS *Great Britain*
Mr C Taylor	Dartington Hall Trust
Jean-Marie Teutonico	English Heritage
Steven Thomas	Historic Landscape Management
Frank Thomson	National Trust
John Thorneycroft	English Heritage
Robin Turner	National Trust for Scotland
Anne Upson	A O C Archaeology
William Wake	National Trust
Jack Warshaw	Conservation Architecture & Planning
Mark Watson	Historic Scotland
Humphrey Welfare	Royal Commission on the Historical Monuments of England
Juliet West	English Heritage
Richard Wheeler	National Trust
Kevin White	Southampton City Council
Tony Whitehead	Defence Estate Organisation
The Very Revd R Willis	Dean of Hereford
Jan Wills	Gloucestershire County Council
Caroline Wilson	Julian Harrap Architects
Kate Wilson	English Heritage
Linda Wood	Sheffield Hallam University
Colonel M J Woodcock	Exeter Cathedral
Ms S Woodcock	National Trust
Dr Roger Wools	Roger Wools & Associates
Lucy Worsley	English Heritage
A D Wright	A & E Wright Architects
Christopher Young	English Heritage

Acknowledgements

The conference was organised jointly by Kate Clark, Martin Cherry, David Thackray, and Jason Wood. Jane Lawrence and Susie Zumpe undertook most of the hard work before the conference and throughout the event itself.

Sponsorship for the conference was generously provided by the National Trust, by WS Atkins, and by English Heritage. The Heritage Lottery Fund and ICOMOS UK also lent their support to the event.

St John's College, Oxford, provided an excellent conference venue, and ably demonstrated how new architecture can be accommodated within historic places. We are grateful to the many conservation professionals who made presentations at the conference and allowed them to be reproduced in this volume, as well as to Simon Cane of the Manchester Museum of Science and Industry and Chris Smith of English Heritage. Paul Finch, Editor of the *Architects' Journal*, braved the bread rolls to give a memorable after-dinner talk.

Editing and compilation of this publication was undertaken by Kate Clark and Kate Owen. It was designed by SJM Design Consultancy.

The views expressed in this publication are those of the individual authors and not necessarily those of English Heritage or of the organisations the authors represent.

The editors and publisher also wish to thank the following for kind permission to reproduce illustrations (further reproduction is not permitted without the prior approval of the organisations concerned):

Kate Clark: pages 27, 35, and 36

Nigel Corrie: page 47

Countryside Commission: pages 76, 78, 79, 80, and 81

English Heritage Photographic Library: pages xxii, 4, 5, 33, 34, 47, 96, 103, 104, 131, 135, 144, and 150, and front and back covers

Heritage Lottery Fund: page 21

Horniman Museum and Gardens: page 24

Inskip & Jenkins Architects: pages 49, 50, 51, 52, 53, 54, and 55

James Semple Kerr: pages 9, 15, 16, 17 (top), and 19

Mitchell Library, State Library of New South Wales, Sydney, Australia (reference V5B/FREM/4): page 17 (bottom)

David Moore: page 10

The National Trust Photographic Library/Chris King: pages 63 and 64

The National Trust Photographic Library/Nick Meers: page 62

The National Trust Photographic Library/Ian Shaw: page 61

NSW Public Works and Services Department: page 11

Peddle Thorp & Walker (photographed by Patrick Bingham-Hall): page 12

Royal Commission on the Historical Monuments of England (© Crown copyright): pages 44 (right) and 70

Skyscan Balloon Photography: page xxii

The SS *Great Britain* Project: page 22

The Zoological Society of London: page 44 (left and centre)

Background to the conference

Kate Clark, English Heritage

This volume is a set of proceedings of a conference entitled 'Conservation Plans for Historic Places', held at St John's College, Oxford, on 27 and 28 March 1998. The conference brought together people from different areas of heritage conservation to debate the use of Conservation Plans and coincided with the launch of *Conservation Plans for Historic Places*, published by the Heritage Lottery Fund.

The conference was structured in two parts. On the first day papers were given by representatives from the main bodies and professions involved with Conservation Plans — the Heritage Lottery Fund, English Heritage, the National Trust, and the Countryside Commission, as well as planning, museums, architecture, and project management. The second day was built around a series of debates, chaired by different conservation professionals and led off by two short presentations before being opened to the floor. The final session involved three thoughtful philosophical pieces. James Semple Kerr opened the conference with a keynote paper, and ended it with a wise, relevant but gently reproachful conclusion.

Most of the papers published here are edited transcriptions of what was said at the conference rather than more considered formal written papers. We chose to do this partly because of the difficulty most professionals have in finding time to write, and partly because the result is a more immediate text. The discussion was edited to focus on the most substantive points.

In order to make sense of the conference, it is important to read *Conservation Plans for Historic Places*, the document launched at the conference (further copies are available from the Heritage Lottery Fund, telephone 0171 591 6000). Other key references on conservation and management planning can be found in the Appendix and Bibliography at the back of this volume.

Understanding sites

The idea for the conference began with the Institute of Field Archaeologists' Buildings Special Interest Group (IFABSIG). Archaeology is an infinitely flexible methodology, which makes it possible to 'read' the fabric of a site, whether or not documents survive. Set up to explore the application of these techniques to historic buildings, the IFABSIG had already held a successful conference on buildings archaeology in Chester in January 1993.

Five years later, however, we were frustrated by the slow take-up of buildings archaeology. The Chester conference had set out principles and approaches very clearly (Wood 1994), and much had happened since then to reinforce this message: PPG 15 had been published, which provided unequivocal guidance on the need for good information in support of applications for listed building consent; the Association of Local Government Archaeological Officers (ALGAO) had published a guidance note on the subject, and English Heritage's guidance to grant applicants stressed the need for understanding in advance of work; and IHBC had been launched with a new emphasis on recording and understanding sites as one of the key areas of competence for conservation officers.

Yet we were still hampered by the perception that understanding or recording a site was something that happened — if it happened at all — after key decisions had already been taken, and usually as a condition of consent. Recording was still seen as a punishment for bad applicants, rather than a beneficial process that could avoid damage to sites. Sites were being recorded *because* they were being damaged, not *before* they were damaged.

A number of factors lay behind the slow adoption of these measures. The first was a lack of awareness of the potential of the fabric of a building to tell us about the past. A second factor may be a reluctance to realise how easy it is for conservation — often done with the best of intentions — to damage buildings. Once the potential of a building to tell us about the past is recognised, then the ease with which that potential can be damaged becomes apparent. An early decorative scheme may be scraped off, datable original timbers replaced, original fixtures removed or lost, old doors upgraded for fire protection, the historic service areas knocked about and disfigured by modern heating. This is not to say that buildings or sites should be frozen in time, but simply to suggest that the better the building has been read, the easier it is to accommodate change without damage. These arguments apply as easily to landscapes, to the countryside, and to large museum objects as they do to historic buildings. Managing such sites is difficult, and the better the fabric and significance of the site is understood, the easier it is to avoid inadvertent damage or loss.

As a group, then, we felt that it would be timely to bring different professions together in order to generate dialogue about how conservation could make better use of the skills involved in reading historic fabric, whether of buildings or landscapes.

The Heritage Lottery Fund guidance

Our deliberations coincided with the preparation of *Conservation Plans for Historic Places*, a guidance note issued by the Heritage Lottery Fund.

The Heritage Lottery Fund was set up with a very broad remit which enabled it to fund work to buildings, landscapes, archaeology, ecology, museums, and libraries. Two of the primary criteria on which decisions were made were 'heritage merit' and 'heritage benefit'. It was soon apparent that difficult decisions would be helped by the adoption of a consistent approach both to assessing heritage merit, and also to demonstrating an applicant's commitment to the care of a site.

There were also cases when more than one type of heritage merit or significance needed to be considered together — a building in a historic landscape, a collection in a historic building, or archaeology in the countryside. Such sites might already have a collections policy or a landscape restoration plan, but it was rare for these to be brought together. Whilst it might not normally matter to have different documents for different aspects of a site's significance, problems arose when these areas of significance came into conflict.

The HLF, National Trust, and others were already making informal use of the Conservation Plan methodology, a formula used in Australia mainly on sites of European importance in response to the Burra Charter. The approach is perhaps best set out in *The Conservation Plan*, written by James Semple Kerr for the National Trust for New South Wales (Kerr 1996a), although it has much in common with similar methodologies in Britain and abroad.

Stokesay Castle, Shropshire, the finest and best-preserved thirteenth-century fortified manor house in England, is now in the care of English Heritage. The castle provides a good example of how a monument needs to be considered within its wider landscape setting

Whilst this document provides very sensible guidance, it was felt that it had to be adapted to the United Kingdom context. Any new document would have to build on the existing published guidelines on managing landscapes, the countryside, archaeology, and museums, and arise out of the United Kingdom legislation (*see* 'Further reading' section in the Appendix below).

At the same time, a United Kingdom version would have to integrate these approaches for sites that had more than one type of heritage. The Countryside Commission, English Heritage, and English Nature had already jointly made a strong case for integrated planning at a strategic and local plan level (Countryside Commission *et al* 1993), and the same principle needed to be extended to the level of the single site.

One of the most influential concepts in conservation over the last two decades has been that of 'sustainability'. Over the past few years 'heritage' conservation has learnt much from 'green' conservation about the need to change attitudes. Sustainability sees development and conservation as part of the same process. If conservation is to succeed, the economic dimension needs to be addressed, whilst at a local level community involvement is central to sustaining conservation initiatives. Sustainability emphasises the need for a long-term view, which in itself requires an understanding not just of what is important but also of what is happening to those places. Unless we understand how the heritage is being lost or damaged, and what factors are contributing to those processes, we will not be able to manage it, let alone hand it on to future generations. Effective heritage site management involves both knowing what is important and understanding how that importance is vulnerable to loss.

Thus, *Conservation Plans for Historic Places* began with James Semple Kerr's work, and still owes a tremendous debt to Jim's good sense and experience. We tried to adapt his basic framework so that it was compatible with the best existing practice in British conservation and the new ideas coming out of sustainability. The document was commissioned from English Heritage by the HLF, but the preparation involved much wider internal and external consultation. We are grateful for the comments and input from all of those who assisted.

Conclusion

Formal bookings for the Oxford conference opened on a Monday, and by the Friday of the same week the event was oversubscribed. The level of interest and the range of bodies represented at the conference show that Conservation Planning is a matter of concern across the whole heritage spectrum. The conference was a lively event and debate ranged from the positive and supportive to the negative and cynical, and in editing this volume we have tried to give a fair representation of the views exercised at the conference.

Since the conference, things have of course moved on, and a large number of Plans have been prepared or are underway. In order to keep the debate moving, we have added an Epilogue at the end of this volume, setting out some of the lessons that have been learnt. Finally, to assist those who are in the process of commissioning Conservation Plans, we have included a section on commissioning a Plan and provided a model brief which can be adapted to different circumstances.

In conclusion, as Kerr notes:

This ... is therefore about gathering, analysing and assessing information that bears upon policy decisions and on the processes of making those decisions. It offers a common ground for debate, a method and a common language to help resolve differences and achieve a balance between the old and the new. The result of these processes is a Conservation Plan (1996a, iv).

Conservation Plans versus Management Plans

There was much debate at the conference about the relationship between Management Plans and Conservation Plans.

A Conservation Plan sets out 'why a place is significant and how that significance will be retained in any future use, alteration, development or management'. The Conservation Plan process begins with understanding the site and moves logically through an assessment of significance, to understanding how that significance might be vulnerable and thus what policies or guidelines are needed to retain that significance.

Once a Conservation Plan is in place, specific strategies or actions can follow. These might include management strategies, options appraisals, feasibility studies, work plans, development opportunities, and financial arrangements. The Conservation Plan can be the first stage of a Management Plan, but not vice versa. The precise terminology is not important — what matters is that as site managers, we should do our best to hand on the significance of what we have inherited to future generations.

Assessment

- Understand site
- Assess significance
- Define issues
- Set policy

Action

- Management prescriptions
- Budgets and action
- Options appraisal
- Feasibility study
- Business planning

CONSERVATION PLAN

MANAGEMENT PLAN

SESSION ONE

INTRODUCTION TO THE GUIDANCE ON CONSERVATION PLANS

Chair: Pam Alexander, English Heritage

Introduction to the Conference

Pam Alexander, English Heritage

The title of the conference is 'Conservation Plans for Historic Places: an Interdisciplinary Approach'. A Conservation Plan can provide a framework that integrates, amongst others, archaeological, architectural, historical, landscape, art historical, countryside, museum, collections, technological, and ecological issues. It can provide a forum in which diverse professions, all concerned to achieve positive outcomes for the historic environment, can work together. It can provide a framework, too, for discussing with other partners — the owners and users of the buildings and landscapes — the significance of historic places for them and for their organisations.

At its simplest, a Conservation Plan explains why a site is significant, how that significance is vulnerable, and, from there, states policies for management now and in the future. Conservation Plans are not new, of course, and indeed understanding sites at the outset has always played a central role in English Heritage's conservation philosophy, both in relation to our own properties and monuments and in our advice to others. We are very pleased, however, that the Heritage Lottery Fund has given Conservation Plans a new impetus, through the publication of its guidance note, *Conservation Plans for Historic Places*, and through its encouragement of the production of such Plans by grant applicants, including ourselves.

I would like to focus very briefly on three aspects of the role of Conservation Plans and consider ways in which we could integrate them into our own work at English Heritage:

- their role in overall *strategy* for managing change in the historic environment;
- their function as a *tool*, to be used in *partnership*, and not as an end in themselves; and
- the *dynamic* nature of the process.

1 Conservation Plans and current strategic initiatives

Identifying character and diversity has always been central to our work. It is the basis for assessing the impact of change and attempting to manage it so as to conserve and add value. Conservation Area Appraisals are one way of doing this for towns; archaeological assessments, landscape plans, and building assessments are some of the other tools that can be used. Conservation Plans provide a single integrated approach, which can be used for individual properties, monuments, and landscapes. English Heritage is currently looking at the application of Conservation Plans in three key areas of its work:

- the development and management of its own properties;
- the assessment of applications for conservation grants; and
- the identification of future opportunities for important Buildings at Risk.

Developing our properties

First, we have already begun to introduce Conservation Plans at our own sites. We are responsible for the management of 409 extremely diverse properties in our care, from the humps and bumps of prehistoric burial mounds to Stonehenge, and from Dover Castle to Lindisfarne Priory to Osborne House and its royal collection on the Isle of Wight.

In April 1997, strongly urged on by the HLF, we prepared our first formal Conservation Plan, for Whitby Abbey headland. Preparing the Conservation Plan enabled us to bring together the issues and to help to identify, together with our partners — the local authority and other owners — a future for the site and a substantial HLF bid.

In July last year, just after I had arrived at English Heritage, I joined some 40 of our staff at an internal seminar to debate the wider use of Conservation Plans at our own properties. We have decided to develop and use them where they are likely to have the most immediate influence on the management of change, at those sites where we need to plan major new works.

Conservation Plans are underway for Wrest Park Gardens, Belsay Hall, Scarborough Castle, Fortress Falmouth, Witley Court, and Bolsover Castle. New projects coming forward at our key development sites will be preceded by a Conservation Plan.

English Heritage is currently reshaping and reorganising its activities into nine regional offices in order to build much closer links between staff in the Historic Properties and Conservation Divisions and to be able to engage effectively with local authorities, local owners, and the Regional Development Agencies (RDAs) as well as local communities. Developing Conservation Plans will provide a way of working with our partners in a more structured and integrated way. One of our first tasks will be to establish targets and a timetable for delivery.

Conservation grants

English Heritage also has an annual £35 million programme of grants to owners of properties — sacred and secular — in need of repair. Understanding must be the first step in any repair programme. We already grant-aid building analysis and recording, landscape surveys, and other

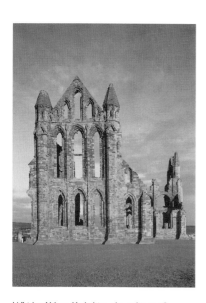

Whitby Abbey, Yorkshire, the subject of English Heritage's first formal Conservation Plan

The east front of Belsay Hall, Northumberland, built by Sir Charles Monck to his own designs between 1810 and 1817. A Conservation Plan is currently underway for this English Heritage property

investigation, where it is needed to progress repair. At Ironbridge we have grant-aided a major programme of recording to inform the restoration of key monuments such as the Bedlam Furnaces. In future, we could consider grant-aiding Conservation Plans to help the owners of major monuments of this kind.

At both Ironbridge and Hadrian's Wall we and our partners have successfully pioneered the development of Management Plans for World Heritage Sites (WHS), now produced for Greenwich and Avebury, too, and soon to begin at Stonehenge. The Conservation Plan nests easily within this framework, a Conservation Plan for an individual building complementing the Management Plan for a World Heritage Site as a whole.

In 1995 we published advice on *Developing Guidelines for the Management of Listed Buildings*. This note sets out ways in which we can begin to manage change better in listed buildings. Guidelines were produced, for example, in 1992 for the Willis Corroon building in Ipswich. The approach is currently in use in Nottingham, where Boots is considering producing Management Guidelines for its own property in order to assist with future management of the building and with applications for statutory consent. This project is very similar in spirit and approach to the Conservation Plan.

Buildings at Risk

Finally, in relation to our own strategic objectives, in May this year [1998] we will be publishing the first illustrated list of Grade I and II* Buildings at Risk across England. This will take the form of nine illustrated registers covering the nine RDA regions. Our regions will then work closely with local authorities and owners to identify possible futures for these 1500 or so important buildings, and there may be a role here for Conservation Plans as well.

To look back at a building successfully rescued from very serious risk, at The Crescent in Buxton we worked with the building's owners on a series of documents aimed at establishing the need for public investment; defining a development brief for the site; and identifying marketing opportunities. The Development Brief defined the importance of the site and established principles for conservation. It was very close to what we have now defined as a Conservation Plan.

The Crescent, Buxton, Derbyshire, photographed in 1992 when it faced an uncertain future

Not every building at risk needs a Conservation Plan by any means —
for most buildings, an understanding of what they are and why they are
important will be enough to inform change. We must use Conservation
Plans where they will be most useful — for example, at sites with more
than one type of heritage to conserve, for buildings where a new use may
be difficult to identify, and for the most complex sites.

2 Conservation Plans: a tool in partnership

Conservation Plans are simply a tool. This is my second point. They are
one of many *different* tools that can be used to understand and manage the
historic environment, and are not to be seen as ends in themselves.

Any tool can be misused, and we recognise that the Conservation Plan
process should not be abused. There is no point in producing hefty
documents that no one can read or use, or documents that tell us what we
already know. Conservation Plans should only be used when and where
they are appropriate. I hope that over the next two days the debate will
help us to clarify this question — when and where will they be of genuine
benefit to the conservation process?

3 Managing change — a dynamic process

Thirdly, Conservation Plans are about managing change, not resisting it.
But doing so in an informed, planned, and sensitive way, taking account
of all the interests involved and adding value to the heritage and to its
surroundings. This is a dynamic, not a one-off, process.

The issues are complex. Different heritage interests may conflict;
ancient materials are expensive and complex to repair and maintain. The
second half of this century has brought greater threats to the environment
alongside greater concern for it; an expectation of higher standards of
access, interpretation, and facilities alongside a dislike of visual intrusion,
other people's traffic, and over-commercialisation. The balances are
delicate indeed, and they will change radically — and often swiftly — over
time as new techniques appear and markets change.

Conservation Plans are one way in which these different concerns can
be balanced. By ensuring that we understand a site at the outset — why it
is important, what threats there are to its significance, and what we need
to do to care for that significance now and in the future — we will help to
ensure that the sites we pass on to future generations are as important as
the ones we inherit, and that we have added value, not removed it.

The better we understand the constraints and opportunities provided
by a historic building, the easier it is to manage change. A good
understanding of the significance of a building can be used to identify and
make possible what may be quite radical new uses.

Conclusion

Conservation is a dynamic process: all sites change over time.
Conservation Plans can help us to manage that change, by keeping a
record of what we want to do and why we want to do it, and then of what
we have done.

Some of you may feel that Conservation Plans are an additional
bureaucratic burden, others may wonder why they have taken so long to
be introduced. Many of you already go through this process, either
explicitly or implicitly every time you work in a historic environment.

Either way, over the next 48 hours we should explore how and where
Conservation Plans can help all of us to care more effectively for the
historic environment.

Opening Address:
the Conservation Plan

James Semple Kerr, Conservation Consultant

A new approach to an old concept

The Conservation Plan is a process that seeks to guide the future development of a place through an understanding of its significance. The objective is to evolve policies to guide work that are feasible as well as compatible with the retention, reinforcement, and even revelation of significance. These twin concepts of compatibility and feasibility are the bases on which the policies are built.

'An English sculptor's home', north of Kymeton, Victoria, New South Wales, Australia

While there may be nothing new in this concept, its presentation in a co-ordinated written document has been extraordinarily useful. First, the policies, their supporting arguments, and evidence can be reviewed, tested, and adjusted. It is surprising how quickly woolly thinking can be exposed when committed to paper. Second, because the Conservation Plan policies have been tailored to a particular place, it not only provides useful guidance when planning new work, but also simplifies the process of assessing the impact of proposals that affect the place. Both are of immediate benefit to client and reassuring to any funding body involved.

As an example I have tabled a copy of the Sydney Opera House Conservation Plan (Kerr 1996b) and a copy of an assessment of proposed work based on that Conservation Plan. The latter is sub-titled 'statement of the heritage impact of the proposed Broadwalk Studio redevelopment intended to provide an assembly area for the concert hall, a venue for "new music" and associated access and facilities'. It demonstrates just how strongly the impact assessment is based on the Conservation Plan and how much time and money is saved by the existence of the Conservation Plan.

A Conservation Plan is something of a paradox. It must have a scholarly basis yet be prepared in a commercial context using finite resources — and whatever techniques and sources of information are

Sydney Opera House seen behind the masts of a replica of the Bounty

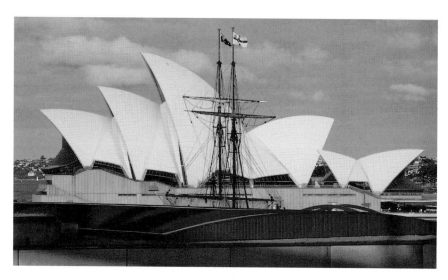

most appropriate, expeditious, and economical. As well as developing policies based on an understanding of the place, it should so engage the reader that the policies evolved become persuasive as well as practicable. There is therefore an underlying marketing objective, which must be tempered by the integrity of the practitioner.

I assume you will have draft papers from English Heritage dealing with the Conservation Plan process and that those matters will have an airing over the next two days. So instead of focusing on the mechanics of the Plan, this talk is about the virtues which help rescue Conservation Plans from oblivion:

- flexibility rather than standardisation;
- co-ordination rather than disciplinary demarcation;
- simplicity, clarity, and relevance rather than bulk, density, complexity, fragmentation, and esoteric jargon.

The objective is to make the Plan readable rather than impenetrable and to offer ways of solving relevant problems.

Sequence, integrity, and confidentiality

Irrespective of the nature of the place and its problems, there is a basic sequence appropriate to the preparation of a Conservation Plan. The first stage is an assessment of significance based on an adequate understanding of the place through a co-ordinated analysis of relevant documentary, oral, and physical evidence. The second stage contains the policies to guide the future treatment of the place. It takes into consideration the practical issues that bear on the place as well as an understanding of the nature and, where necessary, the levels of significance.

This separation has its uses: it allows assessment of significance to be made away from extraneous pressures and thus helps preserve the integrity of the process. Anyone who has worked in the conservation trade for any length of time will be aware of the occasional pressures to understate (or overstate) the level of significance of a particular item. Such pressure may be subtle or blatant, but the intention is almost always to render the assessment compatible with an intended proposal, or even an objection to a proposal. The reverse sequence is obligatory: that is, making the proposal compatible with the retention of significance.

There is a further value in maintaining a distinct separation of the two stages. It was nicely illustrated by an Australian Department of the Environment campaign in 1978, which defined Heritage as 'things we want to keep'. The campaign helped to muddle assessment and management issues, and to polarise attitudes to conservation.

Heritage is what we inherit. It includes things we do, and do not, want to keep as well as things we want to modify or develop further — urban disaster as well as architectural masterpieces, surface salination as well as surviving old forest, and genetic predisposition to certain diseases as well as creative talent. To illustrate: the 'circle' or 'bullring' at Parramatta Gaol was a heritage structure of exceptional significance. The proposed continuation of the gaol in its original use, however, made the demolition in 1985 of the circle both a social necessity and an acceptable heritage option.

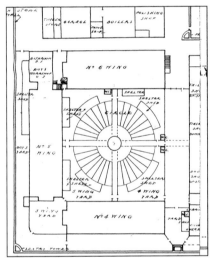  

Parramatta Correctional Centre: the oldest gaol in original use in Australia.
(above left) A 1939 plan of the radial exercise yard, variously known as the 'circus' or 'bullring';
(above centre) the gaol before redevelopment took place, showing the 'circus' or 'bullring' (oblique air photograph taken in the late 1960s or early 1970s);
(above right) the gaol in 1994 (oblique air photograph taken by John Lugg on 21 June 1994)

My reservation about the use of the seemingly innocent phrase 'things that we want to keep' stems from the erroneous but real public perception that when a thing is heritage it must be kept. An unintended result has been a stiffening of institutional resistance to any assessment process, and particularly listing, for fear of inflexible consequences. Developer-inspired excisions from the city of Sydney list confirm the point. Such difficulties reinforce the value of a two-stage Conservation Plan in which assessments of significance may be seen to be untainted by expediency. A flexible second stage can then provide an opportunity for all aspects to be considered before developing policies.

Assessments should not be confidential. What is done openly is more likely to be done with integrity — and more competently. Government agencies and developers are inclined to include confidentiality clauses in their standard contracts for Conservation Plans. In the case of the agencies this is due to habit and precedent rather than necessity, and it is my experience that such clauses are easily removed. Sensitive defence installations and high-security prisons can be an exception. The Conservation Plans for two such prisons that I was commissioned to do at Goulburn and Parramatta (in 1994 and 1995) were published immediately on completion — simple and non-technical plans or diagrams being adequate for the report.

Commercial developers are somewhat different. There can be reasons for short-term confidentiality, but it should only be for a stated time. The more experienced developers tend to choose conservation practitioners with reputations for competence and integrity who are likely to have the respect of the approving authority. Some others prefer more amenable creatures who will give them what they want. The latter submissions necessitate a time-consuming review process by the relevant authority.

The sequence of Conservation Plan preceding the concept stage of development proposal is ideal but not common. Most Conservation Plans down under are still commissioned in response to a proposal or premature political decision and are carried out to a tight schedule. The Capitol in Sydney's Haymarket was an example. The Conservation Plan (Kerr 1992) for this last reasonably intact atmospheric cinema or 'picture palace' in Australia was prepared at the same time as a revised application to local government for the development of the block in which it was situated.

Interior of the Capitol Theatre, Sydney

I had the pleasure of simultaneously investigating and assessing significance and enunciating policy, at the weekly prayer meeting of the 14 sub-consultants engaged by the project architects, Peddle Thorp. The revised development application and the Conservation Plan were submitted in tandem. It was a process that makes me doubly appreciative of your Heritage Lottery Fund, which presumably allows a less hurried approach to conservation planning — at least in theory. Doubtless, market forces and short-term political expediency are not entirely absent even in your relatively utopian situation.

Flexibility

In the last few months English Heritage has produced draft model 'briefs' and 'templates' for Conservation Plans. All rightly emphasise the need to adapt them to 'your requirements and the needs of your particular site'. Retaining such flexibility is an essential part of the process of structuring and presenting a Conservation Plan. It applies equally to assessment and policy sections and enables the report to be presented in as brief, clear, and simple a way as the complexity of the place permits.

Beware the mania for standardisation: standard briefs, standard criteria for assessment, and standard structures for Conservation Plans. Where they have been enforced, the results have mostly been depressingly repetitive and long-winded. Instead, all aspects of the Plan should be tailored to fit the nature, complexities, and problems of the particular place. It is the opposite approach to that of compiling and storing a list or inventory. In the latter case, standard criteria can be tolerated and even useful for their computer-friendly and accessible characteristics.

Similarly, there should be no standard way to set out the important link between policy and the data and argument on which it is based. The link may be presented in terms of traditional 'issues and opportunities', or as factors to be taken into consideration, as described in *The Conservation Plan* (Kerr 1996a), or even in terms of the vulnerability of the place. Whatever is most simple, direct, and easy to follow is appropriate.

Parramatta Gaol was the oldest and longest serving penal establishment in Australia when its Conservation Plan was completed in 1995. It was a major complex, including 50 to 60 penal, industrial, and residential structures both above and below ground together with landscaped and specimen-planted riverlands. Its policy section was kept simple by incorporating evidence, argument, policy, and any qualification or implementation of policy under each aspect or element of the place. The policy for the removal of intrusive elements is a basic example (Kerr 1995).

Removal of intrusive elements

A number of elements have been identified as intrusive in this policy section. Examples include the additions to the former female hospital (Figures 39 and 57), upper verandah additions to the 1901 governor's and gaoler's house (Figure 44).

Policy 8.1 *Elements identified as intrusive in this conservation plan should be removed or modified.*

Where the element is necessary to the function of the establishment, action may be deferred until new developments or change of use make the element redundant or suitable for modification. Occasionally, intrusive elements are also significant ...

Being a former administrator, I understand the apparent advantages of standardisation, but I believe its disadvantages heavily outweigh its advantages.

Co-ordination

Most places or sites require a multi-disciplinary approach. However, the more disciplines and people involved, the more difficult it is to evolve a coherent product. The most useless Plans are those that are virtually a collection of separate analyses or essays by persons from every conceivably applicable discipline. Antipodean cellars are full of them. There has to be a balance.

The objective should be ... to engage the minimum number of persons having the necessary range of skills between them directly relevant to the assessment of the particular place. Whatever the arrangement, multiple contributions will need to be co-ordinated (Kerr 1996a, 18).

In these days of cross-disciplinary education, relevant skills are not confined to traditional disciplines and increasing numbers of practitioners within those disciplines are multi-skilled. This can mean that careful selection will result in teams shrinking rather than expanding — making the whole process less unwieldy. If this is also becoming true of the United Kingdom, it may mean some reduction in time and cost for Conservation Plan work.

It is a truth universally acknowledged that the number of experts needed for any job directly corresponds to the funds available. Happily, there are solutions, regardless of the size of your cast. The first is the team system proposed in the English Heritage drafts I have just read. All espouse the multi-disciplinary team and emphasise the role of the co-ordinator — 'someone with the breadth of experience and imagination to understand the various issues and to pull them together in a balanced way' (English Heritage 1997a, 2).

The same draft added a zealous note:

> no one — not even an experienced conservation architect — can write a Conservation Plan by themselves. It is a team effort, and might well include:
>
> an architectural historian …
> archaeologist …
> architect …
> landscape architect/archaeologist …
> specialists …
> engineer …
> planner …
> operations manager/director.

The writer was quite properly reacting to those Plans that are limited in their vision to a single aspect of a site, for example, the architectural fabric. Nevertheless, care is needed to prevent this laudable approach being translated into a level of resource utilisation, fragmentation, and detail, which is more likely to produce a fat pup than a lean running dog. Team selection is a matter of flexibility, balance, and choosing the right people with the right skills — not necessarily the 'right' disciplines.

There is an alternative model of equal strengths and weaknesses. It might be called the star system, as it involves complete control of all aspects by a single experienced person who draws on such expert assistance as is necessary to fill gaps and who writes the entire Plan. Its advantages are easy co-ordination, economy, complete continuity, and quality control. Accurate acknowledgement of all assistance is essential to both systems.

Of my 14 published assessments and Conservation Plans, only one, Yungaba Immigration Barracks in Queensland (Kerr 1993), was basically a team effort. As I never met the other team members, it was a very odd example. The other 13 reports were classic star-system jobs. Starting with a specialist knowledge of prisons and asylums, I gradually extended my range. For example, before tackling nineteenth-century fortifications, I spent time in the Royal Engineer Corps Library, Brompton, the Royal Artillery Institution Library and Museum, Woolwich, the Public Record Office, Kew, and the United Services Institution Library, Sydney. As I had earlier been a gunnery rating in the Navy, it was like the proverbial duckling taking to water and a fine basis for work on Sydney Harbour fortifications.

Where neither time nor interest permitted such preparations, as in the assessment of the riverlands west of Australia's longest serving gaol at Parramatta, I prepared a base map and worked over the area with a botanical expert. This filled out a sufficient understanding of structures above and below ground as well as remnant natural vegetation and exotic plantings of the late nineteenth century.

The obvious difference between 'team' and 'star' is that the former is multi-disciplinary and the latter cross-disciplinary. Cross-disciplinary only works if you have people who have built up the breadth of knowledge and techniques but who remain aware of their areas of ignorance and hence know when to seek help — and then to acknowledge all assistance fully. As all respected authors know, acknowledging sources not only retains friends and self-respect, but it also fingers the culprit if that part of the exercise has flaws. Whether 'team' or 'star', many a Conservation Plan has foundered on the time-honoured public service principle of never putting your name to anything, especially your own work.

When a Conservation Plan is a team effort, effective co-ordination is vital. This is nowhere more apparent than in the interpretation and analysis of evidence. In this modern age historians, architectural historians, and architects involved in the investigation of a place who are not trained to recognise and 'read' physical fabrics (and graphic images) as core documents are condemned to being a few bob short of a pound.

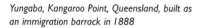

Yungaba, Kangaroo Point, Queensland, built as an immigration barrack in 1888

As well as Nikolaus Pevsner's famous pronouncement about cathedrals being architecture unlike bicycle sheds, some of you may remember his more laudable emphasis on the physical fabric of a place as a document to be 'read' and interpreted. It was his practice to deposit his mixed bag of students at an undisclosed, unknown, and complex building at sparrow fart on a Saturday morning and to require an analysis of its building history by nightfall. Lunch had to be carried and no one was to leave the site. Pevsner himself prowled round to encourage diligent application and discourage truancy. The evidence had to be located and analysed without intervention and it gave his students a great respect for the reliability of the actual fabric as primary evidence as well as a sharp awareness that it could be incomplete. It also emphasised how useful prior documentary research would have been in helping with interpretation.

Where documentary, oral, and physical evidence is not analysed by a single person, it is essential that those involved work as a team and feed off one another in the interpretation of that evidence. For example, an architect of the Sydney School trained in 'aesthetics' and 'gut feelings' might be unimpressed by Gladesville Psychiatric Hospital's dovecot made out of salvaged timber. An accompanying documentary researcher would take one look at the prickly Doric column and recall the complaint of the keeper of the Gladesville (then Tarban Creek) Asylum following its opening in 1838:

> the patients shin up the verandah posts of the airing yards and escape over the roof (Digby to Colonial Secretary, 29.1.1844 and 21.3.1844, ML, MSS 20/1).

Prickly Doric columns (1838) supporting a dovecote in the grounds of Gladesville Asylum, New South Wales, Australia

Colonial Architect Mortimer Lewis responded by having the posts (or rather columns) 'studded with tenterhooks' as a discouragement (ibid), information which throws new light on both the dovecot as a fabric for interpretation and as a source of otherwise vanished evidence of the precise nature of the verandah columns.

Neglect of the written word can be equally deleterious to the work of engineers. Before commencing the redevelopment of the south-western part of Parramatta Gaol, a geo-technical investigation was commissioned. It involved boring test holes to understand sub-surface strata before determining the type of structure that could be appropriately superimposed. The holes delivered divergent results and presented a somewhat incomprehensible picture. The documentary research required for a Conservation Plan would have revealed the early location of a deep pool, an underground tank, and an erratic escarpment base, all covered by a process of cut and fill. This knowledge would have permitted boreholes to be located to give maximum relevant data and a clearer overall picture.

The reason I so strongly emphasise co-ordination is the defective structure of so many current Conservation Plans. They contain a section on documentary history by an historian, an analysis of the fabric by an architect, and, depending on the thematic complexity of the place, a range of separate specialised inputs from other disciplines. Without a combined analysis of evidence, it is a half-baked approach, which delivers reports of almost useless volume rather than a succinct understanding of the place.

As mentioned, optimum results are obtained by involving the fewest persons having the relevant skills for the job and by ensuring that evidence from all sources is analysed in a combined operation and set out in a co-ordinated narrative.

Consultation and the resolution of conflict

One of the major benefits of the Conservation Plan process is its potential for the resolution or, at least, reduction of conflict by consultation with, and involvement of, interested parties. The process can be effective at both assessment and policy stages if the parties are listened to attentively and their suggestions either worked into the text or acknowledged by an argument which sets out clearly why one of several alternative solutions may be preferable. It is an informal process by which a competent and experienced practitioner becomes both conciliator and arbitrator.

Regardless of relative reputation and expertise, the practitioner must be listener and negotiator, not dictator. Once he or she assumes the mantle of Moses handing down the tablets to the children of Israel, he or she is a dead duck — and so, most likely, is the Plan.

At least four and perhaps six of my Conservation Plans were commissioned because the client saw it as an opportunity for resolving awkward local situations. The first was the Governor General's residence in Sydney, Admiralty House, where there was a polite dispute over responsibility and jurisdiction. Both the house and the Commonwealth Public Works Department had received a mauling from a Governor General's wife, and officers from the Works Department sought a rational argument to protect the house and give them appropriate jurisdiction (Kerr 1987).

Different, but similarly awkward, situations had arisen at Sydney Observatory, Tamworth Gaol, the Sydney Opera House, and Juniper Hall — the last being the aptly named 1824 home of a convict who made his pile distilling gin. It follows that those who draft Conservation Plans should display a nice balance of integrity and diplomacy as well as knowledge and experience. It is important to work at getting the tone right. Partisan, dogmatic or naive passages can irritate to the point where the draft never reaches the public eye. After all, the client has ultimate control over the Conservation Plan and can not only ignore it but also commission a replacement.

Fremantle Prison was a case in point. The complex is now part of a proposed serial World Heritage listing of Australian convict sites. It was disestablished in November 1991 after nearly 150 years of occupation as a purpose-built gaol (erected by its inmates). In the previous three years so many reports had been written by so many experts that I received a late-night distress call: 'if we send them all to you, will you write a policy for the place?' They arrived airfreight two days later and weighed 16.75kg.

Reports on Fremantle Prison prepared in the five years prior to December 1992

The Convict Establishment, Fremantle, watercolour by T H J Browne, 1864

The policy development process at Fremantle was made difficult by conflicting demands of potential and established users, local and state government agencies, and watchdog societies — most of whom were represented on a very large steering committee. A process of individual consultation and policy adjustment resulted in the full committee endorsing the final draft without dissension and without losing the thrust of the policies. It was published within a month and the 1100 or so copies will sell out in nice time to make way for the revised version, which should be published in June (Kerr 1998). All my Conservation Plans recommend periodic revision — and this one was needed after six years of changed use as a tourist attraction and leased premises.

Conservation Plan revision need not be expensive. It usually only involves the policy stage. In 1992, Fremantle Prison, for example, required a fee of about £7600 and expenses of £2000. The 1998 revision fee will be £2200, with expenses unchanged. The expenses are due to the fact that Fremantle is as far from Sydney as Moscow is from Oxford.

Three months is an average time for the preparation of a Conservation Plan. Large complexes such as Parramatta Gaol and associated lands may take five or six. Plans that extend past six months are usually no longer Conservation Plans.

Irrespective of the processes and parties involved in the preparation of a Conservation Plan, it is finally the practitioner (or team co-ordinator) who must shape and take responsibility for its content. If approached without a preconceived agenda, evolved with skill, acquired contextual knowledge, and integrity, and drafted with precision and clarity, the Plan will make a strong and positive contribution to the future of the place.

As the most interested party, the client should be kept in touch with the progress of the Plan and should be involved in its evolution. Springing a completed Plan on a client may lead to nasty surprises for both practitioner and client. The provision of drafts of both the first and second stages of a Plan for discussion and comment is a basic requirement. It is also my practice to provide drafts of key policies for informal comment. In this way policies can be improved and their relevance sharpened. Acceptance of the final draft can then become a formality.

A word of caution: the client contact for a practitioner should be an individual of some ability, understanding of the client's requirements, and adequate seniority. I have seen many projects go astray because the client has not taken reasonable care in choosing its representative.

The brief and commissioning process

Inadequate or muddled briefs and contractual agreements will disable a Conservation Plan. The worst of these pests is the detailed standard brief designed to cover a multitude of situations and often applicable to none. Like criteria for significance, each brief and agreement should be tailored to cover the issues relevant to the particular place and circumstances.

Where a client has an established working relationship with a practitioner, and knows from previous experience what will be produced, the relevant issues can be covered in a single page. The Parramatta Correctional Centre letter of agreement provides a suitable example. It covered:

> role of the practitioner
> role of the client
> practitioner's contact
> schedule of work
> remuneration
> publication and copyright
> indemnity of client
> status of practitioner

Contracts between less familiar parties, or which are going to tender, will need to be more precise in setting out the scope and intensity of the work expected. They should not, however, prescribe structures or criteria to be adopted in the report unless able to be designed with a precise knowledge of the particular place and issues involved.

Selecting the lowest tender for a Conservation Plan (even from a select list) frequently produces dismal results. Two of my recent jobs were directly commissioned by clients after such an experience. It effectively doubled their cost and the time taken to complete the work. A carefully prepared brief directly relevant to the place, and interviews with the persons actually doing the work, are necessary preliminaries to reducing the risk of tendering.

Dissemination, publication, and costs

The preparation of a Conservation Plan usually involves a limited number of people, yet it is important for the future care of the place that the Plan is widely disseminated and, where appropriate, published. Apart from the fact that it can both interest and instruct all persons involved in the use and care of the place, publication of seminal Plans plays an important part in advancing skills and typological knowledge of practitioners (and students) in the industry. It is in the interest of government and local government agencies and other funding bodies to advance the quality of conservation practitioners and hence Conservation Plans. Perhaps the situation is better in England but at home Conservation Plans range from abysmal to good. It is, however, much better than it was a decade ago and access to examples of what is done well has made a distinct impact.

The Conservation Plan as story

You can read about the mechanics of preparation in *The Conservation Plan* (Kerr 1996a). The concept I want to leave you with today is that of the Conservation Plan as story. It is a story that reveals the cultural values and character of the participants and the way these have shaped the fabric and function of the place. In one respect, however, it exceeds the traditional story-line — as well as telling of past development and present significance, it goes on to propose how the story should be continued in the future.

While the techniques and knowledge of all relevant disciplines should be brought to bear on the contents of the Plan, it is the traditional skills of story-telling that will convey its message to the reader and user. Continuity of structure, clarity of style, precision and economy of words, and, because of the need to include some relatively indigestible material, variations of pace are all necessary attributes. The whole is made immediate and comprehensible by the intimate relationship of text and supporting graphics. The production of a Conservation Plan in comic strip form remains my unrealised (and perhaps unrealisable) ideal.

Finally, as a Conservation Plan is a guide to the future, it is a beginning — not an end. It is vital that Plans make provision for the continuation of conservation advice and informed supervision of work. The Molong (New South Wales) mason, John Cotter, strikingly illustrated the need for future supervision when he carved his own gravestone, leaving a space for the date of his death and his age. His assistant or successor faithfully carried out the accompanying instruction and inscribed on the stone:

WHAT WAS HIS AGE
WHEN HE DIED
IN YEARS MONTHS
WEEKS AND DAYS

Headstone of John Cotter, a Londoner, mostly carved by himself. Molong Cemetery, New South Wales, Australia

Conservation Plans and the Heritage Lottery Fund

Stephen Johnson, Heritage Lottery Fund

The refurbishment of the Grade II* Adams Building, in the Lace Market in Nottingham, is now all but complete. A Conservation Plan was produced to help inform the process of adaptation of the building offering key facilities for Clarendon College of Further Education

The awareness of the need for Conservation Plans for some of our most significant heritage assets has taken a while to dawn. For some time now, statutory agencies have wanted those who propose change to any heritage asset to assess properly the full impact of what they propose to do. Provisions in PPG 16, which deals purely with the archaeological heritage, are already in place to ensure that decisions on planning matters by local authorities are not taken without background information about the importance of the site in question, and, therefore, take full account of its significance. Similar provisions exist in PPG 15, dealing with the built heritage, for statements on the impact of proposed changes to a building to accompany the application for listed building consent.

This, of course, makes perfect sense: no one should allow significant change to take place to an important historic asset without as clear a view as possible of the implications that the change will bring with it. This applies, whether the proposals are to convert a country house into a major hotel and conference centre, to site a car park and new visitor centre in a tucked-away corner of a major historic landscape, or to rearrange the interior of an important historic building to make it more accessible to today's users. Even in the relatively uncertain world of archaeological excavation, a research design — at least a quasi-prediction of what will be found — is an absolute requirement before an archaeologist starts to dig.

So the question today is not why do we need a Conservation Plan, but rather, why has it taken us so long to realise we need a Conservation Plan? Part of the answer to that, of course, is that the Heritage Lottery Fund (HLF) is a relative newcomer to the heritage world. In the space of only three brief years, HLF Trustees have already made grants of over £1 billion available throughout the country to projects large and small in all five of our main heritage sectors: historic buildings; museums; archives and libraries; land and industrial; and maritime or transport. These were areas in which the National Heritage Memorial Fund had 15 years of expertise before the lottery tail was grafted on to it in 1994. At that point, vistas of being able to do all sorts of things unheard of before opened up in front of everyone's eyes. Major problem buildings, up until now apparently beyond hope of assistance because of the scale of resources required, could suddenly hope for salvation; museums, long starved of cash for much needed developments, could hope to provide the new facilities which would improve their outreach to the public and guarantee a more sustainable future; owners of portions of our maritime heritage have also seized on the opportunity, as witnessed by the recent rumbustious Select Committee hearing about HMS *Cavalier*. The HLF has had to grow up fast and start to define its own identity, its own agenda, and its own priorities.

Let us not forget how uniquely placed the HLF actually is. We have the ability to fund projects that support anything — within the broad definition of the United Kingdom's cultural and natural heritage. Since March 1998, when the powers approved by Parliament in 1997 came into force, we have been able to make grants to any owner of heritage property — not just the public or charitable sectors we have supported to date: our Trustees have, however, indicated that they propose for the time being at least to give a low priority to direct applications to us from private owners or commercial companies. So the field is wide, and the ability is there to take a holistic approach towards buildings, their settings, their contents, the educational and visitor outreach they can stimulate as well as the geology, flora, and fauna of their environs. It is not a question of knowing what to support; it is a problem both to choose how to limit support but also how to identify the significant elements of a programme to support in order to ensure the right things start to happen. Make no mistake about it: the field is impossibly wide, and with a budget of some £250 million a year to deploy, our Trustees are going to have to be very careful in making their decisions.

Clearly, this ability to take an overall view is critical, but it comes at a price. First, because we can contribute to all aspects of a project, applicants expect us to do so: this, of course, puts up — surprisingly often into seven or eight figures — the amount of grant requested. Sheer mathematics show that with a budget split into individual sectors and with other demands on our resources from specific initiatives, no more than £50 million is going to be available in 1998/9 for any of the major funding sectors of historic buildings or museums; somewhat less will be awarded to urban parks or countryside projects. In one sense, this is a good thing: it will be more difficult for our funding to be all-embracing and we will all have to think harder about the benefit of lottery funding and the careful way in which it can be deployed. Hence the reason for wanting to reinforce the messages that the only sensible way to approach important heritage sites is so far as possible to understand them first, to translate that understanding into an assessment of the significance, and to ensure that proposals put forward for improvements to the site reflect that assessment.

Nor is this an untried route. Our Urban Parks programme has been based on the premise that no restoration plan for a historic park is possible unless we have a view of the landscape gardener or architect's original intentions in order properly to inform an approach to dealing with urban parks for tomorrow in a way that fully reflects an appreciation of its past. Equally, we have already started to ask some of our higher profile clients to provide Conservation Plans for sites or buildings for which grants have been requested or awarded. Among these are the Royal Academy, the British Museum — to examine the overall impact of the proposals for an education centre in Smirke's Great Court — and the National Trust, examining the plans for the refurbishment of Hardwick Hall in the context of the management requirements of the estate overall.

Even more progress has been made at Whitby, where English Heritage has produced a Conservation Plan evaluating the site and which is therefore available to inform the proposed approach to improving the visitor's experience of the medieval abbey, abbey house, and the banqueting hall, which have far too long been disjointed. Work on the Conservation Plan has cast light on the archaeology of the pre-Norman abbey, the abbey layout itself, and the seventeenth-century house and its surrounding gardens, and has enabled English Heritage to assess the implications of its proposals for the headland.

So the Conservation Plan is a tool, or a discipline. Logically, in any approach to a major heritage site, it is a first step — an attitude of mind, which puts the recognition, and protection of what is of most significance about that resource paramount in our forward planning about it. As ever, in such circumstances, the theology is that of today: we can only recognise

A Conservation Plan has helped determine the treatment of the vessel SS Great Britain and its historic site at the former Great Western Steamship Company Dockyard in Bristol

as significant those aspects which current research has helped us to record and evaluate. But this gives us — the HLF — our first problem. Whilst we think it entirely appropriate that our major heritage agencies, with their staff and skills resources and specialist abilities, should go through the Conservation Plan approach before embarking on any new enterprise — improving the visitor's experience at Stonehenge springs to mind — it is less easy to define how far down this route we can expect smaller organisations, with fewer resources of staff or expertise, to go before putting forward proposals for the HLF's support. In the end, we have decided that we will normally expect to see a Conservation Plan produced for any project costing more than £500,000. Where it would help to plan for an appropriate treatment for a heritage asset, we would also encourage those who have projects of smaller size to subject themselves to the discipline.

The problem arises from our two-stage process. Because our budgets for larger scale projects in 1998/9 will be limited, we have decided to introduce a two-stage process for projects of over £500,000. This will enable us to reach early and strategic decisions on the projects that Trustees wish to support — based on our criteria and priorities — from a less complicated and detailed first-stage application. Even though less complicated, we will still require a substantial amount of information and supporting documentation to go with a first-stage submission, but after a great deal of thought, we have decided not to make the formulation of a full Conservation Plan a requirement at our first stage. What we will require, however, is a relatively brief conservation statement to show some of the issues that would need to be fully explored and addressed if the project progresses to Stage Two. I should, of course, point out that we do not expect to provide any funding for applicants to work up their Stage One submissions to us: if they qualify for and require funding for developing their proposals once they pass Stage One, we would consider making a contribution.

But this means, of course, that as part of a project to which we give the amber light of a 'Stage One pass', we may also, in due course, contribute to the formulation of the Conservation Plan — but only once the project is steaming ahead after negotiating the ice floes. We hope that this is a practical and pragmatic response to this requirement, without putting too heavy a burden on Stage One applicants, but providing HLF and our own advisers with sufficient information to be able to reach a sensible early conclusion about the merits of each case submitted to us.

What can I say about a Conservation Plan that has not already been said by James Semple Kerr? I suppose it is just this: I am not interested in the HLF forcing the production of another new document for the sake of form; not interested in codification of knowledge for its own sake. The point is to focus on attitude and respect. The attitude says, 'we will observe to the best of our abilities what is there and use the best of our knowledge to understand and interpret it'. Respect recognises what is there, and uses its known values to plan for the future; it does not force solutions that cause unnecessary damage, and will always try to mitigate or eliminate substantive loss of integrity or harmful impact. To this I would also add practicality. Unless the Conservation Plan can be delivered and gives a clear means of doing so, it is not much help, and will be destined to sit on the shelf with other well-meaning documents.

I mentioned earlier the HLF's agenda, its identity, and its priorities. For 1998/9, in our new application pack (which will incorporate details of the two-stage process), we have attempted to set out our stall in a new way. The traditional divisions are there — natural habitats, urban green spaces, historic buildings and sites, museums, historic libraries, and the industrial heritage. But there are some interlopers — for example, we will from April onwards be able to fund archaeological projects (which we have chosen to focus quite tightly on areas not covered by others) and we will be launching our new Townscapes Heritage Initiative — support for conservation areas throughout the United Kingdom — as well as continuing with our Local Heritage Initiative. Many of these categories, however, are not meant to be mutually exclusive, and our assessment processes do not treat them in this way. We expect countryside projects to have regard for the archaeological as well as the ecological significance of sites; museums, libraries, and archives should have regard to the heritage significance of the building in which they are housed.

A major award of a grant from the Heritage Lottery Fund to the Grade II* Horniman Museum in London was dependent on the production of a Conservation Plan detailing the future treatment of the museum and its collections, dovetailing with a Historic Landscape Restoration Plan for the Horniman Park

We are also increasingly focusing on the qualities of wider public benefits. This may involve looking, for example, at the extent to which access to the heritage can be improved, either physically or in compiling and providing public access to information in any medium relating to an important aspect of the history, natural history or landscape of the United Kingdom. Projects we support can now be capital or revenue, and projects will need to demonstrate how they help preserve or enhance, broaden access or increase understanding or enjoyment of the heritage. If we can secure a double or triple dividend by our funding, that is all to the good.

Our widened powers, and the new opportunities we have to give support to a very broad definition of heritage, make the task of deploying the money from the National Lottery to the heritage sector a challenging and exciting one. Throw into that pot the need to square our consciences with regard to regional equity, the requirement to think about community involvement in lottery projects, the pressures on us from some quarters to consider factors such social deprivation in awarding grants, and the constant need to be alert that we do not allow private gain to accrue from lottery grants, and you start to appreciate the icebergs which can be in the path of even the most watertight — or should I say Titanic — of projects. This is precisely what makes it so exciting.

And why choosing to do the right projects for the right reasons is so important. The Conservation Plan is part of the navigating equipment to help us be certain that lottery funds, directed at this or that aspect of a major scheme, are not going to disturb the quiet equilibrium of our national heritage treasures. We shall all be learning, once again, as we press ahead down this course, but I commend its use to you all and am pleased at this occasion to be able to launch our new document to its intent and thoroughly engaged audience.

Introduction to the Heritage Lottery Fund Guidance

Kate Clark, English Heritage

Wigmore Castle, Herefordshire, where conservation involves caring both for the monument and for its associated flora

Introduction

At its simplest, a Conservation Plan is a document that states why a site is significant, how that significance is vulnerable, and puts forward policies for retaining its significance. It is the first stage in managing any site. It is not, however, and does not claim to be, a full Management Plan, any more than it is likely fully to meet either the requirements of building recording on a project, the day-to-day needs of collections management, or the design brief for an architect or an archaeological mitigation strategy.

It is a tool for a job, and the job is, as James Semple Kerr says, to understand what is important about a site and what to do about it. Moreover, it is only the first stage in the process of understanding and managing heritage significance, which should be a continuing process throughout our stewardship of any site.

I want first to explain some of the background to the timing of this current initiative. Secondly, I want to work through the Heritage Lottery Fund (HLF) guidance document with you, to try to explain why it is as it is — warts and all — and why we have drafted it in the way we did. Finally, I want to ring some very loud warning bells, not because I think that Conservation Plans are a bad idea, but because I am worried about what may happen if we abuse what I believe to be an important opportunity created by the HLF.

1 Background to the guidance

Why has this guidance been necessary?
The HLF's remit is:

> to improve the quality of life by safeguarding and enhancing the heritage of buildings, objects and the environment, whether man-made or natural, which have been important in the formation of the character and identity of the United Kingdom.

This remit does, of course, cut straight across each of our existing heritage areas, which have traditionally been dealt with in Britain by different agencies and different funding regimes.

English Heritage, Historic Scotland, and CADW deal with monuments. The same agencies deal with listed buildings but by means of different legislation; gardens and landscapes are dealt with by the Countryside Commission and sometimes by other land agencies; local authorities deal with archaeology, landscapes, and listed buildings; the Museums and Galleries Commission deals with museums and large objects, and so on.

In practice, most sites have more than one type of heritage asset. Monuments have ecosystems and wildlife; museums care for sites as well as objects. Libraries keep books in historic buildings; buildings themselves can rarely be divorced from their historic landscapes; ships are berthed in Conservation Areas, and wildlife can be found in urban settings.

Whilst this might not matter most of the time, it is surprising how easy it is to damage the heritage when one is considering new projects or new work. This is not usually deliberate damage — it is the type of inadvertent damage that occurs when trying to balance one interest against another and is why managing change in the heritage can be such a difficult process.

In deciding how to spend its money, the HLF has a duty to safeguard and enhance this heritage. This means it has to ensure that each of the different competing heritage issues has been balanced out in the projects that it funds. Unfortunately, each of the different heritage professions in this country have their own procedures for managing change. There are several different Acts, a larger number of relevant government policy guidance notes, and a plethora of individual guidance documents for land and built heritage issues (see table opposite). Conservation Plans are intended to enable the HLF to ask for a single, integrated assessment at an early stage in the grant-application process.

This, then, was the background to the request from the HLF to help with drafting a guidance note on Conservation Plans. In particular, the Fund wanted to bring together the different heritage issues at an early stage in the application process in order to help it make decisions.

The starting point for the document was, of course, James Semple Kerr's seminal document on the Conservation Plan, which has had the advantage of being in use for many years. But I was also conscious that there was already a long tradition of site assessment in the United Kingdom, and that he did not necessarily bring into the picture the full range of issues that the HLF needed. So I turned to some of the existing guidance material, in particular, to Land Management Plans, Unesco World Heritage Site Plans, the standard for buildings and archaeological assessments published by the Institute for Field Archaeology (IFA), the RIBA project stages, and guidelines about sustainable development and the care of collections. Wherever possible, I have tried to make the document compatible with these other documents — although it does not, of course, replace them.

In drafting the guidance note, I was fortunate to be supported by a HLF working party and by the HLF's team of special advisers who were able to ensure that the document covered all aspects of the HLF's remit, particularly in areas where I had absolutely no expertise. I am also grateful for the comments and criticism of the many people who were consulted on the draft. Yes, it has been a controversial process and I think it will be useful if some of that controversy comes out at this conference. But, equally, it has been an enriching process, and I hope that whatever happens with the HLF in the long term, we will not lose the impetus and opportunity for working together which the HLF has created.

2 The Conservation Plan process

What, then, is a Conservation Plan, and what does it contain?

The first point to make is that a Conservation Plan is about the significance of a site. It is not about visitor projections, the feasibility of a scheme, a business appraisal or even the very important day-to-day management regime. Nor is it a document that says why a particular scheme is a good idea.

A comparison of guidance documents for land and built heritage issues

The Conservation Plan process	Countryside Commission management guidelines	Landscape restoration plans	RIBA stages	Archaeological practice	World Heritage Site guidelines	Sustainability
Understanding the site Documents Description of fabric Survey	Site assessment Description of site	Establish and describe historic importance of site Survey	Inception/feasibility	Desk-top assessment of site/building/landscape Field survey or recording	**Survey:** methodical inspection, survey, and documentation of resource, historical setting, and physical environment Inventory and documentation	Improve understanding of a site
Assessing significance	Evaluation				**Definition:** critical historical definition and assessment of object and setting, giving significance	
Vulnerability/defining issues	Constraints and modifiers	Analyse effects of changes in the landscape			**Analysis:** scientific analysis of material substance and structural system, with a view towards conservation	Identify present and future forces for change affecting resource
Policy	Vision Policy Objectives		Design brief?	Advice by County Archaeologist	**Strategy:** long- and short-term programmes for conservation and management of change, including regular inspections, cyclical maintenance, and environmental control Formulation of objectives	Make informed judgements about level of change without unacceptable damage Set objectives, including the thresholds and limits of acceptable change
Strategy Restoration proposals Outline proposals for scheme Revisit existing scheme Management proposals	Operational plan Management strategies Programmes	Proposals for restoration of historic character and features. Ensure design and location of modern additions will enhance historic character and public's enjoyment	Outline proposals	Archaeological evaluation in advance of specific scheme	See above	Define sustainable strategy, plans
Detailed development of project or scheme	Projects or tasks Determination of priorities Work plan	See above	Detailed design		Definition of projects Work programmes	
Business Plan	Financial plan	Costed proposals	Quantity survey	Specification/project design for site work	Identification of resources	
Site work and mitigation	Site work and monitoring	Site work and monitoring	Supervision of site work	Monitoring of work Mitigation — excavation or recording	Execution of works	Monitor change
Review (review of Plan)	Review, revision of plan on annual and long-term basis			Preparation of final report or publication, and integration of results into general understanding of site	Revision of site description and re-evaluation; formulation of revised objectives and reconsideration of constraints	

Sources: Countryside Commission, 1998 *Site Management Planning: a guide*; English Heritage, 1997 *Sustaining the Historic Environment: new perspectives on the future*; Feilden, B, and Jokilehto, J, 1993 *Management Guidelines for World Heritage Sites*; HLF brief for urban parks and gardens; IFA standard and guidance on archaeological desk-top assessments, building analysis and recording, and excavation; Kerr, J S, 1996 *The Conservation Plan: a guide to the preparation of Conservation Plans for places of European cultural significance*

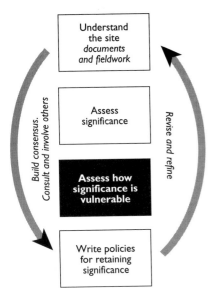

The Conservation Plan process

A Conservation Plan is simply about the significance of the site under consideration. It is about what is significant, how that significance is vulnerable, and what policies need to be put in place to retain that significance.

Essentially, a Conservation Plan has four main sections, and it should be realised that what is important about a Plan is not its detailed contents: rather, it is the logical process that you need to go through to produce the final result. It would be impossible to present the contents of a Conservation Plan in any other order than the prescribed one, as to do otherwise would be to break the intellectual chain.

Understanding the site

The bedrock of any Conservation Plan is knowing what is there, which involves looking at the site on the ground. To any of us working in the conservation field, this seems an obvious procedure. Yet it is surprising how many applications come in without this basic information. What is on the site we are trying to conserve? Have we looked at everything — at archaeology, buildings, wildlife, collections, technology? Many applications for funding relate to a single aspect of a site — perhaps a collection, for example — but their implications for the site are much wider. Knowing what is there is a vital first step.

Assessing significance

The second step is to be clear about why the site is important. Of course the importance of sites is reflected in their designations: whether they are a listed building, a Site of Special Scientific Interest, an Area of Outstanding Natural Beauty or an ancient monument. But designation documents rarely inform decisions about where a new car park might be positioned, or whether an outbuilding can be demolished.

The second stage in a Plan, then, is to look explicitly at the significance of the site. This can be done as a whole, but also at the level of each of the different elements on the ground. How important are the galleries, the decorative scheme, those earthworks in the garden, the collection of stuffed pit ponies?

Vulnerability

The third stage in the process is thinking about what is happening to that significance. This is the section that is usually highlighted in Management Plans as 'Opportunities or Threats?'. When preparing a Conservation Plan, it is important to assess the vulnerability of the significance of a site.

Conservation policy

Finally, we get to the meat of the document, conservation policies: what policies you and your organisation will adopt to care for the significance of the site. This is not about the policy you may have for a new visitor centre or for increasing revenue, but rather, what policies you have for caring for the site. How you will make sure that the significance is not vulnerable; that we do not continue to do things that will damage the site; how you will ensure that what is passed on to future generations is as important as what we have inherited. Policies can also include opportunities for new work and for enhancing the site.

Once all of this has been done, it is possible to go down a number of different directions. If you are proposing new work at a site, you can brief an architect to develop a scheme. If your application to the HLF to purchase land is successful, you may need to complete the process by working up a full Management Plan. If you are some way from finalising a scheme, you may need to carry out archaeological surveys or other investigative work.

Either way, what is important is that there is now a benchmark statement of what is at the site, why it is important, and what needs to be done to retain that importance as a first step in the application process.

Conservation Plans for Historic Places

Heritage Lottery Fund guidance on the preparation of Conservation Plans

3 Contents of the guidance

I think it would be useful now to work through the contents of the guidance. We have the rest of today and tomorrow to debate issues, to wrangle about the pros and cons of Conservation Plans, to argue over terminology, and to discuss the relationship between Conservation Plans and Management Plans.

In writing any guidance note it is almost impossible to find the right balance. In this one there was the question of who should we be addressing — an applicant faced with what looks like another bureaucratic demand? A conservation architect who really does not see why this needs to be written down? A land manager who does it every day but to rather a different formula? The consultant who would be writing a Plan?

In the end we tried to address an informed applicant — somebody who was likely to be going for a larger scheme. We tried to steer a line between jargon and accessibility, which means, inevitably, that heritage professionals will be upset about terminology, and applicants may find it too difficult.

The other balance we tried to strike was between prescriptiveness and openness. How could we provide enough of a formula so that the HLF would get the information it needed to make decisions rapidly and effectively, without pushing heritage professionals into an inappropriate straightjacket? We have been criticised from both sides on this, but our final decision was that it is easier to have a relatively detailed prescription that can be adapted intelligently, than to have something which was too open.

In setting out the document, we took the HLF guidance on preparing business plans as a model. It was structured in three main parts: 'Getting Started'; 'Contents of a Plan'; and 'After Drafting'. We have also produced a checklist for the contents of a Plan.

It may be useful quickly to run through each of the sections of the document and touch on some of the issues they raise, which those of us in the heritage sector will need to watch out for.

One of the longest and most contentious debates we had was over the name of the document. Almost everybody objected to it: to the word 'conservation'; to the word 'plan'; to the combination of both. At the end of the day, however, we stuck with it: the title is in international use and has meaning beyond the bounds of the United Kingdom.

Introduction

Ironically, this was one of the most difficult aspects of the document to write. One of our longest debates was over which sites need Conservation Plans and which do not. In general, our conclusion was that complex sites with more than one type of heritage asset were most usefully served by a Plan. We were aware that there are well-established procedures for Landscape Restoration and Land Management Plans, and have said that these remain the most appropriate documents for designed landscapes and natural sites.

We also had a long debate about words. Should we have definitions? Should we use the words 'site' or 'asset'? Did we need a jargon buster? In the end, we took the minimalist approach.

1 Getting Started

This section is aimed at an applicant or site manager, using the model of the Business Plan.

One of the most common misconceptions about a Conservation Plan is that it is something you can buy off the shelf from a consultant, rather like a packet of cereal or, perhaps more appropriately, an insurance policy. In fact, preparing a Conservation Plan is nothing like that. We felt that it was worth taking time to help people plan the document.

Somewhere in the editing process we lost the title 'Benefits of a Conservation Plan'. Again, many people — including those who should know better — see Conservation Plans as a bureaucratic demand, something you have to endure if you want HLF money.

So the first message to get across was that a Conservation Plan is a beneficial concept. Even if no money is forthcoming from the HLF, a Conservation Plan should be something that is useful in the long run, to the owner or manager of a site and to heritage agencies. It is like having a risk assessment.

The Conservation Plan and your project

The second problem we faced was that people were often being asked for Conservation Plans after a scheme had been agreed. The net result has been that, in effect, the cart is before the horse, and applicants are often locked into schemes that a Conservation Plan might then show to be inappropriate.

It was essential to get across the message that for a Conservation Plan to be useful it needs to be done early in the process, before key decisions are taken and before applicants are committed to spending money on schemes that may never happen.

Who should prepare a Plan?

This is a thorny issue. Those involved in landscape restoration plans and building recording, for example, know that there are probably only a handful of people in the country who are good at analysing buildings and landscapes. But often those people do not have the design or business skills needed to work up a scheme. So finding the right skills is difficult.

There is also the question of how you balance the need for the involvement of the site owner and their existing professional advisers — such as, for example, a Cathedral Architect, who may have a deep knowledge of the site — with the need for an outside view. Many applicants, quite reasonably, do not want to pay an unknown expert to come and tell them about their site. On the other hand, an outside view is often necessary in order to step back from the issues or even the politics of a site.

The answer seems to lie in very close involvement by the existing heritage professionals in preparing a brief for a Plan and in managing the process to make sure that the document is useful for them, but using an outsider to draw all of the issues together.

Plan the stages

Earlier this year I was involved in preparing a Conservation Plan for Whitby Abbey. My experience demonstrated something that I have long suspected was true, and that is, once you have the text for a Plan you are only half way there. Layout, consultation, illustrations, and negotiation are all essential.

The production of a Conservation Plan needs to be managed. In particular, I would highlight the need for a brief for a Plan. The document we have here is clearly not a brief — it is simply an introduction to the process. In Australia the production of standard briefs is a contentious matter. On the one hand you need to create a level playing field for consultants; on the other, as I know from my involvement with archaeology and building recording, standard briefs can kill initiative and intelligence stone dead. What we have done for the HLF is to produce the beginnings of a standard brief, but with fairly open checklists for each heritage sector. The aim is to provide applicants or their advisers with a starting point.

The other tricky issue is the process of tendering. It is obviously important to be able to demonstrate value for money, but tendering a Conservation Plan can be like tendering elastic: you can always produce a Conservation Plan more cheaply. In Australia, some agencies work by announcing a fixed sum for a project, and then asking for bids. This is one of the issues we might look at later in discussion.

Consultation

The strength of a Plan is proportional to the amount of support it has gained. Some of us in the heritage have grown a little complacent. We tend to assume that we know best, and if our expertise is challenged, we slog it out with the applicant at a public inquiry. Conservation Plans provide an opportunity to consult at an early stage in the development of a project, to draw people together before key decisions are taken. This, I think, is one of the most welcome aspects of Conservation Plans. It is important, therefore, to plan for consultation, and to build it into the process.

The requirement for consultation does, however, place a burden on those persons being consulted. Those of us who work in the statutory agencies have to be prepared to put time into reading Plans. If this seems unacceptable to those of us with an already overwhelming caseload, I can only suggest looking at the analogy with the statutory planning process. There, the emphasis has moved from individual applications to development plans with wide consultation.

Consultation has been essential to defining the future of Stonehenge

Brodsworth Hall, South Yorkshire: the level of detail in a Plan should match the decisions it will be used to inform

Detail

The amount of detail included in a Plan is perhaps the most difficult aspect of the document to manage. How do we prevent Plans from becoming great, undigested telephone books, containing 'history by the metre'?

This brings us back to the brief. The key to defining the amount of detail lies in being clear about where we want to be at the end of the Conservation Plan. What decisions do we want to be able to take? From this, it is possible to establish what information we need, both now and later. You don't need the microscopic paint analysis for the Conservation Plan, although the Plan may tell you that you need it before you design your interiors. Equally, you may not need a detailed earthwork survey for the landscape, but you will need it before you finalise the decision on where to place the new car park.

A Conservation Plan is a tool for a job. Inevitably, it will contain enough information to get to the point of an HLF decision on a scheme, but not enough to prioritise next year's maintenance budget. Nor is it a finite process. The Conservation Plan becomes out of date almost as soon as it has been prepared and will need to be revised in due course.

Presentation

Yet another area of debate. On the one hand you have architects who produce A3 plans that are a delight to read and cost a fortune to copy, and on the other, the bureaucrats, with an A4 filing system. On balance, we felt that to gain maximum effect Plans should be copied as widely as possible and therefore A4 won.

We also debated whether or not it was reasonable to expect applicants to produce work of a desk-top publishing quality. I feel strongly that Plans need to be read and in my experience nobody reads anything without pictures. This is an additional expense, but one that brings overwhelming advantages in terms of accessibility.

Adoption

This is a critical issue. It is easy to commission a Plan, submit it to the HLF, get the money, and then put the Plan on the shelf. If a Plan has any meaning at all, it has to be formally adopted. And that in itself can be a difficult and time-consuming process.

2 The content of a Plan

Summary

This is a straightforward overview of the results of the Conservation Plan.

Background

We felt it was essential to know when and why a Plan was written. I have already seen Plans that do not tell you who wrote them, why, and when. What may seem obvious today will be less apparent in 30 years' time.

Understanding the site

This is where the question of detail becomes most problematic. It is also where, from my point of view, the lack of professional skills is most obvious.

Most sites already have a huge amount of information in place. Cathedrals typically will have volumes of material, often published in the nineteenth century, on the detail of the sculpture, the date of the nave, the location of the earlier building, and so on.

Some of the most trenchant criticisms I have encountered come from people who are well aware of this and ask how can you reasonably write down what is known for a major British site.

Against that, I have never yet come across a site where our level of knowledge is not biased. Whitby was the site of one of the most important Saxon excavations in Britain. Yet we had no idea of the extent of the Saxon site. The stonework of the church is much studied, but where was the medieval precinct? The garden was mapped in the late seventeenth century, but was that the garden that was built? There are excellent accounts of the site in the nineteenth century, but English Heritage had few files dating from before 1990.

I strongly suspect that this is not untypical. The job of the Conservation Plan therefore is to look at the broad picture, from earliest times to the present day, to identify what we know and what we do not know. It was important at Whitby to be clear that we do not know the extent of the Saxon site — especially important if we were planning a new sewage system, for example.

The practical solution, which I used at Whitby and which seems to have worked elsewhere, is to produce a survey or gazetteer, which covers the whole site and irons out any of the gaps in our existing knowledge. Whether you use site compartments, rooms, buildings or features does not matter. The main aim is to have a basic level of data that covers everything. It is quite useful if this information is in the form of room data sheets or tables, which builders or site managers can use and be comfortable with.

Sometimes, of course, more detail is needed. If at the end of a Conservation Plan you know that a particular decision is needed because things will otherwise come to a halt, you may need to pull in more information now. At Whitby a detailed earthwork survey of one small area was commissioned because we needed to make a decision about an access road.

In practice, many Plans will face the issue of the combination of a need for an overall helicopter view with the need to solve a specific problem. Try as we might, Plans are not always 'scheme-free', objective documents. They are usually written with a rough idea for a scheme at the back of someone's mind. This is fine, but it does mean that it is rather more difficult to manage the level of information needed in a Plan.

The Conservation Plan process can often throw up information about hitherto unknown structures. The Rocket House on the headland at Whitby is an example of a minor structure which nevertheless played a significant role in the historic relationship between the headland and the sea. The Conservation Plan enabled English Heritage to include such structures in an overview of the headland as a whole

Assessment of significance

The fourth section of the Plan consists of the assessment of significance or heritage merit. I predict that this section alone will generate a huge amount of debate.

The 'Assessment of Significance' is needed for three reasons. Firstly, a designation document is not detailed enough to make day-to-day decisions about a site. Secondly, significance may encompass many different values that do not always come together — ecology and archaeology, for example. Thirdly, there are often ways in which a site is important that are not found in the designation.

We have asked here both for a general statement about the significance of the site as a whole and for a more detailed breakdown of the significance of each of the elements of the site identified in the section on 'Understanding the Site'. There is bound to be debate about how we do this, and I hope Martin Cherry will pick up on this point later.

Vulnerability

Masonry at Whitby Abbey: Conservation Plans can also help to prioritise programmes of repair

This is an area where, rightly or wrongly, we have departed in title (although not in approach) from the James Semple Kerr model, drawing instead on the approach used by the Countryside Commission in the first stage of its Management Plans and also on the lessons of sustainability.

This partly arose from my debate with a project manager at Whitby over conservation policies. He naturally argued that our policy for the site should be to build a visitor centre. I was adamant that our policies should be broad principles. He then asked: 'What is wrong with the policies in PPGs 15 and 16?'.

Somehow, we need to be able to generate policies that are more than just general motherhood and apple-pie ones, but at the same time avoid writing a Plan that is, in effect, a '*post-hoc* justification for a scheme'.

Sustainability asks us to take a longer term view of sites: to look at what is happening to them now and in the future, and to begin to think about the cumulative impact of individual decisions.

It was this that generated the idea of vulnerability — of thinking about how significance was vulnerable as a first step in writing policy.

In this section of the Plan it is important not just to write a list of all the issues concerning the site — and, looking at the guidance again, I am slightly worried about how this will be interpreted — but instead to look at the effect of these on the significance of the site. How does the lack of resources affect the significance of the site? How does demand for public access create problems? Have we always managed the site in the best possible way?

Conservation policies

Here, at last, is the meat of the Plan, the section that will either give the HLF and its advisers confidence that an applicant is genuinely committed to conservation and has a clear idea of what responsibilities that involves, or reveal that they are just gold digging.

Conservation policies are extremely difficult to write. You have to know the relevant legislation and government guidance; you have to know the site and understand the competing issues; and you have to be able to write something that is specific enough to be useful without being too prescriptive.

It is not easy to produce such a document, and the test will only come in 5 or 10 years' time when we come to review what has happened to sites in the meantime, and find out whether Conservation Plans were useful or not.

As ever, the temptation is to write '*post-hoc*' policies, which support the scheme you first thought of. This is certainly the risk that could arise if we were to use Conservation Plans in the statutory process, and it is already emerging as a real risk for the HLF.

Appendices

Finally, we come to the appendices. We are all familiar with the idea of HLF applications arriving on a truck. I have tried to encourage applicants to use appendices to reduce the detail presented in the main Plan. A good

Plan will inevitably draw upon a huge amount of information, some of which should be presented in detail, such as copies of designation maps or a bibliography. But not all of it is needed by any means, and appendices should be used ruthlessly to keep the main text to a minimum.

3 After drafting

Perhaps one of the sources of much of the criticism of the Conservation Plan approach has been because of the variety of different things that can happen in the heritage management process.

It is one thing to draw up a Management Plan for a site where your responsibilities are fairly static — caring for the landscape or an acquired object, managing existing visitors, creating interpretation aids. It is a very different matter to plan a major intervention such as new visitor facilities, a major refurbishment of a building, extensive landscape restoration, or the construction of a new car park.

This was why we drew the line where we did between a Conservation Plan and a Management Plan. It was not because we misunderstood Management Plans at all. It was simply that in response to the particular circumstances of the HLF procedures, some information is required before a grant can be made, and other information can come later. A Conservation Plan can slot easily into the first stage of a Management Plan, but not the other way round. Equally, a Conservation Plan can help draw up a design brief for an architect.

Once a Plan is in place, it is up to the applicant and their advisers what happens next. If an existing scheme is already on the cards, it is possible to go back and assess the scheme against the Plan. If a Management Plan is needed, the first part of the work is already in place. If a new scheme is to be worked up, the Conservation Plan provides the parameters.

Either way, a Conservation Plan is only a first step. Of course it is not a Management Plan, any more than it is an archaeological assessment, building recording or collections policy. Instead, it is the high-level view — an initial bringing together of different heritage interests. And the most important feature is that this bringing together happens early in the process — before ideas are set, money spent on elaborate schemes, time invested in abortive proposals.

> These issues have been developed further since the Oxford conference: see the Epilogue and Appendix.

A health warning

I am not suggesting for a moment that Conservation Plans are a universal heritage panacea. They are not, and it is already evident that there is room for abuse in the system. That abuse will only happen, however, if we let it and if we fail to manage the process.

Some of my own personal worries are:

1 Conservation Plans simply become a money-spinning exercise

If Conservation Plans are linked to HLF funding, and HLF funds are diminishing, unsuccessful applicants who have prepared a Conservation Plan may see the whole procedure as a waste of time. We can only avoid this if we are clear about the intrinsic value of Plans.

2 Conservation Plans become automated

Cynics could easily develop a standard template on the word-processor. Every Plan would be the same except for the name of the site. Writing good Conservation Plans is in fact extremely difficult. It takes time and understanding, commitment, and emotional energy.

In order to make sure that Plans are useful, we have to manage the process. We should only ask for Plans where they are useful, and send back Plans that are no help.

3 We in the various heritage sectors may undermine the process

This is already beginning to happen — heritage professionals who say we don't quite understand it, or we don't like the terminology, so we will view the whole enterprise with suspicion. We must work together, not retreat into our own specialist domains.

4 They are cynically exploited by clients

A developer could see the Plan simply as a document that demonstrates why their scheme is the best possible one. It is up to the statutory agencies to guard against this. After all, it is we who will have to take responsibility if the wrong decision is made.

5 We are all buried under mountains of paper

James Semple Kerr remarked that most people only read the Plans they write themselves. I suspect he is correct.

Conclusions

Conservation Plans are not new. They are simply a version of the good practice which all of us, in any heritage profession, should have been employing for many years, whatever individual terminology we choose to use. Some of us do it explicitly in the form of Management Plans or assessments; some of us do it implicitly. In an organisation such as English Heritage, our own files are, in a sense, Conservation Plans.

However, I also believe that it is easy to fall into bad habits. For historic sites at least, we are far worse than our Victorian forebears at setting out what it is that we have done. We do not always write down what we have done and why we have done it. There are often no records of modern work.

At the end of the day, the Conservation Plan initiative has come about because the HLF needs to be sure that its money will be of benefit to the heritage. It is a question of stewardship and sustainability — ensuring that we pass on the best of today's environment to future generations. Managing change is a complex process. Every day we make decisions about what is and is not acceptable; what is and is not important; what we can afford to lose and what we should fight for. I believe that the initiative taken by the HLF is a brave one. Whatever happens with the HLF in the long term, I hope that this is an initiative which will begin to change the way we work in Conservation, which will bring the natural and heritage sectors closer together, and help us to manage and sustain the historic environment.

In England at least — I do not feel competent to speak for Northern Ireland, Wales, and Scotland — we have already made great strides in working with different agencies at the level of the statutory planning process. Conservation Plans should provide another opportunity to build on these achievements at the level of the individual site.

I know that there are important debates to be had. But I hope we can get beyond terminology and sectarianism, and use the opportunity provided by the HLF to move forward. It will not be easy, but I believe it will be worth it.

Delegate

There is no mention in here as far as I can see of the publication of Conservation Plans, and yet it is an issue that James Semple Kerr has talked about quite widely. Is it going to be a requirement that Conservation Plans are published?

Kate Clark, English Heritage

I think it is very important that Conservation Plans should be available in the public domain. One problem that we will have to face is the issue of confidentiality, which we are really only just beginning to work through.

Stephen Johnson, Heritage Lottery Fund

I think the whole issue of public relations is one that the HLF must look at. Much of the documentation that is submitted to us is of a private nature and the basis of an application for a grant. We need to think through as an organisation how much of that material we should, or could, make public. At the moment, therefore, I don't think I can fully answer that question.

Chair

We have spent a lot of time this morning talking about how Conservation Plans may be used to apply for grants, but, extending the field of discussion, it would be very useful to gain a wider understanding of the significance of the historic places through the publication of such Plans. I think it would be regrettable if they were available only within professional circles and not circulated for wider use.

Delegate

Stephen, you mentioned the two-stage application process. Conservation Plans can take some time to prepare, even along the lines that James Kerr was describing. What will be the recommended timescale for submitting Stage One, and when can you move on to the second stage?

Stephen Johnson, Heritage Lottery Fund

We would prefer the Conservation Plan to be produced as one process, but I have to make clear that there is no mechanism I can think of whereby we could fund people to produce that detailed documentation, even though the site may only require a report of 24 pages. The role of the HLF does not extend to helping applicants submit applications for grants.

The time-scale between a Stage One pass, if you like, and a Stage Two submission is entirely up to the applicant. It is the applicant's responsibility to determine what needs to be done between these two stages, and I would expect a great deal of work to be necessary. Not just in terms of conservation work but also developing a scheme, producing architectural drawings if required, and so on, right up to the stage where it is possible to apply for listed building consent, planning permission or whatever.

I'd like to end by saying that when our Trustees award a grant, that's where the work begins, not where it finishes! I'm afraid many of our applicants think that having been awarded the grant, then that's the end of the process. We have got to make it clear to them that the real work starts once they get past Stage One, and that is when they are going to feel the pressure.

SESSION TWO

LEARNING FROM EXPERIENCE

Chair: Philip Whitbourn, ICOMOS UK

Benefits of Assessment — Conservation Plans and Statutory Bodies

Paul Drury, Conservation Consultant

I have been asked to consider the potential value of Conservation Plans to those national and local statutory bodies that exercise some control over elements of the historic environment. Just as Conservation Plans start by looking back to provide a basis for looking forward, I want to start by looking at how statutory control has developed in the United Kingdom, and where current trends may be leading us.

The development of statutory management of the historic environment

Statutory preservation in the United Kingdom began just over a century ago, with the Ancient Monuments Act of 1882; in other words, relatively late by European standards. An assessment of significance has been implicit in selection from the outset, as well as an intention that the future of things identified should be influenced by that assessment. Why else do it? So the basic principle of the Conservation Plan is implicit in practically all legislative protection of the immovable cultural heritage. What has really changed since 1882 is that the scope of protection has expanded hugely; there are explicit and increasingly comprehensive statements of the basis of selection; and the procedures for doing so have become diverse and complex. Conservation Plans can be seen as the next step in this process.

Statutory protection implies substantial significance, for it confers protection under the law. But of course the definition of what is sufficiently valuable or special to warrant protection continues to expand, usually because the existence or character of something we have previously taken for granted becomes threatened by the force of progress. We began with ancient monuments, historic buildings followed in 1947, and, with increasing emphasis on context and setting, conservation areas in 1967, parks later, and battlefields later still. We have gone from the particular to the general, with an increasing emphasis on the management of the historic environment as a whole, exemplified by countryside *characterisation* rather than classification and grading. A draft European Landscape Convention (CLRAE 1998) has recently emerged, which advocates the sustainable management of the whole historic environment; its definition of 'landscape' is the whole surface area of the land.

This change in the scope of protection obviously implies that there is a continuous process of change in the assessment of significance or value. Considered in relation to a time-scale of little more than a century since the first legislation, the change has been very rapid, particularly in the last 30 years. So value judgement, which is what we are talking about, cannot be objectively right or wrong. At best, at any point in time, it can be consistent; it can summarise the view of a peer group of similar background and outlook.

Two things, in my experience, are absolutely certain. The same group will not come to the same view at a different time, and groups working on different value systems will not agree at all. Setting value judgements of different aspects of a site against one another to arrive at a balanced view thus tend to be particularly problematic. The only certainty is that those who come afterwards, and indeed we ourselves revisiting the same issues, will disagree. There can be few of us who have not looked back at something we did even five years ago and thought, good grief, did I write that?

The story of statutory designation can be seen as a widening appreciation of the nature and extent of what is significant and special, beginning with prehistoric monuments and reaching buildings constructed only a decade ago through increasingly rapid steps. The designating authorities are constantly striving, with new categories and new lists, to catch up with ever-widening definitions (or ever-falling thresholds, depending on your point of view) which are essentially generated by public opinion, I think, rather than specialist self-interest.

In a sense the heritage has become more democratic. It is not just the 'high heritage' of the great houses and cathedrals, the sites of nationally important events. It has become much more about the collective memory and identity of all social and regional groups, attaching significance to tangible survivals or expressions of their culture, past and indeed present. There is recognition that sites have many layers and degrees of cultural value and meaning; different meanings, and so different priorities, for particular groups of people.

The changing face of London Zoo: the zoological gardens in 1829 (above left); The Lion House, 1875–7 (above centre); replaced by The New Lion Terraces, 1972–6 (above right), reflecting changing attitudes to animal curation

Let us consider, for example, London Zoo (Guillery 1993), with which I am currently involved. Lying within a Grade-I designated landscape, it is also important in terms of many of the individual buildings that have been listed. It is important in the history of zoo keeping and zoology, for it was the first modern, scientific, zoological garden. Its very function of keeping and presenting animals itself tends polarise, indeed politicise, people's judgements. For some it evokes fond memories of a London childhood, for some it is a scientific institution unreasonably constrained by (heritage) conservation, whilst for others it represents shameful degradation of fellow creatures. Heritage is not limited to things that produce a universally positive response. It will mean different things to different people. Its common denominator is precisely that it does have meaning, and therefore tends to provoke a response, often an emotional as much as an intellectual one. If you don't believe me, look at the Balkans — which is perhaps not a bad analogy, given the way some defenders of the rights of animals play the game.

But one thing is clear: people tend to place increasing importance on local distinctiveness and local identity. Spike Milligan was once asked why he was crouching under a table. He replied, 'Everybody's got to be somewhere'. The local environment will have some value for most people; it will be special to them. I think that the rate of change has highlighted for most people the loss of their cultural context; it can no longer be taken for granted, but must be actively defended.

In statutory protection, I believe that we are moving towards a view of the past not as a thing apart, but as the framework within which we all live and work. And having gone from the particular to the general in our approach to identification and designation, I see an increasing realisation of the need for a holistic view of the sustainable management of the whole cultural landscape, based on knowledge of its evolution, and appreciating the wide range of values it embodies. We are looking to understand how we got to where we are, not for its own sake, or to prevent change, but primarily to guide positive change. Most people realise that the historic environment, in that very broad definition of the draft European Landscape Convention, has always been in a state of change, and that preservation is not an option on a large scale. This leads to a very positive question: 'How do we want it to change in the future?'.

That is, I think, a positive 'spin' on conservation, that it is not just about imposing a 'presumption in favour of preservation' (to quote the legislation), and high-quality thresholds for intervention, on ever-expanding parts of the historic environment. The flip side of that kind of designation of some areas is implicit downgrading and degradation of the rest. And arguably it is the most damaged areas that are in greatest need of a presumption that change should preserve or enhance environmental quality. This is increasingly a live political issue in any district where designations cover more than about half of the whole, as in some London boroughs. And in Jersey, where there are no conservation areas, they are looking at skipping that whole step and considering that all development should preserve or enhance the island context.

If I am right in this projection of trends, the next decade or two is likely to see a more sophisticated approach to managing our environment, where an understanding of its evolution, and the values — emotional, historical, architectural, aesthetic — attached to things inherited is a strong influence on deciding how to sustain and enhance environmental quality. In 1999/2000, perhaps to mark how far we have travelled in the 25 years since European Architectural Heritage Year, the Council of Europe will be running a campaign, 'Europe, a Common Heritage', which should emphasise this very broad, holistic concept of heritage. This sort of approach, already evident in archaeological and landscape studies, is likely to lead to fewer specific designations and greater integration of the value of cultural heritage into planning strategies. Alternative scenarios, of a kind of creeping heritage paralysis rooted in a desire to resist change of any kind, or a reaction against heritage conservation, are, I think, less attractive and so actually less likely in an increasingly sophisticated world.

Conservation Plans and statutory control

What has all this got to do with Conservation Plans? First, the logic, the intellectual rigour of understanding, assessing significance, defining issues, drafting policies, and assessing proposals against them, in other words, the Conservation Plan process, is undeniably the conceptual and intellectual approach that is needed for the cultural landscape as a whole. And not surprisingly, reduced to such bare elements, the process is very similar indeed to the making of statutory plans within our town and country planning system. If I am right about an increasing emphasis on the historic or cultural dimension of the environment as a whole, understanding that dimension and assessing its significance will become much more important in the survey stage and cyclical process of review of statutory plans. And indeed it is already happening, tending to apply the principles of conservation-area management that English Heritage has advocated over the past few years (English Heritage 1995a) to a broader canvas. But there is one, I think crucial, difference in emphasis at this broad level from that which has come over so far in our Conservation Plans; there must be at least as much emphasis on opportunities for beneficial change as on identifying constraints.

Other speakers have emphasised the need, in an old and complex country, to establish levels of information gathering and presentation appropriate to the scale, level, and purpose of a Conservation Plan, so the result is effective. We also need to be aware that the simple act of amassing facts about something can appear to invest it with importance, particularly to the layman. If I describe a building as a Victorian brick privy, it conveys very little implication of importance. If I manage to find out who designed it and when, and describe it as a brick privy designed by John Smith and constructed in the spring of 1888 at a cost of £1 3s 4d, the attribution and information seem to add to its status. Establishing a complex building history by archaeological analysis can have the same effect. The more you delve into the facts, the more important your subject can be made to appear, particularly in relation to other comparable (or indeed more important), but less well-described, examples of the same type. This is a trap into which we must not fall.

The concept of the Conservation Plan is less familiar or formalised in relation to the control of works to listed buildings rather than Conservation Areas (but see English Heritage 1995b). I remember saying about 15 years ago, as an English Heritage Inspector, that alterations to a listed building should be based on an understanding and assessment of the importance of the building both as a whole and in its elements. But that requirement is only implicit in our legislation. It merely requires consent to be obtained for work that would affect the character of a building of special architectural and historic interest. DoE Circular 8/87 emphasised the need for local authorities to take advice from 'skilled persons' when considering applications. In paragraph 90, it offered some criteria for assessing proposals, but really gave us very little support if challenged.

Only with the introduction of PPG 15, in 1994, do we have an explicit requirement for applicants to justify their proposals:

> They will need to show why works that would affect the character of a listed building are desirable or necessary. They should provide the local planning authority with full information to enable them to assess the likely impact of their proposals on the special architectural or historic interest of the building and on its setting.

Note that the onus is on the applicant, not the planning authority, to do so. One might ask why it took so long. The distinction maintained in the post-war years between the detailed study and understanding of historic buildings by the Royal Commission, selection for protection by the Ministry of Housing and Local Government and its successors, and decisions about what happened to them by the planning authorities and the Secretary of State, certainly produced a fragmented, pragmatic, and rather ill-informed system. Things have, of course, improved hugely; but I still think we have some way to go in the integration of the key responsibilities for these processes.

Conservation Plans potentially offer a more rigorous approach to this question within the statutory framework, setting the definition of the issues and establishing the policies between assessment on the one hand and the proposals on the other. I do not know whether or not it is true in Australia, but in the United Kingdom, we already have layers of planning and conservation policy, indeed layer upon layer: national policy, statutory planning policies in every local authority, and usually supplementary guidance for conservation areas within that. Site-specific policies can, of course, provide a finer grain of detail, interpretation or application, but what would be their status? Are local planning authorities to be expected to adopt them as supplementary guidance, as some speakers have suggested? Will they tend to generate conflict with, in legal terms, the higher levels of the hierarchy? Is it desirable, indeed, to proliferate over-lapping layers of policy in this way? And a concern that was raised in response to English Heritage's advisory note, *Developing Guidelines for the Management of Listed Buildings* (1995b), which in essence sought to apply the conservation-area management model to very large, complex, often modern buildings is still relevant — what are the resource implications for local authorities?

A key issue for Conservation Plans is certainly value in relation to resource input. This has been covered very well by other speakers, but I think that if the approach is to be advocated as part of the statutory process in the next revision of PPG 15, we will have to accept that the application of site-specific Conservation Plans will need to be confined to heritage assets of considerable complexity, whether of evolution or of the issues, particularly conflicting issues, which they raise. They may perhaps be no more than 5% or so of protected buildings and monuments as a whole.

Listed building management guidelines have been prepared for sites such as the Willis Corroon building in Ipswich

The serious problem is assessment, the value judgements. I think we need to be very aware of the limitations and pitfalls. It is obvious that assessment of significance is valid at a point in time, but that is not a fundamental problem in the statutory process, because decisions are always based on the balance of advantage at the time. That is why statutory plans are reviewed, and unimplemented consents must be renewed, after five years. So I certainly underline very strongly the message that has come over this morning — if you have a Conservation Plan, you must review it every five years, because an out-of-date Plan may well be worse than none at all. It should be a long-term commitment towards the stewardship of the site.

Related to the issue of value judgements is the fact that there is no such thing as a totally objective view. A professional view should be balanced, but it is almost certainly not wholly unbiased because everyone, even at the subconscious level, has an agenda. The point is recognised in the Heritage Lottery Fund (HLF) guidance (Heritage Lottery Fund 1998). If you want an assessment and policies that are as balanced or unbiased as possible, I believe that there must be players outside the body responsible for the site or building and its consultant team involved in refining the Plan, either as part of an advisory group or through formal consultation. I certainly don't want to encourage the use of the methodology and structure of Conservation Plans to give a spurious credibility to what is, in reality, purely advocacy for a particular proposal.

Conclusions

As appreciation of the value of the historic, cultural dimension of the environment increases, so the knowledge-based approach to its management through the planning process will grow. Conservation will become much more central to the mainstream planning process. From the statutory point of view, I believe that Conservation Plans for larger historic entities are likely to be more valuable than smaller, less complex ones, and those guided by a wide range of interests more valuable than those overseen by the owner alone.

For those complex entities, the existence of a Conservation Plan will undoubtedly make assessment of statutory applications much easier; provided, of course, that the Plan is not so long and so detailed as to be incomprehensible or effectively inaccessible. But do not be surprised if local authorities and English Heritage put more weight on the facts than on the assessment and the policies. The main value of Conservation Plans is, I believe, complementary to the planning process. They should provide the basis of a management strategy for those who have stewardship of major historic sites and places.

Caveats

Last week I was at another conference, listening to a very sad story about a city in one of the Baltic States with roofs falling in. The person who recounted it ended by saying that they had stopped all work until they have the right plan for the future of this city. I think we must avoid at all costs the danger of delaying action until we have the perfect plan; not least because the perfect plan, like all planning policies, is always looking back to the last battle, not forward to the next one. Issues will constantly change and so will assessment of overall significance, particularly the balance between elements of it.

The HLF guidance is written, I think, very much with sites in mind where maintaining the evidential value of a monument is the paramount concern; for 'conservation' to an extent read 'preservation'. So I come back to the point I made earlier — if Conservation Plans are to be of wider value, which means outside the kind of site that the HLF is funding, more care needs to be given to identifying opportunities for positive change, as well as to constraints. I believe *Conservation Area Practice*, a guidance note produced by English Heritage (1995a), better addresses that balance.

Finally, and perhaps against my own interests in the private sector, can I emphasise that we must all keep value for money and priorities clearly within our sights? If historic buildings have holes in their roofs, mending them, I think, has got to be a greater priority for scarce resources than paying me to write a Plan that concludes that you should have mended the roof five years ago!

Conservation Plans and the Architect

Peter Inskip, Inskip & Jenkins Architects

It would be most unfortunate if Conservation Plans in this country became solely a requirement of the Heritage Lottery Fund (HLF) as part of the process of awarding grants. Conservation Plans are there to help protect the building or the place, and should be available to all, not just the conservation lobby. They are the most wonderful tool, and their preparation informs the architect and the client just as much as a drawing does in the development of a design for a new building. Conservation Plans reveal the unexpected and invariably act as a catalyst to lateral thought.

Our recent commission to prepare a Conservation Plan for Battersea Power Station has as its objective the definition of the cultural significance of the site to ensure that it is retained within a commercial development that covers an area of 34 acres in central London. Three primary areas of significance are present, and each one is vulnerable. Firstly, Battersea has significance as a great landmark — and vistas need to be maintained. Secondly, there is the architectural design of Theo Halliday and the contributions made by Sir Giles Gilbert Scott, who was called in as consultant architect because the site was seen to be so sensitive. Scott was never happy with the building, but it is the forerunner of Bankside and, if you compare it with Fulham, it was undoubtedly successful. Finally, it was the first centralised generating station in London and as such the pioneer of a new building type.

Battersea Power Station: within the roofless boiler house, 1998

Obviously, one needs to understand how the building and the site worked: the riverside cranes show how coal was moved from the barges to the great coal beds beside the river and then up into the building, which was arranged symmetrically with turbine halls and switch rooms on each side of a central boilerhouse. Constructed in two periods either side of the Second World War, both phases can be seen as innovatory: the first in its provision of water washing to remove the sulphur from the gases; the second as it supplied district heating to Churchill Gardens on the opposite bank of the Thames. The great problem, of course, is that it is now ruinous, with the boilerhouse roofless and the building seriously damaged. With a proper assessment of significance, a rational and positive approach will be possible.

We have been working with Conservation Plans in our practice since 1990, and this came about from two sources. Firstly, the Australian contingent in the office who brought news of the Antipodean approach. But it also came to us from the way we were approaching the repair of buildings on site. We had found tremendous advantages in introducing building repair conservation techniques previously reserved for museum objects. When we were working on the repair of the Grenville Column at Stowe (with Trevor Proudfoot of Cliveden Conservation) it was not a big step to decide that the whole monument should be considered as a sculpture, rather than just the statue of Heroic Beauty (by Van Nost) at its head; or to extend the work on the conservation of the seventeenth-century furniture to that of the architectural joinery at Chastleton. This brought us to the world of museum conservation reports, where one sets out the significance of a work of art, considers its needs, and makes recommendations. Why weren't we doing the same for buildings?

We still see the analysis of fabric as an all-important tool. This is a document that places beside an assessment of what is present, the history of the building. All available historical illustrations and archival records are thus co-ordinated with the object. From this, one can determine the significance of a structure and make recommendations to ensure retention of that significance.

An example of this is provided by the Eating Room at Mogerhanger, designed by Soane in 1811 and used as a hospital since 1919. Each room is analysed in turn on a systematic basis, taking the ceiling, cornice, walls, and so on, down to the floor. We record this information in a tabulated form, with the first column effectively providing an inventory description of the element as it exists: the presence of the dado with Soane's favourite sunk moulding concealed beneath the later wallpaper; the French doors that replaced the sash window in the 1930s; and the imprint of the columns removed in the 1960s that remains on the floor and the beam. Against this, one sets out all the historical records relating to that element. By historical records, one means all documentation that survives from the time of a building's construction to the present day, as the whole of the building history is essential, particularly recent events. In our example at Mogerhanger, we have the columns shown in the original drawings, gilded and elaborated in the mid-nineteenth century and removed in the 1960s to gain more bed space. Oral evidence records that they were not thrown away and they were eventually discovered, having been concealed for 30 years at the back of an outbuilding.

Mogerhanger, Bedfordshire: Sir John Soane, 1811

The third column in the table sets out significance. The importance of the columns to Soane's scheme is obviously significant, whereas the hatch of 1908 is intrusive when seen in relation to how much of Soane's design remains intact. The final column in the table gives recommendations in the light of current conditions and resources. These recommendations need to be short, medium, and long term because it is unrealistic to expect that all conservation policies can be implemented immediately and will in fact be carried out as opportunities become available.

Of course, analysing a Soane house is easy because there is such wonderful material in the Soane Museum, with the architect's original drawings, journals, daybooks, and accounts. His drawing of the Eating Room particularly was of great importance in confirming and dating the visual evidence. All this material showed how much of the building remained intact — an extremely important factor in establishing significance — and in the light of that evidence it was possible to make a case to the Department of Culture, Media and Sports that the building should be upgraded to Grade I. This helped greatly in raising the profile of the house for our clients — an evangelical Christian group who had bought the house purely for the space it contained, without any realisation of the importance of the building — and it meant that a wider range of grants was available for the property.

The study of the historical documents also revealed something extremely important about the significance of Mogerhanger, a small house, probably of the 1750s, which had been bought in 1791 by Godfrey Thornton, a director of the Bank of England. It was natural, therefore, that he should ask Soane to help with what Repton described as 'Mr. Thornton's sporting lodge' in Bedfordshire. Soane's alterations of 1792 were very simple and modest, but what was of interest is that the architect was back at the house in 1797 with proposals for an eating room. When Stephen Thornton inherited the house in 1805, Soane returned in the following year to make yet more alterations, and he eventually carried out a complete recasting of the house in 1811. In fact, by 1817 he had worked on houses for both Godfrey Thornton and all three of his sons. What we see is a house where there was a deep personal relationship between the architect and his client and at Mogerhanger the Thorntons were gradually led into the world of serious architecture. Whilst the house of 1792 is an unassuming villa, the house of 1811 employs a judicious massing of elements to give an impression of great scale and the semicircular portico reflects the very latest archaeological discoveries. This is also confirmed when one analyses the original external decorations and we find that the joinery of 1792 is painted stone white, whereas in 1811 the windows are black. It is crucial to understanding the significance of Mogerhanger, and with so many of Soane's buildings now demolished or converted out of recognition, it becomes a building of the greatest importance, providing an interpretation for us of all those lost structures, not only in the Bank of England but in the Palace of Westminster as well.

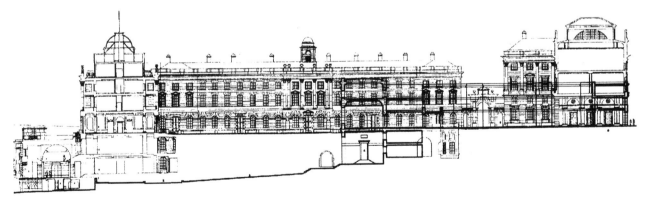

Plan of Somerset House, The Strand, with Old Somerset House overlaid

Investigations to analyse a building are not restricted to visual examination or archival research, but, in order to interpret sites, should also exploit the architect's ability to draw. We all know Canaletto and Kip's views of Old Somerset House, which was constructed by the Lord Protector in the 1550s and extensively extended in the seventeenth century to be the Royal Dower House and a veritable 'treasury of English architectural genius'. I don't think, however, that most people are aware of the dramatic change in level that lay between the Upper Court, opening on to the Strand, and the Privy Garden south of the New Gallery that was often attributed to Inigo Jones in the eighteenth century. We know that the level of the Strand had never changed, and the archaeological discovery of the walkway along the Tudor river wall located the level of the river frontage. By drawing a section through the site, one could see how the gallery had masked a two-storey change of level, and it was this that inspired Chambers' rebuilding of 1776. The basements below the new North Wing were excavated and the spoil deposited on the south half of the site to raise the Great Court. In effect, Somerset House is a six-storey building around a terrace built up two storeys above the level of the garden through which seventeenth-century courtiers strolled, and it is that level that today is represented by the lowest basement area. Significance, therefore, had to be seen to lie very much in Somerset House being a great feat of civil engineering.

Chastleton House, Oxfordshire: the glazing

At Chastleton House in Oxfordshire, recently acquired by the National Trust, only an extremely limited amount of archival or topographical information was available and our analysis of fabric had to be based much more on detailed visual investigations. But it was particularly thorough and went beyond the building, for it extended from the setting of the house to the contents. This ensured the holistic approach that is one of the great advantages of preparing a Conservation Plan. With the house itself, an analysis of the glazing showed that it correlated with the history of the occupancy of Chastleton over three centuries: the remarkable crown glass is restricted to the limited areas of the house occupied by the bachelor squire, John Jones, in the second half of the eighteenth century, while rooms at the top of the building that were not used at that time remained with their earlier plain glazing. Material analysis revealed that although the design was highly sophisticated, the house was constructed with very basic materials, such as clay plasters. With the furniture, each piece was related to the historic inventories so that they could be traced through the rooms in the seventeenth, eighteenth, and nineteenth centuries. On a larger scale, the historic garden identified as a remarkable survival of the seventeenth century could be shown to have been totally replanted in 1833 and substantially replanted around 1910, when many of the topiary animals were transmogrified and the surrounding myrtle hedge replaced with Edwardian yew.

The assessment of significance completely altered the perception of the property from that of an untouched seventeenth-century house to one that had been continuously altered throughout its history, but always respecting its antiquarian interest. The high point of Chastleton has come to be seen as the reign of John Henry Whitmore Jones in the second quarter of the nineteenth century, with the contributions of the eighteenth and twentieth centuries also being recognised as significant. The conservation policies that were developed as a result of our analysis proposed that Chastleton should be maintained as found. This principle was not only applied to the fabric of the building, but to the furniture and the garden as well. The consistency of approach that was achieved was attributed to the clear conservation policies established within the Conservation Plan following the analysis of fabric.

If the assessment of Chastleton resulted in policies that determined a conservative approach to the site, that carried out at the Temple of Concord in the landscape gardens at Stowe determined one of restoration. We all knew that the Temple of Concord and Victory was an important building but I do not think that anyone anticipated how beautiful it was, or the depth of thought that had gone into its development. Stowe is a site of innovation and the Temple of Concord was the first major neo-classical temple in Europe. Significance lay in the development of the building in the eighteenth century, which was based on aesthetic decisions, not in the nineteenth and twentieth-century alterations, which were guided by economies elsewhere. The sale of the statues from the pediments in 1922, and the removal of the columns for reuse in the new school chapel and the subsequent walling up of the peristyle in 1927, undoubtedly had a devastating impact, which needed to be recorded, but the cultural significance of the Temple did not lie with those alterations and was indeed concealed by those changes. The conservation policy of taking the building back to its state at the end of the eighteenth century was therefore appropriate and instrumental to recovering a monument of international significance.

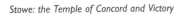

Stowe: the Temple of Concord and Victory

Again, the analysis of materials was important in showing that much of the original fabric still survived. Paint scrapes suggested that the doors were originally brown but paint analysis revealed that the Prussian blue and gold described by Monsieur Lapatie in 1777 lay beneath the brown. While everyone was enthusiastic about the use of limewash on the stone and renders, the disposition of the gilding was not what was expected by twentieth-century eyes: our experience was coloured by the nineteenth-century manner of gilding, which good taste suggested would be a better solution. However, we did not waver from the policies established in the Plan and when the doors were complete, everyone agreed that the eighteenth-century gilding looked amazing.

Stowe: the restoration of the Temple of Concord and Victory, by Inskip & Jenkins, 1998

Stowe House was a casualty of the Great War and the foundation of Stowe School in 1923 saved it from demolition. The school generously gave the gardens to the National Trust 10 years ago, but retained the mansion. Since then, the school's governors have adopted a series of sound conservation policies in order to look after the heritage in their care. One aim is to recover the quality of the external courts, which entails the removal of inappropriate ancillary buildings and boilerhouses as well as the proper management of cars on the site, especially on the North Front. The potential impact of schoolchildren on the historic interiors has been recognised and restrictions placed on the use of rooms, and it has been agreed that the philosophy of repair for the school should be the same as that practised by the National Trust in the grounds in order to achieve a balanced site. We have prepared a framework Conservation Plan so that the problem of the vast house can be considered in a reasonable time scale. The house has been considered as an entity and the building has then been divided into some 21 sections, with a detailed Conservation Plan developed for each part as repairs progress. This has to be the way in which a large site is approached, and it is how we have tackled the whole of the Stowe estate (and our work on Somerset House). It is important to realise that significance does not necessarily follow the boundaries of property ownership, and a

Conservation Plan must be all-encompassing if it is to be successful. Significance can easily become vulnerable from what happens on a neighbouring site. The Conservation Plan for Stowe takes in the properties of not only the school and the National Trust, but diverse others. As an example of this, while the majority of the Western Garden at Stowe is the property of the National Trust, its northern section is inextricably interwoven into the property of the school.

The Western Garden lay, as its name indicates, to the west of Stowe House and the north end was organised around Coucher's Obelisk, arranged axially with Vanbrugh's Temple of Bacchus. It was one of the greatest formal gardens of the eighteenth century and was in fact Lord Cobham's Garden of Love — which, the more you study the iconographic programme, was a Garden of Vice. Today Clough Williams-Ellis's Chatham House of 1924 occupies the site of the obelisk, carefully aligned with the Great Cross Walk, and, behind it, the chapel, by Lorimer, stands on the site of the Temple of Bacchus. The expansion of the school progressed in an ordered fashion across the north of the Western Garden, but after 1950 it was characterised by a series of *ad hoc* developments, which bore no relationship to the underlying garden structure.

(above left) *Stowe: Coucher's Obelisk, Bridgeman, 1739*

(above right) *Stowe: Chatham House on the site of Coucher's Obelisk, Clough Williams-Ellis, 1924*

The preparation of the Conservation Plan for Stowe School is one of the most interesting that we have done as the revelation of the cultural significance of the site provides an opportunity to make sense of a 'place' that has virtually lost all its meaning. The historical time line for Stowe spans 300 years and a quarter of that time has been spent under the aegis of Stowe School. The school saved Stowe in 1923 and it is the school that makes the house viable, for without a compatible use no historic building can be considered secure. There are, therefore, two layers of significance that need to be respected. Lord Cobham's formal garden, designed by Bridgeman and Vanbrugh in the 1720s, was developed by his nephew, Earl Temple, towards the Picturesque from 1749 onwards, and by the time of his death in 1779 the gardens to the west of the house were a series of character areas around the Home Park. The upper and lower flower gardens lay immediately to the west of the house, and beyond this lay Lady Temple's Spinney with the Temple of Bacchus to its south and Nelson's Seat to the north. Lees Bastion and Pyramid Wood completed the northern boundary of Home Park, and this was enclosed by Nelson's Walk, which ran along the whole of the northern edge back to Nelson's Seat. After Lord Temple, Stowe continued to be developed to keep apace with aesthetic changes and reached its zenith by 1797, but the next century was characterised by decline.

In the twentieth century, Stowe School has made a contribution to the significance of the site with buildings by Clough Williams-Ellis, Lorimer, and Fielding-Dodd. Their success has been dependent on their relationship to the underlying character areas and it is clear that respecting the landscape structure could also provide a framework within which future developments could occur. Boundaries of character areas should not be straddled, and the sequence of character areas needs to be respected. A thorough 'understanding of the place', as James Semple Kerr quite rightly refers to it, will provide a holistic approach that can accommodate the interests of both the school and the National Trust.

When we started using Conservation Plans 10 years ago, our Antipodean colleagues reported on the excitement of the preparation of a Plan for an early brewery. This in turn, however, lay on the site of a sacred Aborigine place that could be 10,000 years old. I like to think there are parallels at Stowe — Stowe School is obviously our brewery and below that we have the sacred grove.

Conservation Plans and the National Trust

David Thackray, the National Trust

In this paper I intend to introduce the National Trust's current involvement with Conservation Plans through my perceptions of the Conservation Plan philosophy and rationale, by reviewing the Trust's long involvement with the preparation of various forms of management plans, and by outlining its recent involvement with the preparation of 'Statements of Significance'.

In the two years leading up to its centenary in 1995, the National Trust undertook a review of its conservation policies and attitudes, involving a wide range of staff and outside experts and relating particularly to its work in the countryside. This was known as the Countryside Policy Review, and was a very valuable, reflective process; it was a privilege to be able to spend time in structured thinking, debate, and research — but a very necessary privilege for an organisation with nationally important responsibilities for the preservation of buildings, habitats, and landscapes. Nor was it a review focused exclusively on the countryside; it also looked at the Trust's wider role in society and at the many perceptions of its many constituencies.

This review culminated in a major centenary conference, held in Manchester, and the publication of a detailed consultative report entitled *Linking People and Place* (Russell 1995). The report developed many important precepts, amongst which were the recognition of the importance of research and consultation to guide and inform the Trust's policy development and management practices. It also helped to focus the organisation on the importance of sustainable approaches to development and management, both on its own properties and in the wider world affecting them or influenced by them, and the need to develop and embrace environmental principles to help to achieve this.

Recognising the Trust's role as an important practitioner in conservation, the Countryside Policy Review explored what it meant by conservation and adopted a definition first expounded by Alan Holland and Kate Rawles of Lancaster University, which it found to be of great help: 'Conservation is about negotiating the transition from past to future in such a way as to secure the transfer of *maximum significance*' (my italics) (Holland and Rawles 1993).

This statement is, I believe, particularly valuable, as it embraces the continuum from the past to the future and asks us to decide, responsibly, what is important or significant about our own inherited heritage and the contributions we are making to our own culture, which we want to share with the future. In this it reflects the conservation principles of the Burra Charter, a seminal document, which also profoundly influenced the thinking of our Countryside Policy Review. Indeed, the Burra Charter's first conservation principle embraces much of the Holland and Rawles definition. It states: 'There are places worth keeping because they enrich our lives — by helping us understand the past; by contributing to the richness of the present environment; and because we expect them to be of value to future generations' (Marquis-Kyle and Walker 1996, 15).

The Burra Charter goes on to consider 'cultural significance', which it defines in its subsequent conservation principle: 'the cultural significance of a place is embodied in its fabric, its setting and its contents; in the associated documents; in its use; and in people's memory and association with the place' (Marquis-Kyle and Walker 1996, 15).

It is this wide definition of 'cultural significance' that underpins the Trust's various approaches to the development of 'Conservation Plans' for its properties, for it is in this breadth of definition that we can accommodate the range of significance or values that might apply to any one place, from international and national significance to local identity and local distinctiveness. It challenges us to ask the question 'Significant to whom?', and admonishes us to consider scientific and academic values alongside aesthetic, spiritual, and associative meanings; important both to the expert and to the people who live and work in a place, as well as those who may visit as tourists and enjoy its special qualities.

I have dwelt on this process of thinking that stemmed from our Countryside Policy Review because it highlights some important principles, but by no means all, which are inherent in the Conservation Plan process, and which must help underpin our conservation policy. In summary, these include the following points:

- the first is that conservation is based on understanding, derived not just from research and survey, but from consultation and a wider dialogue;
- the second is that the fulfilment of the responsibilities of conservation, for it is a very responsible activity ('negotiating the transition from past to future'), depends on our assessment of the significance of a place;
- the third of these principles is the fact that significance embraces a wide range of meanings and values; scientific and technical, aesthetic, and spiritual, and reflects the interests of all who have an interest in a place.

Now, if these principles are so fundamental in the Conservation Plan process, why is it that the phrase 'Conservation Plan' is not yet widely accepted in our current usage? I think that this is in part a matter of terms. We have a long history of 'management plans' for our properties, and although our Management Plans (and we are now in the third generation of these) were well informed, and their objectives often embraced the preservation of the significant components of a property, they were focused on operational guidelines and very often did not derive these guidelines from a 'vision' or conservation policy for the place, based on its significance.

However, and whatever the semantic problems we might be experiencing, the latest Management Plan guidelines (drafted in 1996) that the Trust has adopted do embrace much of the Conservation Plan process which we are considering at this conference. These new guidelines were developed following a period of consultation with the managers of properties, and reflect a consensus of opinion about what is needed to guide and inform property management. This consultation identified that there is a 'real desire for concise guidelines giving a clear overall framework for the process, but which are non-prescriptive and flexible allowing for the different needs of different properties' (National Trust 1996a, B3.2, para 1.2).

In particular, the new guidelines state:

> One point particularly worth emphasising is the need for the
> management plan to identify the essential and enduring significance
> or meaning of a property, as expressed by Oliver Rackham in *The
> Last Forest* (1989) [which it then quotes]: 'We cannot guarantee
> that our successors will be men of goodwill or of steadfast purpose,
> but we can tell them what we propose and why. This is what a
> management plan is for. It needs to be descriptive; not just a bald
> list of biological or archaeological features, but to mention
> everything that is special or wonderful or beautiful, and above all to
> set out the meaning of the place.' This must be the starting point
> for a plan, and from which all else flows. It is the key to achieving
> genuine continuity of purpose and management, highlighted
> recently as one of the prime objectives of the Trust (National Trust
> 1996a, B3.2, para 1.3).

These latest Management Plan guidelines refer to this section of the plan
process as 'the Strategy Plan' (yet another term), which, it states, 'should
need little subsequent alteration, although it should be reviewed on a
rolling annual basis to refresh memories and make any adjustments
needed in the light of changed circumstances'. It then goes on to describe
the process required to produce this part of the plan, and I will further
quote from this, because it is important to reflect on the similarities
between this process and the Conservation Plan.

> The Strategy Plan should contain:
>
> • First, a description summarising the **significant aspects of the
>   property**. This is *the* most important part, as all else flows from
>   it. Consultation should take place at this initial stage, and should
>   be as broad as possible to establish both lay and academic views
>   of, for example, regional staff, National Trust advisers, local
>   residents, visitors, and tenants.
> • Next, a **long-term vision** of what the Trust is seeking to achieve
>   at the property, setting long-term, ideal, strategic objectives.
> • It should contain an analysis of constraints and opportunities that
>   will affect the management of the property and the achievement
>   of the strategic objectives ('the Issues').
> • **Statements of policy** about specific management aspects of the
>   property.
> • **Short to medium-term objectives**, looking three to five years
>   ahead, geared to achieving the long-term strategic objectives
>   (National Trust 1996a, Section 3, paras 3.1 to 3.5).

We can recognise some of the elements of the Conservation Plan process
in these guidelines, and, indeed, the subsequent sections in the Trust's
Management Plan guidelines, including the Financial Plan and the
Annual Implementation/Action Plan, echo the final part of the
Conservation Plan process — Implementation and Review. What, most
importantly, is missing from these guidelines is acknowledgement of the
whole process of gaining understanding of the site, derived from
appropriate survey and research. Although this is inherent in the way that
the Trust works with its various technical survey processes —
archaeological, biological, and vernacular buildings surveys amongst
others — I believe it is important that guidelines should make proper

reference to this, to integrate it formally into the process (it is all too easy for those who do not understand the importance of this to ignore it), because it is essential for informing summaries of significance.

Since these latest Management Plan guidelines were drafted, there has been further debate on the means of achieving 'Statements of Significance' that form the starting point of a plan. A National Strategic Plan has identified the requirement to produce these statements for all properties by the year 2001 (National Trust 1998a). There is a continuing debate as to who should have the responsibility for drafting these, but there is little doubt that the Property Manager should manage and co-ordinate the process, following wide, interdisciplinary consultation, and drawing together and reconciling different values. Recent guidelines on the preparation of Statements of Significance identify the need for survey and research as well as discussion and consultation (National Trust 1998b). These guidelines also identify a number of factors, special qualities or physical attributes which need to be taken into account. They include:

- an **assessment of aesthetic qualities**;
- the **recognition of natural features and processes**;
- **acknowledgement of cultural features**;
- and of **socio-economic activities**;
- **associations**;
- and other **special characteristics**, such as access, individuality, distinctiveness, rarity, typicality, or craftsmanship.

The guidelines advise the careful evaluation of the assembled and possibly diverse views on significance — before a statement is prepared — and make recommendations as to the means of achieving this. The ensuing statement should recognise and summarise all contributions of views and values, but not necessarily prioritise the key qualities requiring protection or enhancement, and should lead, through consideration of the issues affecting a place, to the formulation of management and conservation policy objectives. It needs to be flexible and capable of modification to incorporate new information or changing perceptions of value, and should be reviewed periodically.

This process has already been adopted with some enthusiasm, but in some instances without the rigour of the Conservation Plan process of which these Statements of Significance form part. This is worrying, given our requirement to produce Statements of Significance for all properties within the next two years. We need to be alert to the danger that in forcing the pace of such a process, the resulting Statements may be over-brief, ill informed, and anodyne. Unless there is a requirement to identify where further information is needed, to inform our understanding of the place or property, then there will be no mechanism for establishing priorities to undertake this additional work. Clearly, many of these statements can be no more than initial commentaries based solely on present levels of knowledge, but we know from many years' experience of carrying out detailed surveys and evaluations that the present level of understanding about the core qualities of a place, the architectural importance of a historic house or designed landscape, for example, or the scenic attributes of a piece of coastline or upland, may hide many other unrealised values.

Having just described the similarities between the Trust's latest Management Plan process and Conservation Plans, and having also touched briefly on our requirement to produce summary 'Statements of

Significance' for each of the Trust's properties, I must say something about the Conservation Plans themselves that are being increasingly developed for properties.

'Guidelines for long-term Conservation Plans for historic parks and gardens' (National Trust 1997) have been in use for a number of years, and updated periodically. They have a stated and very clear purpose:

> A Conservation Plan helps us to understand the significance of a garden and its components and to propose appropriate management strategies to ensure their preservation and renewal in perpetuity. The Plan describes the ideal, long-term vision for the landscape and then details the practical steps to be taken in the medium term towards achieving this (National Trust 1997, 1).

These Garden Conservation Plans feed into property management plans, and it is Trust policy to produce them for all parks and gardens (National Trust 1997, 1). They do follow very closely the format and spirit of the Conservation Plan guidelines, which we are considering here. They are based on and follow from park and garden surveys, and set out a 'clear, concise, practicable' vision for a number of years, the duration depending on the sort of process that is being addressed in the Plan — up to 200 years for long, cyclical processes such as avenue replanting. Most importantly, these guidelines recognise that 'only by working through the separate subject areas can a feeling for the whole property be built up'. They state: 'the Plan should attempt to succinctly convey the "spirit of the place" using descriptive language, quotations, illustrations, etc' (National Trust 1997, 1).

I would like to illustrate the detailed application of Conservation Plans within the Trust by two brief examples. (We have already heard from Peter Inskip of his approaches at both Chastleton and Stowe.) In neither

Biddulph Grange Gardens, Staffordshire. The Chinese bridge in the China Garden at Biddulph after restoration

case can I go into much detail; all I want to do is to show how understanding, derived from survey, research, and consultation, has contributed to a process which has included the assessment of the significance of the places, the development of a conservation philosophy, and has informed detailed and developing conservation management.

Biddulph Grange Garden

The summary Statement of Significance for Biddulph (National Trust 1996b) begins with the following statements:

> Biddulph Grange Garden has been very aptly described as 'not a typical Victorian Garden yet very much a Garden of its time'. Certainly, it reflects the enthusiastic eclecticism (and perhaps even imperialism) of mid-nineteenth-century Britain, but is at the same time an intensely individual garden (ibid, Section 2).

Biddulph Grange Gardens, Staffordshire. A view of the Dahlia Walk and Shelter House looking from the West Terrace, after rediscovery of the Dahlia Walk by archaeological excavation

The Conservation Plan was achieved through historical and horticultural research, and by dividing the Garden into 'Character Areas', for each of which 'a Character Sketch was drafted, identifying its particular qualities — the effects, features and moods that the creator of the garden was trying to achieve' (ibid, Section 1). Its current state was then considered, together with any constraints, before a programme of work, itself supported by further research, including archaeological excavation, was identified for the area.

Llanerchaeron House, Ceredigion

At Llanerchaeron, a Conservation Plan is being developed to 'conserve the estate for what it is, a rare survival of a nucleus of a small but significant Welsh agricultural estate in an intact and unspoilt condition, set in a very beautiful area of countryside' (National Trust 1996c, project aims). It is important for its history, architecture, nature conservation, outstanding natural beauty, community values, and associations. These

Llanerchaeron, Ceredigion. A detail from the Home Farm: a view across the cobbled courtyard with a horse cart standing in front of the farm outbuildings. Llanerchaeron is a rare survivor of a Welsh gentry estate and was acquired by the National Trust without endowment

sorts of estates have all but disappeared elsewhere in Wales, and there is an opportunity to preserve for this and future generations something which in the past has played a major part in the social, economic, and cultural development of rural communities in Wales (ibid). The National Trust was left this estate, without supporting finance, in 1989, and is now seeking funding to conserve and regenerate the core and essence of the estate. The Trust has been working closely with the local community, CADW, and the Countryside Council for Wales to achieve an understanding of the importance of the place. The Conservation Plan (which is linked to a Heritage Lottery Fund application) draws upon a detailed programme of biological survey, historical research, and archaeological survey of all the buildings. These include the villa designed by John Nash in 1794–6, but based on an earlier building of which much of the core fabric remains. A complex and fascinating Home Farm with a full range of farm buildings, probably also by Nash, has been subject to the same degree of survey to guide initial, urgent repairs, and for which separate evaluations of significance have been drafted. The house is surrounded by landscape grounds and a small park laid out in the 'picturesque' style; again, a detailed park and garden survey has been undertaken, together with an assessment of the wider landscape context, its aesthetic and vernacular qualities. The house is listed Grade II★, and the estate contains other listed buildings, three Sites of Special Scientific Interest, and other important vernacular buildings.

Llanerchaeron, Ceredigion. Llanerchaeron house, park, and surrounding estate, including farmland and woodland in the Aeron Valley, with the sea in the distance

A summary assessment of the significance of the whole is being developed based on the detailed surveys and evaluations. The Plan is supported by further condition surveys, and a further assessment of the opportunities that it will provide for public benefit; not just for visitors, but for the local community as well, in terms of training in conservation skills, employment, the maintenance of the highest environmental standards, and habitat improvement and management. In addition, the estate is also home to two important collections of artefacts, the Geler Jones collection of predominantly local, agricultural machinery, which is very well at home in this setting, and the Pamela Ward collection of fine art objects, which will enhance the house when its conservation is complete. Both are themselves the subjects of detailed cataloguing and assessments of their conservation requirements.

Conclusion

This rapid overview of some of the variety of planning processes, Management Plans, Statements of Significance, and even Conservation Plans for parks and gardens, still ignores others which I am unable to mention: in particular, Whole Farm Plans and Landscape Assessments, both based on well-established methodologies, closely related to the Conservation Plan approach, and both in use within the National Trust. Surely we need, at the very least, to develop a common language of conservation which we all understand, to develop a generic structure of conservation planning to which all these various models relate. This conference offers a clear avenue for consideration of this point, and the Conservation Plan methodology a clear, rational, and flexible approach, which is capable of use for buildings and monuments, habitats and ecosystems, and for wider landscapes. For all of these, it is important to identify what is significant about the place, physically, in its entirety or as the sum of its identifiable components, and also what may be, less tangibly, its 'Spirit of Place'. Unless we have an approach that is based on understanding what is significant, and is itself not wooden and overly mechanistic, we are in danger of standardisation and mediocrity in our management, which will continue to undermine the links between people and place, and which will continue to cause damage to our historic landscapes, buildings, and habitats.

Conservation Plans — an Edinburgh Perspective

James Simpson, Simpson & Brown Architects

I live and work in Edinburgh, but I was brought up in the small Borders town of Duns, from where John Duns Scotus preceded me to Oxford, almost exactly 700 years ago. Duns Scotus was concerned to differentiate between faith and reason, and between religion and philosophy, which is a dangerous thing to do in any age. So if I gently question one or two aspects of the Burra Doctrine, tentatively suggest ways in which the liturgy of the Conservation Plan might be made to seem more relevant, or the linguistic orthodoxy of the 'cult of the significant place' more comprehensible to the people, you will probably call me a Scots heretic, or at least a 'Dunce' — a term originally applied by his contemporaries to Duns Scotus.

I have long been interested in conservation theory and it is about 30 years since I first read Harold Plenderleith's *The Conservation of Antiquities and Works of Art*. A standard work, but not what every architecture student was reading in the 1960s. Plenderleith was the first Director of ICCROM. He and Charles Peterson from Philadelphia were present at the signing of the Venice Charter in 1966. The Duke of Grafton, then Lord Euston, is the only other anglophone I know to have been present. They told me that the British and American delegations had not supported the Venice Charter, which had been fairly hastily conceived in French and Italian by Raymond Lemaire and Piero Gazzolo, and, in Peterson's phrase, 'railroaded through'. Plus ça change!

The point about this anecdote is that it may help us to see the Venice Charter in proportion. It was a critical milestone in the evolution of conservation theory, but it was not the New Testament any more than William Morris was Moses and the manifesto of the Society for the Protection of Ancient Buildings the Ten Commandments.

The world has changed out of all recognition since 1966. Then, in the aftermath of two world wars, self-confident brave new world modernism was in total charge and, in theory at least, the entire building stock was scheduled for replacement, much of it by the end of the century. Even the contemporary 'Civic Amenities Act' was not, we were repeatedly assured, about the preservation of buildings, but about the conservation of the character of places. The Venice Charter was not written with reference to the ordinary building stock at all, nor even to historic buildings in everyday and long-term use. The International Charter is about cultural monuments, 'monumenti di cultura', 'monuments de culture', in the European or — as I think Bernard Feilden might have it — in the Latin sense.

The language and philosophy of the Venice Charter are those of the museum and the principles are drawn directly from textbooks such as Plenderleith's own *The Conservation of Antiquities and Works of Art*. Its whole basis was that at a time when many buildings, including much urban fabric and much architecture, was likely to be swept away, it was necessary to ensure the preservation of those monuments which represented the high points, or which were key to our understanding, of our culture; monuments, in fact, of cultural significance.

The fact that the artefacts under consideration might be architecture, gardens or great composite sites was neither here nor there; they might just as well have been sculpture, furniture or textiles, or the famous polar bear before the hearth of the great library at Newhailes. They were just objects, whose sole *raison d'être* was their cultural significance. Architecture, living, working everyday architecture, with 'Commodity, Firmness and Delight', was not what the Charter was about, and architects, by and large — most of whom were only concerned with new buildings anyway — saw it as no business of theirs.

It is also worth reminding ourselves that in 1966 the science of ecology and the concept of environmentalism were in their infancy. We had not then begun to think that by resource extraction and consumption, by burning and using up, by discarding and polluting, by breeding, travelling, and genetic engineering, we could destroy whole habitats and species by the thousand, change the climate, and raise the level of the sea. Although one man who had, it occurred to me only many years later, was Peter Whiston, the Edinburgh architect who started the postgraduate course in what was then called 'Environmental Conservation' at the Edinburgh College of Art.

It was a remarkable document that came out of Burra, that small mining town in South Australia, in 1979. Remarkable not least because what was presumably intended by ICOMOS Australia to be a development of the International Venice Charter, which would set a suitable framework for the conservation of monuments and sites, or rather, places of European cultural significance, was clearly adopted in late 1970s Australia with enthusiasm, and carried back by evangelical young Australian conservation architects to Europe, to the United Kingdom in particular, and, no doubt, to many other parts of the world.

There is no doubt in my mind that the Conservation Plan is an enormously useful and important concept, which is here to stay. It is not, of course, a static concept. 'The Conservation Plan is not meant to be a "bible"', James Semple Kerr wrote in the introduction to the third edition of *The Conservation Plan*, 'but a guide, accessible to all, and subject to frequent revision'. We have, in fact, been producing a very similar sort of document for about 15 years, our name for which was a 'Strategy Plan' or a 'Strategy Report'. A Simpson & Brown 'Strategy Report' always included: a detailed historical and architectural account of the building or site, sometimes based on new research; drawings as existing, based on a new measured survey if necessary; a detailed condition report; and an analysis of requirements and opportunities leading to the recommendation of a strategy for the future of the building or site, usually with costs. What these reports did not do was systematically to lay out the various components of cultural significance, and to synthesise them into a statement, though I firmly believe that the analysis was present, if not explicit.

Nonetheless, I welcome the discipline of the Conservation Plan methodology and format. Work undertaken at such buildings as William Adam's Arniston House, St Paul's Cathedral, Dundee, Alderman Fenwick's House in Newcastle, and Taymouth Castle in Perthshire, has, since the 1970s, been based on our proto-Conservation Plan, Strategy Report approach. We now have a number of entirely orthodox Conservation Plans on the stocks. We completed one last month for the buildings by Joseph Paxton and others in Baxter Park, one of the principal public parks in Dundee. It is all there, in about 100 pages, well researched, well described, drawn, and presented; I did not make any contribution to it myself and I think it is an excellent document. We are in the process of preparing a Conservation Plan for the ruin of the great eighteenth-century house and all the garden buildings within the landscape policies of Penicuik House, in parallel with a Management Plan and the development of a Visitor Strategy and a Business Plan for the landscape itself, one of the greatest in Scotland.

We have a captive Australian who writes Conservation Plans, Jane MacKenzie. Putting together Jane's experience with our own, we find nothing particularly difficult or daunting, and, if one believes in a scholarly approach to architecture and conservation, as we do, it is just wonderful to be funded to do the job properly.

There is, on the other hand, nothing magic about a Conservation Plan and I am going to conclude by highlighting what I consider to be problems and by suggesting ways in which the methodology needs to be developed.

Firstly: one does not practise architecture, or conservation, by numbers. Charters, principles, and methodologies do not provide all the answers. I am told that there has been a trend in Australia whereby specialised conservation practices spend a high proportion of their time writing Conservation Plans, which are then often handed over to general practice or downright commercial architects, who then carry out the work, almost literally by numbers, following the guidance laid down in the Plans. This fits with the American trend towards competitive tendering at every stage of a job, so that one architect does the design, another the working drawings, a third the post-contract work, and so on. I would regard trends of this sort as being disastrous, both for our buildings and sites and for offices like ours. One does not practise architecture or conservation by numbers.

Secondly: except in the case of monuments, buildings or sites whose existence is their only justification, and which have no demanding use, decisions cannot be predicated on cultural criteria alone. If a building or site is to be genuinely sustainable, economic and environmental criteria must be considered as well, and all of these in an integrated way.

Thirdly: the scale and ambition of a Conservation Plan needs to be appropriate. Even when there are large quantities of material, the importance of a building or site may be easily assessed on the basis of a limited number of simple facts. A proper balance must be struck.

Fourthly: the Conservation Plan is not the only methodology relevant to architecture and conservation. The forthcoming British Standard Guide (*British Standard Guide to the Principles of the Conservation of Historic Buildings*) also provides for the continuous care of buildings and sites on the basis of quinquennial inspections, the establishment of conservation manuals, and the maintenance of logbooks.

What I hope for and will be working towards, in the long term, is the addition of economic and environmental criteria to the analysis, and the replacement of the 'Statement of Cultural Significance' with a 'Statement of Values' and an 'Analysis of Objectives', leading to a broader, more balanced, and more integrated conservation policy. For as Architecture is about Commodity and Firmness as well as about Delight, so is Conservation about Economics and Environment as well as about Culture.

Let us welcome and delight in the elevation of heritage and culture, and the translation of everything into archaeological terms. But let us beware of the sort of tunnel vision that leads to an agriculture and food policy which takes no account either of ecology and environment or of practical economics and the needs of the rural population. Let us develop the Conservation Plan methodology, created by James Semple Kerr in the land of Oz, in our own way, with a sense of proportion, balance, breadth, common sense, and an enlightened clarity of vision.

Conservation Plans for Museums and Galleries

Kate Clark, English Heritage

Introduction

Over the past year several major museums and galleries have been putting Conservation Plans into place and a number of other Plans have emerged for historic properties which include collections. Since the time of the Oxford conference, we have learned a great deal about the application of the Conservation Planning process to the museum context.

Museums and galleries — like any other branch of the heritage — have perfectly well developed existing procedures for understanding and managing their holdings. Collections management plans, collections policies, forward plans, and the whole emphasis historically placed by museums and galleries on documentation already contribute directly to the care of museums and their contents. In many ways the principles of the Conservation Plan have their origins in established practice on the treatment of objects. But, in common with other conservation professions, museum and gallery staff are understandably more comfortable (more confident?) in dealing with their own area of expertise. This might not matter, except that many museums house collections in historic buildings that have been adapted for the purpose. Elsewhere, many of the most famous galleries and museums in Britain are housed in purpose-built buildings that have become of historic interest in their own right. Thus, the management of a collection is often also a matter of managing a building and indeed a wider site.

This is relatively easy where values are compatible: a Victorian collection housed in a Victorian building, sculptures in a designed landscape, the contents of a jeweller's workshop housed in the conserved original building. But when the collection and the building embody different values or a different aesthetic — hanging a modern collection in an older building with an ornate interior, for example — there can be conflicts.

Even where the building and the collection work comfortably together, other issues arise — the modern requirements for environmental control can conflict with the fabric of a historic building; the changing educational role of museums can create a demand for spaces which were never provided in the original building. Visitor requirements can also put undue strain on a historic building or site. Floors most typically can come under pressure and may require replacement in order to meet modern health and safety requirements — yet those floors may have been part of the original building and be of interest in their own right. Historic glass in roof-lights can pose an unacceptable public safety risk, yet its replacement with modern toughened glass can diminish the historic interest and aesthetics of the building. The provision of cafés and toilets is another constant issue of concern.

Ironically, in some cases the interest in the historic building lies in evidence for historic collections care. At the Royal Academy in London, cast-iron grilles and an ingenious system of ducts at cornice level kept air moving around the galleries. This system is no longer adequate for modern requirements, yet the physical evidence provides a rare documentary record of Victorian curatorial practice. Retaining such evidence may be as important as retaining items in the collection.

Conservation Plans in museums

A number of major museums and galleries are in the process of putting Conservation Plans in place, including the National Museums and Galleries of Merseyside, the Bowes Museum (County Durham), the British Museum, the Fitzwilliam Museum (Cambridge), Dulwich Picture Gallery, and the Royal Academy. In several instances it is probably fair to say that the requirement for the Conservation Plan came from the Heritage Lottery Fund and was greeted with a degree of ambivalence by curatorial and management staff, who initially saw it as an unnecessary replication of existing information. As the Plan developed and staff were drawn into the process, the benefits became more apparent. Often those benefits were unexpected — at one site it became clear that the whole exercise of collating information about the site was in itself positive. The knowledge and experience of front-line staff is essential to the preparation of the Plan and the act of bringing it together draws them actively into the planning process.

Each Plan has also generated debate — over lighting, signage or the value of twentieth-century changes, for example. Conflicts that might otherwise be swept under the carpet have been brought out into the open, if not always resolved. And, despite initial confidence over the extent to which a site was already understood, every Conservation Plan has provided new insights.

The Conservation Plan for the British Museum has been prepared by a team from PMT, led by Michael Morrison. The experience of Nigel Sunter in fabric analysis was particularly useful in unpicking the complex series of changes that the building had undergone through time. In order to make the material more digestible, the consultants were asked to produce a 'Handy Guide', which would be given to front-line maintenance staff to help in the day-to-day care of the fabric

When are Conservation Plans useful to museums?

Not every museum requires a full Conservation Plan. There are some circumstances, however, when the process can be particularly useful, as, for example, in the case of museums or galleries in historic buildings that:

- are protected in their own right and are particularly sensitive or complex;
- are associated with complex holdings (for example, groups of structures);
- have sharply divided management frameworks (for example, for building and site) where better communication is essential;
- are facing major changes;
- create ongoing difficulties with access or collections care.

Conservation issues

Some common threads have emerged from the preparation of Conservation Plans for museums, and suggest a number of policy areas that should be addressed. It is useful to try to identify such issues at the outset of the Plan process, so that you can make sure that the information to be gathered is targeted towards real problems.

Conflicts between buildings and collections

It is difficult to meet modern curatorial standards of care in a historic building. In order to maintain appropriate lighting levels and stable environmental conditions, and to provide adequate security, new equipment is required which may have to be accommodated within roof spaces, in wall cavities or, if free-standing, can intrude into buildings. Sometimes this equipment requires the replacement of existing fixtures such as case fittings or locks. In order to resolve such conflicts, the Conservation Plan has to identify the significance of existing solutions, and also to explore the potential impact of any new work.

Occasionally, those conflicts may be fundamentally irreconcilable, such as the use of some timbers in historic libraries. In such cases either the building may have to be altered or the collections rehoused — decisions which in their own right can have knock-on effects for other elements of the site. Again, careful research into the significance of each, and an assessment of issues in the wider context of the site as a whole, must precede any decisions.

Sometimes modern museum practice may have to recognise that a fairly flexible approach to the application of conservation standards in the context of historic buildings may be more appropriate.

Ancillary spaces

Ancillary spaces such as basements and roof spaces are often used for boiler plant and other equipment. At many sites a fairly cavalier approach has been adopted to the creation in such areas of new ducts or the removal of old material by comparison with the attention given, for example, to galleries. Yet these spaces may be of interest in their own right, perhaps as historic service areas or because they incorporate the remains of earlier buildings. Conservation Plans can usefully focus on ill-understood parts of a building and ensure that they are brought into the planning process.

Collections

The Conservation Plan is not just about the fabric of the building — it should take an overview of the significance and issues relating to the whole site and its contents. Where there is already a collections policy and good documentation, this information can be used to understand the history of the collection and its significance. Answers to such questions as how were the collections built up, what are the provenances of the collections, and how much of the collections is firmly associated with the site will be relevant to the Plan. Historic buildings may have items that were associated with the building prior to its becoming a museum; elsewhere, much of the collection may be independent of the site. An overview of the size, condition, and nature of the collections and their importance in a regional or disciplinary context will be relevant to debates over the extent to which the building can accommodate current collections needs, and if there are conflicts, which might take precedence.

For some museums, the buildings themselves have been collected. Re-erected structures in industrial or buildings museums create their own conservation dilemmas; the recreation of a Victorian street in an open-air museum could lead to the loss of an early twentieth-century railway siding. Which is the more significant in the museum context — the visitor experience or the existing (albeit late) railway feature? At the Bowes Museum, for example, recreated historic interiors have been inserted into principal spaces in the building. On the one hand they are products of an early phase in the history of building conservation; on the other they represent outdated and now unacceptable practice. Difficult decisions have to be made about whether they should be retained.

The analysis of significance should encompass everything on the site — from objects to buildings to the site itself in order to generate enough information to make judgements in such cases.

Landscapes

Almost every museum site includes a landscape or setting element that can come under pressure from changing visitor requirements, particularly for parking and access. In the case of the Bowes Museum, the landscape was a formal park created at the same time as the construction of the museum, whereas in a place such as the Ironbridge Gorge, that landscape might be considered to extend well beyond the bounds of the museum, to include all of the industrial remains in the valley. In such cases where the landscape is integral to the significance of the museum, the care and curation of the landscape is as much a curatorial duty as the day-to-day curation of objects. The Conservation Plan can help to define this role, and ensure that policies for the landscape balance policies for the collections or buildings.

Integrated management approaches

Responsibility for the building, for collections, and for associated landscapes often falls to different departments in a large museum, or, for smaller museums, to different local authority sections. This can lead to conflicts, and to varying standards of treatment — policies on conserving objects may, for example, meet higher standards than policies for conserving building fabric. The Conservation Plan should provide an opportunity to bring these areas together and can include robust policies on the importance of a more integrated approach to management. It can be difficult to define where and how far policies in a Conservation Plan should go with regard to management; a useful rule of thumb is that where management issues can be shown to impact directly upon the significance of the site, then a policy is needed — even if that policy points to further development at another time (for example, in a full management review).

Access

The requirement for better physical access to museums is a welcome one, but can be difficult to deliver in the context of a historic building or site. Ramps can intrude into sensitive façades, and the insertion of lifts may damage interiors or floor structures. The understanding of the building and site in the Conservation Plan can provide basic information against which to balance access requirements. It may be that in some areas, physical access would be too damaging to the fabric of the building and therefore alternative forms of intellectual access could be provided. Again, such issues are best debated within a creative overview of the whole site rather than remaining focused on, for example, the front portico. It is essential that any access review is linked to policies in the Conservation Plan and makes use of the data collected for the Plan.

Space planning

Visitors, collections conservation, toilets, and catering needs can all create new demands, which a historic building was never designed to accommodate. Equally, the amount of space required for storage is becoming an increasing problem as museums try to accommodate changing displays as well as the need for access to collections for the purpose of research. The process of understanding the building and aspects of its significance as part of the Conservation Plan can create baseline information against which to explore areas of flexibility and contentious issues such as new build. Space planning is best done within the context of the whole building — indeed the whole site.

Historic sites with collections

Many of the same issues that have been set out here arise at historic properties which include collections that either belong with the building or have been acquired subsequently. Similar issues relating to environmental conditions, security, storage, visitor services, education, and access will arise.

Preparing Conservation Plans for museums

Most museum Conservation Plans have been prepared by firms of architects with experience in historic buildings and Conservation Planning, but all have involved very close working and regular reviews with curatorial and site staff. Indeed, much of the value of the process comes from the way in which it provides staff with an opportunity to discuss issues that extend beyond their own immediate areas of responsibility. The specialist curatorial knowledge of staff will be particularly important in the preparation of the Plan and will not be available outside the museum, so in choosing a consultant it is probably best to approach firms with skills that complement the in-house team.

Conclusion

It is not an easy matter to reconcile the different demands and degrees of significance of buildings, collections, and their sites. Although museums are in many ways already in the forefront of Conservation Planning, through their care and documentation of collections, best curatorial practice is less often extended to associated sites. Yet it is not a great leap of imagination to treat the building or landscape as the largest object in a collection, and to accord it the same degree of care as one might a fine painting. The same ethical concerns over restoration, framing, and hanging will arise, but the canvas over which these issues are debated is a very much wider one. The experience of collections care has much to teach those more used to buildings or landscapes, and the integration of collections management into the Conservation Planning process can only benefit the process overall.

Conservation Plans for Landscapes and Gardens

Paul Walshe, National Heritage Adviser, Countryside Commission

The Countryside Commission very much welcomes both the advice on Conservation Plans recently published by the Heritage Lottery Fund (HLF) and its intention to make the preparation of a Conservation Plan a condition of financial assistance. The introduction to the guidance notes just issued by the HLF (Heritage Lottery Fund 1998) says: 'Sites important for their natural heritage require Land Management Plans which also contain information on the significance of a site and the policies needed to safeguard that significance. Separate guidance on Land Management Plans is published by the countryside agencies'. Both the Countryside Commission and the other government and non-government organisations working in the countryside have published guidelines on the preparation of Management Plans, and a further publication entitled *Site Management Planning: a guide* will be published by the Countryside Commission later this year (Countryside Commission 1998).

This paper discusses the use of Management Plans for landscapes, parks, and gardens. The Countryside Commission has used Management Plans as the medium for understanding the significance of our historic parks and gardens, and for planning their repair, restoration, and future, since the organisation came into being in 1968 out of the old National Parks Commission.

One of its first concerns was the establishment of country parks that would give people an unfettered experience of countryside near to where they lived. These first parks were often in historic parks and gardens, and the Management Plan not only had to restore the parkland and the intentions of its creators but also provide for substantial public access in a way that would ensure that even though people visited in large numbers they could still appreciate and enjoy these landscapes as their original designers had intended. Indeed, in the seventeenth, eighteenth, and nineteenth centuries, their designers had often designed for the general public — Humphrey Repton at Sheringham in Norfolk, and the Hill family at Hawkstone in Shropshire, for example.

This start was continued and stimulated by the losses caused by Dutch Elm Disease in the late 1960s and early 1970s, which resulted in the destruction of many avenues of elms, and by the severe drought of 1976, which killed the peripheral belts of ageing, shallow-rooted trees such as beech. Blenheim, a Grade I historic landscape at Woodstock, and a World Heritage Site, is one such example, losing both its elm avenues and its peripheral belts of trees. A comprehensive Management Plan was produced for Blenheim with a long-term programme of implementation, and each year the Commission helps the estate put into place the next stage.

The end of the 1970s witnessed an increased interest in parks and gardens; a register of parks and gardens of special historic interest was started by English Heritage (then the Historic Buildings Council) under the guidance of Dame Jennifer Jenkins, followed by the other countries of the United Kingdom. The National Trust and the National Trust for Scotland also began to produce Management Plans for the parks and gardens in their ownership, starting with Stourhead, in Wiltshire, in 1978.

The National Heritage Memorial Fund (NHMF), which now incorporates the Heritage Lottery Fund, was set up in 1980 and immediately threw its weight behind Management Plans, requiring their production as a condition of its support. Painshill Park in Surrey provides a suitable example of this approach. Here, Elm Bridge Borough Council, greatly to its credit, purchased the much decayed and overgrown park — a masterpiece of the 1740s created by Charles Hamilton. The NHMF grant-aided the restoration of the park but made it conditional on an agreed Management Plan, which it funded as well.

The NHMF also used its resources to fund the restoration of parks and gardens in the ownership of local authorities and charitable trusts — and the Management Plans underpinning those restorations — which were devastated by the hurricane of October 1987 (affecting the south east, London, and East Anglia) and the storms that hit the West Country and South Wales in January and February 1990. The Fund met the shortfall needed to restore such outstanding historic parks and gardens as those at Petworth and Arundel (in Sussex), Chevening (Kent), Borde Hill, and Dean Park amongst others. At the same time, the government funded the Countryside Commission to set up Task Force Trees with the intention not simply of repairing the damage and replanting the trees within our historic parks and gardens but also of repairing the damage caused by these storms to trees in urban parks, squares, and streets.

Many of the landscape planting schemes initiated in the eighteenth century have only reached maturity in the twentieth century, which in itself raises questions about the management and renewal of this resource

In all this work, there was the temptation simply to replace what was lost but we insisted on the production of comprehensive, historically based Management Plans to guide restoration and to ensure either that we really did want to replant like for like, exactly as it was before, or to ascertain whether there was now the opportunity to correct past mistakes and to return to original decisions about the landscape design. Indeed, in his eighteenth-century Red Book — his Management Plan — for the estate at Henham in Suffolk, the home of the 6th Earl of Stradbroke, the landscape designer Humphrey Repton called for a future generation to put in a large lake once the trees that he planted had reached maturity. Two hundred years later, we put in that lake.

I want now to focus my talk on the 327 heritage landscapes in England — landscapes of outstanding scenic, wildlife, historic, cultural, artistic, and architectural importance — mostly private estates — for which I have responsibility within the Commission. This is a portfolio that contains our finest landscapes and amounts to well over one million acres, twice that held by the National Trust. We are charged with maintaining this heritage for the nation and ensuring that people can enjoy and appreciate it. The way we discharge that responsibility is through the Management Plan.

These landscapes have come under our influence through the conditional exemption from inheritance tax of land and property considered to be of outstanding scenic, historic, scientific, artistic, and architectural importance to the nation's heritage. Any changes which could affect the heritage value of these landscapes and estates, any development, whether it requires planning permission or not, whether it obtains planning permission or not, must have the consent of the Commission.

As an invitation to recognise our national heritage, this system of designation goes deeper and wider than any other system we have, as it works both inside and outside our existing designated areas. Importantly, it has the ability to touch the wealth of small landscapes — distinctive local blends of man and nature with a real sense of place and a cultural, aesthetic, and historic value — that are an integral yet largely unrecognised and unprotected part of the nation's heritage.

This scheme allows us to recognise not only outstanding landscapes, no matter where and no matter what size, but also the importance of buildings in those landscapes. Buildings are an integral part of our countryside and can be a crucial ingredient in its beauty. The Commission can recommend capital tax exemption for buildings that contribute to the outstanding scenic or historic qualities of a landscape. They need not be listed, and can be humble farm buildings, farmhouses, cottages, country houses and parkland buildings, temples, follies, grottoes, and eye-catchers. Or they can include estate villages still substantially in the ownership of a single estate.

It also allows us to exempt buildings that may not contribute to the heritage quality of the landscape but are not seriously detrimental to it, such as many of the farm buildings put up in the 1960s and 1970s and, for that matter, in the 1980s and 1990s. In this way we can both ensure that we do not have holes in the landscape and influence the future of these buildings and their successors.

The Management Plan is the means by which we marshall all this information and work with these landscapes and estates; it constitutes the agreement we have with owners and is the means by which we ensure the conservation of the value that these estates have for us as a nation. Many of these estates have in fact been the subject of 'management plans' for over a hundred years.

We maintain the heritage of these superb landscapes in all their complexity, variety, and diversity through everyday routines: repetitive actions, small and large, performed every day or every month, every year, every decade, every hundred years or so. If these tasks, often simple in themselves, are performed, if estates know that they must perform them and can find the means to do so, then the nation's heritage will largely look after itself. Through this stitch-in-time approach, we can best avoid the constant yawing between neglect and restoration so often found.

We are working to conserve what are largely the products of natural systems — dynamic, changing systems, the result of man constantly working with nature — and the product of that relationship constantly shifts through time as the permutations alter. If you want to keep these products, you must manage these systems so that they continue to produce or sustain the value you want in a landscape.

The relevance of this approach for buildings can readily be seen, but it is equally a principle to apply to landscapes of which buildings are a part. Landscapes too are distinctive, and are the consequences of functional and cultural circumstances.

We can often see this more clearly in countries other than our own, with which we are perhaps too familiar. Take the *pays* in France, for example.

The word *pays* is derived from the Gallo-Roman *pagus*, meaning an area with its own identity. The *pays* explain France, indeed, are France. The *pays* explain why the diversity of France is so much more than merely geographical. Every 30 or 40 kilometres brings a change of landscape, of patterns of settlement and farming, of flora, fauna, and livestock, of folklore, custom, and costume, of dialect, and even of language. The farmhouses and rural buildings of France exhibit an extraordinary diversity and variety simply because they are the physical expressions of the relationship between man and nature, which is unique to each *pays*. They have encompassed and given form to the way people chose to live together, to work their land, ply their trades and crafts, and bring up their children. They are the products of local states of technology, local responses to climate, geology, and geography, and local uses of the natural resources of wood and water, soil and sun. To the traveller they signal departure from one *pays* and arrival in another. They also reflect the cultural and historical inheritance of a *pays*, as they have been constructed out of patterns of thinking and ways of seeing and acting, established long ago when people ceased their nomadic existence, settled down, looked about them, and made the most of what they found.

But this special quality that we care so much about will not survive if we pluck it out of the social, economic, and environmental context that gave rise to it: in such a situation it will become a fish out of water. It must be put back into that water to breathe, to live, to grow; to be part of its place, and to continue to contribute to that sense of place.

The Management Plan for the Chatsworth estate in Derbyshire

Most of the typical elements we associate with our landscape are the result of human impact on the natural environment

We are looking for all places, all sites, estates, and farm holdings to have Management Plans as a requirement of all agricultural support systems: the same Management Plan should be used in support of grant-aid whatever its source, whether we are talking about exemption from inheritance tax or the receipt of grants from conservation agencies or the Heritage Lottery Fund. Every owner should have one for his or her property, in the same way that they have deeds to their property.

We want whole-site Management Plans which cover both what is and what is not of conservation value in itself because of the importance of context, of relationships, of the effect of adjoining development and change on what we want to conserve.

There is also the matter of the point of view. The significance of a group of buildings to an architect or an architectural historian could well be quite different to the significance attached to them by those who have grown up with those buildings. For the former, architectural and historical significance is important but for the latter perhaps the memory, the association, the habitual use of buildings may matter more. For them, the smell, the touch, the sound, the silences of buildings and the way these echo in their memory may be of more relevance to their life.

A stone-built village, characteristic of the landscape of the French Alps

The memories and associations that landscapes have for us are important but so too are the memories and associations that landscapes had for others. People in new housing estates are now looking for the ghosts in their landscape. The thread linking them to the past of the landscape in which they now find themselves has been broken, but they are looking to find the broken ends and bring them together again, to restore the link between the past and the future so that the past can flow through to live in the future.

Wherever possible, the Management Plan should encompass the meaning that landscape has for the people who live and work in it. In the case of villages within landscapes, for example, we might produce a Village Design Statement (published advice on this type of document is available from the Countryside Commission). This is prepared in conjunction with the people who live and work within the village and aims to determine the distinctiveness of the village as understood by them and to involve the community in decisions affecting the future of the village. Our present thinking is that Heritage Landscape Management Plans should be prepared to comply with National Heritage Sustainability standards which we are drawing up for all the elements of a Management Plan. Wherever possible these are prepared on the basis of existing guidance such as that recently published by the Forestry Authority (Forestry Authority 1998), and in the similar document for agriculture about to be published by the Ministry of Agriculture, Fisheries and Food.

The local environment needs to be managed in a way that will retain a sense of the past forces that have created its distinctive identity

The landscape — and not land ownership — should of course determine the boundaries of a Management Plan. Too often owners produce Management Plans for what they own when they should cover the original extent of a historic landscape, a zone of influence or the land within a visual watershed. You may not, in the short term, be able to influence this wider landscape but you should determine how you want to relate to it, and how it should relate to your landscape should the opportunity to influence it ever come your way.

To summarise, the Management Plan is about establishing the context within which day-to-day management and development decisions are made. It is a device that allows the owner and manager to look at the totality of what is owned and managed. The Management Plan is a most useful receptacle for holding and defining the management of woods and forests, arable land and permanent pasture, lakes and rivers, game and wildlife, lawns and beds, hedges, walls, and buildings. But it is also, and most importantly, a means of managing the relationship of these elements to each other and to the whole. In handling the detail we are marshalling and moving the mass.

At the detail level, it sets out not only management prescriptions but also the reasoning behind them. This has two values. First, it ensures continuity and consistency. It is a feeling that whilst a landscape may grow and mature, and bend to the winds of history, whilst there is newness and antiquity, there is an unbroken thread of management and upkeep. It is a quality that seems to stand apart from time and is greatly to be prized and conserved. The existence of this quality accounts in part for the shock we suffered as a result of the devastation of the storms of October 1987 and January 1990. It was unbelievable, but the sad yet silver lining to those horrific experiences is that it brought home the value and the mortality of these landscapes.

Second, a Management Plan allows managers to know whether a management prescription is still valid since they will know whether the reasoning and circumstances which gave rise to it still apply. A Management Plan will also define management objectives and prescriptions that are desirable but are blocked by temporary constraints. For example, the Management Plan can determine that a wood should be of broadleaf composition. However, a constraint on achieving this could be the need to allow an existing crop of conifers to reach their optimum yield. Implementation of that part of the Management Plan would thus need to wait for a period of time. Think of Repton and his planning at the end of the eighteenth century for a lake at Henham to be constructed at the end of the twentieth century.

In looking at these landscapes it is clear that nothing stands still. There is always change, with the past moving into the future in directions determined by the laws of nature and the past decisions of man. The present is simply a fleeting opportunity to touch the rudder. But still a good enough opportunity, as we know all too well, for disastrously changing course if we do not have this historical perspective of knowing where our landscape has come from and where it is going.

Gaining this sense of a continuum by exploring the twists and turns of history, which gave us what we have today, is invaluable. Too often land-use and management decisions are made in ignorance of it, simply, if understandably, responding to the needs of the moment so that a sequence of such decisions, each bolting on to the other, can be seen in time to describe an exponential curve away from an original design concept.

Village Design Statements aim to involve communities in the management of their local landscape

The Management Plan allows us to know better what we are doing, to understand better the wider rippling implications of decisions both through history and through all the functional elements and cultural associations that make up our landscape.

A Management Plan must be seeped in time but preparing it gives us time aside, time out. The decision to produce a Management Plan sweeps the mind for a time of the tyranny of the here and now, the day-to-day pressures and demands tugging at our sleeve. It gives us the essential opportunity to stand back and look at what we have, to understand why it is the way it is today, and to plan better where it is we are taking it.

Bringing Teams Together

Jason Wood, Heritage Consultancy Services

Teamwork

The route to success in preparing and implementing a Conservation Plan lies in a genuine commitment of all involved to working together. Teamwork is paramount, both between the client team, the consultant team, and the design team, and within each of the teams themselves. These teams are not necessarily fixed bodies of people. Their composition is never an absolute. Members may move between the teams as leadership changes hands or as issues get passed back and forth. Consequently, the life span of a particular team is unlikely to be a fixed entity. A Conservation Plan team may begin as a 'twinkling in an eye' of the client and might develop when discussions are opened with statutory consultees or funding bodies. When the consultant is appointed, the responsibility is passed over and the project moves on. Once the Conservation Plan is prepared, certain team members may then play their part in the implementation process.

The client team

Preparing the brief

It is important that the stakeholders are brought together to produce a clear statement of the project's aims and objectives, the scale and intensity of the work, and the resources required to realise it. Preparing the brief is in effect the first stage in the consultation process, and so the question of when to engage the consultant team is an issue here. Whatever the scenario, the consultant team will want to clarify the brief before it can crystallise its thoughts into a plan of action.

Human resources

The human resources required on the client side should not be underestimated. A principal point of contact within the client team should be nominated — who, ideally, should be the chief facilitator, decision maker, and influencer. It is important that this individual be on hand to arrange access to information and to the site (during the Conservation Plan Stage I), and to enter into dialogue (during Stage II). It should be understood that the consultant team does not have unlimited resources.

The consultant team

Shared vision

For partnership to work, the consultant team must lock into the collective vision of the client team and a shared understanding of the end product. It is highly desirable that all members of the consultant team should meet representatives of the client team at the pre-contract stage of the commission.

Composition

In deciding the composition of the consultant team, it is necessary to consider which disciplines should be chosen and what roles are envisaged. Most Conservation Plans will benefit from the wide experience and skills of a variety of specialists, including those outside the umbrella of conservation. Such skills are seldom found in individuals or single practices. Selection of the right people with the right attitudes is the key to building a strong team — perhaps people who have already worked well together or who have a track record of working on projects of a similar scale and nature. In any case, the process of preparing a Conservation Plan will help to develop team cohesion, and building new partnerships and creating new relationships will give the project a unique and fresh approach.

Interdisciplinary approach

The team should be informed, flexible, and above all integrated. There should be consensus across the team and each participant should feel involved. Everyone should be on an equal footing, contributing skills to complement those of others. The aim should be to deliver a unified service built on trust.

Multi-disciplinary skills

A multi-disciplinary skills base is fundamental to this approach. To avoid the team becoming too unwieldy, however, the number of individuals should be limited to the necessary range of core skills. Team members should be competent, efficient, committed, and enthusiastic, with the relevant training and experience and the contextual and comparative knowledge of the subject and period. They should display an ability to gather, analyse, and assess evidence, demonstrate levels of significance, and evolve policies — not just to collate material. Honesty and knowing when to ask for help are also important attributes for the team.

Team management

The role of the team manager is to facilitate the multi-disciplinary approach to deliver the interdisciplinary product. It should not be underestimated what this entails. Indeed, perhaps this role should be considered a speciality in its own right.

Leadership

The manager should be of appropriate seniority and possess considerable interpersonal skills to liaise effectively with client team representatives. As well as demonstrating sufficient technical knowledge, the manager should be familiar with the role, responsibility, and potential of each member of the consultant team. As to which of the conservation professions should fulfil the role of the manager, the purist view would perhaps seek to avoid drawing the individual from those who might make up a leadership element of the likely design team. There are advantages to having the manager detached from possible conflicting interests and able to bring a fresh pair of eyes to the project.

Managing client expectations

In order for the manager properly to be equipped for the task in hand, it is desirable for him/her to build a relationship with the client team through courtship and communication, and an understanding of the context of the work.

Courtship

Close liaison is important to build empathy with the client team. The manager should be dynamic and creative, proactive and responsive, and accessible. He/she should offer reassurance, comfort, and motivation at the right pace to ensure client commitment. However, the courtship should not be consummated! The client team will often have high expectations, but when the honeymoon is over, the manager must be prepared on occasions to challenge the client (particularly private-sector clients) in the best interests of the Conservation Plan, and therefore in the client's best interests.

Communication

Maintaining dialogue with the client team helps to keep the initiative and interest going. This may be achieved through regular progress updates and drip-fed information, as well as the more formal reviews at the agreed incremental milestones.

Context

Understanding the client team's needs and the wider picture requires good intelligence and political acuity to establish what issues are exercising the client's mind and how the team will address them to the client's benefit. The manager should also try to establish the client's current and future aspirations and resources (both actual and procurable).

Managing complexity

Complexity comes in two forms — dealing with a mountain of information and dealing with culture clashes. The latter is potentially the most difficult as different disciplines have different perspectives and agenda. It is therefore important for the manager to have a proper understanding of the relative importance of these competing interests and to create a climate for openness and co-operation that will prevail throughout the project. Clear briefing and progressive supervision of the team will help to develop synergies and avoid duplication of effort. All the usual project management rules apply here as in any other complex planning situation. The team should be disciplined and focused and the manager's role is to motivate and empower to maintain continuity and efficiency. Where problems arise, their early identification and highlighting is essential. The manager must be able to handle objections effectively and not be dominated by a single character. He/she should learn to face up to impediments and resolve conflicts, and also shield the client team from any confrontational attitudes.

Managing evolution

Although project management is often a linear process, a Conservation Plan is essentially a research and development exercise and is therefore an iterative, flexible process subject to revision and refinement. Such a situation requires a bespoke approach to planning, timetabling, and monitoring of resources in order to keep to the programme and avoid being diverted from key issues. A staged approach to delivery ensures that the work is fit for the purpose and will ultimately meet the client team's needs. Knowing when to involve the client team is important. Stage I in the Conservation Plan process should be independent, impartial, and try to avoid the politics. Stage II is more of a dialogue where the need for the client team's involvement is more crucial.

Managing delivery

Sound editorial control is necessary to achieve successful delivery. The manager should be single-minded, able to marshal relevant data, and omit inessentials that do not make a contribution to the assessment of significance or the development and implementation of policy. The most critical sections of a Conservation Plan are those dealing with analysis and value. The team members should be encouraged to contribute to the analysis and value decisions rather than abdicating responsibility to the manager. However, at the end of the day, it is the manager who must summon up the will power and imagination to get the thing finished and be brave enough to stop.

Value management

This final section introduces the concept of Value Management (VM) and how this process may facilitate a continuing role for the Conservation Plan team manager in helping to ensure that the Conservation Plan policies are implemented appropriately in the design stage of a project.

Definition

Put simply, Value Management is an approach that aims to establish, at the start of a project, the strategic plan by which the project should develop. It provides a structured framework for discussion to achieve a consensus view, reducing confrontation between team members and leading to more cost-effective solutions. Value Management is based on a practical and workable set of systematic and logical procedures and techniques developed to enhance value through a hierarchical approach to significance-weighted criteria. It thus assists project teams to orchestrate their activities to deliver full value for the client's investment.

Staged approach

The two stages of Value Management are as follows.
    VM1 deals with concept, the concept being to:

- ensure the need for the project is thoroughly analysed before the client is committed;
- establish clear project objectives and ensure that they are understood by all parties;
- identify explicitly the criteria at an early stage;
- provide new insights into possible solutions;
- ensure that the decision-making process is rational and accountable.

VM2 deals with feasibility, and among other things:

- ensures that the outline design proposal is made in accordance with the appropriate criteria;
- verifies that the previously established project objectives are still valid.

Building bridges

Value Management has been developed literally to build bridges (and other major infrastructure works), and has gained credibility in recent years as a mechanism to identify, analyse, and put forward solutions to manage risk. It is now recognised by both government and industry in the United Kingdom as a way of improving the effectiveness of briefing for development projects. Although the use of the term 'value' in Value Management is best not confused with the description of value in the Conservation Plan, it is striking how the preparation and implementation of a Conservation Plan (Stages I and II) mirrors the concept and feasibility process of Value Management (VM1 and VM2).

As a component of the policy for future management, a Conservation Plan could easily form part of the Value Management toolkit (particularly for major developers and other private-sector clients). Value Management, therefore, might be one of the routes by which a Conservation Plan becomes part of the pre-contract element in the management of a project. It follows that Value Management may also be an appropriate mechanism to help build bridges between the consultant team and the design team.

SESSION THREE

CONSERVATION PLANS IN PRACTICE

Chairs: Ingval Maxwell, Historic Scotland
Mike Coupe, English Heritage
Simon Jervis, the National Trust
Gill Chitty, Conservation Consultant

Understanding Sites, Assessing Significance

Chair: Ingval Maxwell, Historic Scotland

Chair

I'd like to open with a short reflection in my role as chairman. When I joined the Ministry of Public Buildings and Works in 1969, I was introduced to the historic buildings repair grant scheme, which operated on the basis of internal partnership. Our historic buildings investigators prepared merit reports, while the ancient monuments architects prepared reports that gave an unbiased view of what the building under consideration required, expressed in terms of the information that the client needed to apply for grants. If necessary, our colleagues in the Ancient Monuments Inspectorate provided advice on the archaeology of the site, while the structural engineers of the Ministry of Public Buildings and Works gave advice on structural aspects. Again, if necessary, our conservation staff would produce an additional report on the conservation requirements of a particular building. There is therefore a certain *déjà vu* in what we are discussing today, and it is good to see that, in many ways, the old process has worked itself through to the formality of Conservation Plans.

Archaeology or Architecture?

Jane Grenville, Department of Archaeology (incorporating the Institute of Advanced Architectural Studies), University of York

There has long been a debate over who is the best person to understand a site — an architect or an archaeologist. The importance of archaeological research in the conservation of historic buildings is a battleground that is beginning to resemble, metaphorically, one of those notorious salients in the First World War — a minute area agonisingly fought over time and time again, the intellectual victory changing hands each time, but the protagonists so exhausted and battered that in the end the purpose of the conflict is lost and it becomes an end in itself. It is a battle of which I am particularly weary myself, since the Institute of Advanced Architectural Studies at the University of York has recently been merged with the Department of Archaeology of which I am a member. The resulting crisis of identity amongst a body of international students to whom association with an archaeology department sent out all the wrong messages to their home countries or sponsoring organisations has generated much heat and, in my mind at least, a certain amount of light, as I hope to show. Before that, however, I would like to comment upon two specifically archaeological contributions to building conservation.

The first is that of technique. Archaeologists trained in the unravelling of stratigraphic sequence in excavation have developed certain ways of looking at buildings and of untangling complicated building sequences. Often this has involved minute recording, and the specification of stone-by-stone drawings is not unusual. These techniques are now widely accepted, as is the view that archaeology is concerned not only with sub-surface deposits and artefacts, but also with the visible material culture of all periods, above and below ground. The building itself must always form the starting point for the drafting of a Conservation Plan, for it is in the fabric that a record of day-to-day decisions taken on site by earlier builders resides. Nevertheless, I suggest that the profession has painted itself into a corner by allowing itself to be identified only in terms of these technical approaches. For, as Paul Drury has noted, and J T Smith argued nearly 10 years ago (Smith 1989), knowledge advances not by the accumulation of more and more facts, but by the posing of better and better questions. I am less concerned, then, with the stale and fruitless debate of whether archaeology or architecture is 'better', than with how interdisciplinary approaches can help us to frame more interesting questions. How, for instance, were those daily decisions of earlier builders made? They were influenced not only by practical factors, but also by social and ideological conditions, which, by patient and careful analysis of the building and its historical context, we may be able to comment upon.

Secondly, archaeologists are particularly at home with the notion of rapid assessment and evaluation of historic significance. The routine of desk-top assessment and field evaluation for sub-surface archaeology was introduced in 1990 by PPG 16, and has bred a generation of professionals who are used to the rapid appraisal of the nature and potential of archaeological remains, by recourse to documentary sources (original documentation and the records of earlier investigations) and to site survey of all types (observation, geophysics, trial trenching). Some of these techniques (most particularly the desk-top documentary trawl) are directly transferable to the study of buildings. Perhaps more critical, however, is the transfer of a mindset: archaeologists are entirely at home with the concept of assessing significance in advance of carrying out conservation works. It is perhaps not surprising that Conservation Plans have been pushed in this country by the archaeological arm of English Heritage. It is not a particular quirk of disciplinary difference that enables archaeologists to see themselves as somehow more competent than architects, architectural historians or conservationists, but simply the result of a habit of mind inculcated by current professional practice, whose genesis I have discussed elsewhere (Grenville 1993), which demands an assessment of significance prior to full-scale work.

This brings me back to the issue of significance, which is central to the process of evaluation, a word at whose very heart lies the concept of value. It is here that an interdisciplinary approach seems to me to be essential, yet as far as I know it is largely within the sphere of academic archaeology that any serious debate about the attribution of value has taken place. Perhaps this is because archaeology, rather like the arts, has tended to be seen as a luxury rather than a necessity in economically straitened times. Archaeologists are therefore accustomed to arguing for the significance of their work for the wider audience. In a paper that has influenced me profoundly, Bill Lipe, a prominent American archaeologist, provided an analytical framework to aid in the assignment of value to the archaeological resource (Lipe 1984). He proposes four categories of value for cultural items: associational, informational, aesthetic, and economic. Associational value is that which a community places on its past for whatever reason — nationalistic, regional identity (or regional chauvinism), local pride, sentimentality, nostalgia. Informational value is that research value that the professional historian (using that term in its broadest sense to embrace all those who study the past) seeks to elucidate, and which has been championed energetically by Martin Carver (Carver

1996). Aesthetic value speaks for itself, yet we remain constantly aware of its subjective and changeable nature. Economic value is represented by the earning power of the cultural item. A historic building may be valuable in its own right as a magnet for cultural tourism (in other words, it may be possible to make money by exploiting the three previous values), but more frequently, it is an unrelated activity contained in the building or the site itself that is economically critical. How many of us have heard a developer dismiss a case for conservation with the words 'it simply doesn't stack up economically'? It is essential that we should be alive to the unspoken assumption here, that in the end all value is subordinate to economic value — conservationists beware!

In working more closely with architectural conservators, as I have done over the last 18 months, I have become more and more convinced of the interdisciplinary nature of this value debate. As an archaeologist trained in the positivist scientific tradition of the 1970s, I have consciously resisted arguments of aesthetic value, yet it is clear that these are critical in any conservation project. Associational value is highly trendy in the contemporary post-modernist theoretical climate of academic archaeology, but it is a matter upon which planners and local architects may be far better placed to comment than archaeologists. Given the techniques of investigation alluded to above, the gathering of informational value may seem to be the most obvious niche for the archaeologist in an interdisciplinary team, but I would argue that the assessment of the significance of information for a wide audience (a critical stage in the development of a Conservation Plan) is a matter for an interdisciplinary team in consultation with the users of the building. Economic value will be well understood by developers, owners, and tenants — it is the job of the Conservation Plan, as I see it, to make the case for associational, informational, and aesthetic value and this can, or at least should, be done only in an interdisciplinary climate. It is not a question of 'Archaeology or Architecture', but rather of 'Archaeology and Architecture'. The contribution of archaeology lies in the technical business of elucidating the constructional history and historical significance of the building, in bringing to that job a professional approach to the business of evaluation, and finally, but no less significantly, in opening the intellectual debate about the definition of *value*.

Beyond Designation — New Approaches to Value and Significance

Martin Cherry, English Heritage

In this talk I want to deal with designations, but I also want to talk about the problems that designations create, in placing us in a kind of mind warp which actually goes against the holistic approach that is at the centre of the evaluation and understanding of sites. I then want to talk about precisely whose values are being reflected in the appraisals and evaluations that we make when carrying out Conservation Plans. Thirdly, moving on from this, I want to talk more about the involvement of the general public outside of the professional expert world and ask the question: should we really worry about opening up the process?

There are problems with designations and this is not surprising given the history of the three main designation processes that we use today in the conservation of historic buildings and archaeological sites: scheduling, listing, and conservation-area appraisals.

Scheduling deals with archaeological sites that basically have no function or viable use for our time. For long, this category has included all sorts of ruins and archaeological deposits of national importance, but now, coming more and more into the equation, is the question: are these sustainable as unoccupied or unviable sites? Listing involves a completely different statutory process. Town and country planning legislation is concerned with identifying buildings of special interest, which probably have some viable use either now or in the future, which will keep them occupied and in use. And finally, late in the day and late in the United Kingdom by comparison with much of Europe, is the conservation area legislation, which, for the first time, looks at a resource in a holistic way. It is ironic that this is the weakest of all the conservation tools that we have, and weaker now than it ever was post-Shimizu.

Listing, which is the area I know best, is bedevilled by this singularity of approach. For many of the years in which listing developed, from the 1940s right up to the 1980s, it had an old-fashioned museum mentality to it. Buildings were looked at in isolation as if they were museum artefacts. The context was not fully realised and now, when the context is more fully appreciated, the law of listing does not allow us to fulfil the potential. Too much is expected from this legislation, which simply cannot be delivered.

A further problem with all these designations is what's left out. Once you draw a line around something, or once you list something as Grade II, it somehow undervalues the undesignated. We have to live in the real world where we must have full protection, but the singular approach means that we start excluding and belittling the things that are left out. There is a subjectivity that runs right the way through all our designation processes from which it is cowardly to run away, however objective modern scheduling and listing tries to be. You can never run away from the fact that it is a judgement, our professional judgement.

But whose values are we actually talking about? My internationally significant, technologically innovative building is someone else's tat. A building that I, as a professional, value very little — one of those tradable assets in sustainability terms — is your cherished local scene. So exactly how do we bring other people into the equation? How can we be certain that our professional values, which we will defend to the hilt, are the only values that need to be taken into account?

If Conservation Plans and the conservation system as a whole is going to be meaningful and effective, then it has got to take other people's values into account.

I therefore want to consider the wider involvement of people who have other sets of values to those in the conservation world. James Semple Kerr adumbrated the essential qualities that all Conservation Plans must have: they must be intelligible; they must be readable; they must have simple pieces of information, such as photographs, next to the appropriate section of text. But he also said that in order to get something done in three months, it is best done by one person or by a very small team. Within this timescale and framework, how can you meaningfully involve those people who also have ownership of the assets that you are trying to assess and appraise?

Bringing people into that process inevitably means extending it to the public at large, at least to those parts of the public that have some form of interest or ownership. It becomes something of a consultation exercise, a team exercise. It is a dialogue and I think the essential fact that you have to have a Conservation Plan before you move on to development means that you have to bring people in at the point of the appraisal of the resource. You can't wait until the development stage before bringing all the other players into the framework.

In 20 years' time, will historians ask: why did Conservation Plans become an issue in the late 1990s? When we look back to the last 10 years of the twentieth century, we will see a sea change in the whole planning system. There will be a move away from designations and controls and movement towards the involvement and persuasion of the public, saying that not only does the public have a shared interest in sustaining the built and archaeological environment, but it also has a pivotal interest and involvement in determining their value and significance.

Should we be frightened of this process? Underlying our tendency not to go out to the public at large is, I think, a certain fear of whether we should actually bring the public into the process more fully.

I would like now to turn to some specific examples where we have involved the general public in the conservation process. Alexander Fleming House, in Lambeth, London, is not one of England's finest post-war listed buildings, although we very much wanted it to be. The proposal to include it in our listings was turned down by the Secretary of State. At the time, it was a building that was loathed, derided, and mocked, but it is a building that I have learned to admire. For many years known as an empty scar in an inhumane landscape, in an extraordinary way, public opinion has, however, come round to thinking rather differently about it. After having been built as a speculative office block, it became first a government office and then fell into semi-dereliction. Today it is in the process of being converted into housing units and all the apartments have been taken up with extraordinary rapidity. Alexander Fleming House is thus an example of a building that was once demonised and is now a place where people actually want to live. It is also a place where the economics has come round in favour of its continued use. There is a meeting of public opinion and economics in favour of conservation.

The Lower Precinct in Coventry was the first pedestrian precinct to be built after the war and is one of the earliest and most significant in Europe. At the time of our involvement in its future, it was run down and unloved, dominated by a building which is now a burger bar — and we all know what the press made of that: 'Oh, you silly burgers!' But this is an instance where we at English Heritage challenged this kind of response

Alexander Fleming House in London is an example of a once-derided building that has become a desirable residential development

from the local media. It was August, the silly season, when these sorts of stories run, and we said: 'why not ask your readers what they think?' I must admit that it was an unscientific poll, but considering that the planners, the newspaper, and those officially involved with this particular building not only said it was a run-down building but also ran it down, it was extremely interesting that the response we received through the press was much more appreciative than you might have expected. In fact, the whole way in which conservation has been treated by the local newspaper and the media generally in the West Midlands and in Coventry is much more positive to the post-war heritage of Coventry, which is, of course, one of its key phases in terms of its architecture and planning.

My final site is very curious, problematic, and challenging. The gunpowder factory site at Waltham Abbey in Essex is an extraordinary, and, in public terms, unknown site. Although the people of Waltham Abbey obviously knew it was there, very little was known about what survived. Indeed, when English Heritage and the Royal Commission on the Historical Monuments of England (RCHME) first went there, we did not know what to make of it either. It was a mysterious site, with many buildings and structures that were unintelligible, and a huge amount of research was needed to make sense of it.

A Conservation Plan was required in order to understand the nature, function, and vulnerability of these buildings, and the problems of sustainability. Now it is designated to the hilt. Almost the whole of the top part of the site is a Site of Special Scientific Interest (SSSI) and a significant area is also a scheduled monument. It has a group of highly significant listed buildings, including some of Grade I status. The entire site is a conservation area, with all sorts of planning constraints attached to it.

This story illustrates the way in which the public was involved in the appraisal process. Jason Wood brought out the importance of consultation at the appraisal stage as well as at the developmental stage. These two processes had to be done together at Waltham Abbey, which is not normally the way you would go about it. Jason also pointed out the importance of the role of facilitator, and I'm glad to say that we have the facilitator of this project here today, in the audience. Dan Bone of Civix played a key role in moving the process from the appraisal point through the development stage to its eventual success as a project that won funding of £9 million from the Heritage Lottery Fund and is now well on the way to being developed as a museum and resource centre.

The key to the success of this particular project lies in understanding the resource of the site concerned, which was achieved initially through the first-class research and analysis carried out by the Royal Commission. Getting all the players around a table on a regular basis, talking to each other, understanding each other's agendas and priorities, and the pressures they were under, helped to move this project to a successful conclusion. Not only have we extraordinary archaeological remains, which are probably unique in Europe, but the naturalists have made equally significant discoveries, from herons and saxifrages to the only surviving habitat in Essex for the smaller brown common vole!

All these competing interests needed to be moderated and facilitated and the key to moving from a Conservation Plan, through Development and Management Plans to success lies not just in the quality of the appraisal or of the development project, but also in the effectiveness with which all those who are involved in producing a successful conclusion work together.

John Preston, Cambridge City Council

The guidance we've been given concerns Conservation Plans for historic places. It doesn't refer, or at least I haven't registered it as referring, to the portable heritage at all. Can Conservation Plans include portable heritage and to what extent is the holistic view going to be genuine?

Kate Clark, English Heritage

Conservation Plans can include what you want them to include. The aim was to try to bring everything together so there is no reason why objects cannot be considered in the same way that ecological issues, for example, can be brought into the equation. The methodology behind Conservation Plans has been designed to be as broad as possible.

David Heath, English Heritage

One of the great advantages of the process of producing a Conservation Plan is that we can get out and talk to people about why a building is particularly significant. This could help us to explain that statutory designation is not just about the front elevation, but rather that it is the whole building that is important. An assessment process can help to inform people as to why we take this position.

My second comment goes back to Jane Grenville's point that archaeology does not stop at the ground. This may well be true, but there are many archaeologists who believe that it does! And there are also archaeologists who believe that if it does get above ground level, then it certainly stops at the primary appearance and does not extend to what subsequently happens to the building. Again, through the assessment process you should be able to help people to understand the cultural significance of the whole site.

Paul Simons, Bath Spa Project

With regard to who the Conservation Plan is for, I would like to quote a recent example from Bath. We are redeveloping the eighteenth-century spa complex, in the middle of a World Heritage Site. We carried out extensive consultation, which has been material in persuading the Millennium Commission to allocate Lottery funding of £7 million.

Essentially, we are restoring five historic buildings, putting most of them to new uses, while Nicholas Grimshaw is designing a new building to be constructed next door to these Grade II and II★ buildings. In a place like Bath, everyone has an opinion about what should be done to the city. Indeed, most people hate anything new and try to stop most forms of development. But the consultation exercise carried out as part of the Conservation Plan process produced a most remarkable and unexpected result: the conclusion that most people did not really care what the new development was going to look like because, above all else, they wanted their spa back. The point I am trying to make is that the Plan should be used for consultation, which should be as wide as it possibly can be, with the involvement of all potential stakeholders.

Chair

I think this emphasises the point that Paul Walshe made yesterday about significance encompassing both the professional assessment and the individual's experience.

Richard Morris, Council for British Archaeology

We were asked whether the guidance relates to standard national designations. One answer is that it does not. That could be a blessing, taking the point made by Jane Grenville that despite what we are saying, what we are doing in many respects reflects a schism between the areas of archaeology and architecture. Small wonder, when we've got PPG 16 to guide us on how we deal with archaeology and PPG 15, which looks at listed buildings. We are dealing with different legislation with different pedigrees, all things that have become institutionalised and are part of the apparatus that we now have to use to deal with conservation issues. The advantage of the Conservation Plan, and of occasions such as this one, is that we can ignore or dissolve these partitions, and gradually come to see an assimilated form of designation that reflects this intellectual unity.

Oran Campbell, Oran Campbell Architecture

I think one of the most valuable things that has come to us from Australia is the use of the word 'place' instead of 'building' or 'site', and the phrase 'cultural significance'. Our legislation emphasises the idea of listed buildings as being of architectural and historical importance. If we look at the concept of cultural significance on the other hand, the whole debate over whether the architect or the archaeologist should lead the process becomes irrelevant.

It also allows us to take into account the atmosphere of a place, which I think is of great importance, having looked after ancient monuments for English Heritage for 10 years and seen the atmosphere of ruined castles and Roman amphitheatres disappear as sites are consolidated, tidied up, and opened to the public. I used to have to fight tooth and nail to prevent sites from being covered in notices, the grass being cut, and the undergrowth cleared. It is better that people be allowed to interpret and understand it for themselves, as if it were their own discovery, rather than making it look as if some bureaucrat has imposed his will upon it.

Henry Owen-John, English Heritage

I would like to come back to the issue of public consultation. I think that we often use the wrong terminology, because what we are looking for is public *participation* in the process. We should not go out to people once ideas have become fairly firmly fixed in a Conservation Plan that has already been partially developed; we need to work out how to draw in local views to feed the process.

One of the exercises that I'm involved with at the moment is called the Countryside Exchange Programme, which brings together professionals from North America and Britain from different disciplines. What normally happens is that four people from North America and four from Britain address a real-life case study for a week and report back to the local community with their conclusions. One of the themes that emerges over and over again from this exercise is that the North Americans are amazed by the strength of our legislative provision, but appalled by our inability to find and draw in members of the public with any kind of community vision. If we are looking for active participation from members of local communities, we can learn from North America. When American professionals come over here, they slot into the facilitating process as if by second nature. They manage to draw out people's views very expertly, without dictating what they are, and very often, as in the experience of Bath, they produce a surprising answer. This answer may be the one we all want, and through this process we are able to close the gulf between professionals and the community.

Chair

I would like now to address the issue of how to avoid standardisation, which is a concern of James Semple Kerr.

James Semple Kerr, Conservation Consultant

I would like to distinguish between the listing and designation process and the Conservation Plan. The listing process obviously puts up with standardised approaches, but the Conservation Plan does not have to. It depends very much on the use of the English language. And as your understanding of a particular place progresses, you then know what questions to ask in relation to assessing significance. It is not until you are some way down the track that you will get the right questions. Thus, you can start by using the checklists and techniques that are in this guide. There is really no problem at all with that approach — you make up your own questions when you start to understand the place. You can then create a succinct, non-repetitive type of statement of significance; if it is a development site, you progress to hierarchies or levels of significance, and it works out fairly well.

Delegate

The Heritage Lottery Fund application system *is* competitive. You need to compete with all the other applications to secure a grant. Every Conservation Plan that is included with an application will naturally hype up the significance of what is proposed. Plans will end up being treated in the same way as the feasibility studies funded a few months ago where every consultant said this is the greatest project since sliced bread!

James Semple Kerr, Conservation Consultant

You've just stolen our thunder for this afternoon! The answer is yes, that will happen, particularly when people are getting into a Conservation Plan area for the first time. As they get to understand the place, they think it is marvellous and they always overestimate its value, its significance or whatever you like to call it, and so this will happen. But it is up to you lot to do something about it. Keep it under control, perhaps by peer pressure.

James Simpson, Simpson & Brown Architects

We are already hyping everything up, as professionals, and the idea that we are somehow going to get objective assessments simply won't work.

Susan MacDonald, English Heritage

It may well be true that everybody beefs up their statements of significance so that they can get their heritage grant, but I think that shows a misunderstanding of what a Conservation Plan is. A Conservation Plan is not about making your building seem the most important one. It is about making sure that the proposals for work are compatible with the conservation policies that are being developed from the statement of significance. I think this is a very positive step that the Heritage Lottery Fund has initiated. If you are inundated with proposals how else can somebody assess, in a short space of time, whether the proposals are actually compatible with the building and not detrimental?

Chair

What is the technique that is most appropriate to understanding the significance of our site? Yesterday people said that flexibility was important, but Paul Drury warned us of the consequence of delving too much into facts. How do we balance this out?

Donald Hankey, Gilmore Hankey Kirke

I am concerned that significance and value is really based on human perception and is intensely different according to who is looking at it. One thing we understand least about, I believe, is our own human value systems. Do we have a language for expressing them?

I think 'value' is a human concept, which relates to our perception about everyday life. Understanding human values in that continuum of anthropological and psychological perceptions is an area of knowledge that we have not begun to address, and I think to some degree relates to the muddle that we have in thinking about it here.

Jane Grenville, University of York

I agree with that. The issue of value and of significance is highly relative and one of the things that I am most concerned with at the moment is the collapse of history generally into hyper-relativism. There is a point at which hyper-relativism can lead to a completely amoral approach to a view of history. On the other hand, relativism should not be confused with pluralism; these are two entirely different things and one of the problems we have is that we tend not to take a very pluralist approach.

Martin Lowe wrote an essay about flats in Sheffield. One of the responses to the furore, similar to the one that Martin Cherry was talking about in the case of the Goldfinger building [Alexander Fleming House], was that a number of people who lived in those flats started to say that they were not so bad after all, that they quite liked them in fact. One of the interesting things to come out of that debate is the idea of reflexivity. It is not just us saying, 'this is good; you must understand that it's good; we know best; we're telling you that it's good'. There is another approach in which we can say, 'we think it's quite good; don't you think you can find something good about it?'. People may then start saying, 'yes, actually we could; it is quite interesting and we do like this'.

It is a question of finding out how these different opinions — what architects think, what archaeologists think, what developers think — bounce off and modify one another. That is an essential part of what we should do, whether you characterise it as a Conservation Plan or simply as part of a development process.

One essay that a student has just written for me dealt with the question: 'What do you consider to be the major developments of twentieth-century architecture?' I was expecting to read about specialist buildings and high rises, but I got an answer that suggested that the past is something that we consciously involve in our thinking about the future. This seems to be important — the heritage is not just some kind of offbeat subject that we as professional architects and archaeologists deal with. It has become incorporated into the way in which people think about how they want their towns and villages to look, what they think the countryside is there for. We must think in terms of that pluralistic approach.

Defining Issues and Policies

Chair: Mike Coupe, English Heritage

Making Conservation Work in an Ecclesiastical Framework

Richard Gem, Cathedrals Fabric Commission for England

St Mary's, Kempley, Gloucestershire, which has just been shown to have the earliest scientifically dated church roof in England (1114–44) and a door of the same date

The Church of England is responsible for some 16,000 buildings. Around 12,000 of these are listed as of special architectural and historic interest, and 30% of all nationally listed Grade I buildings are Church of England parish churches. Church buildings in use may *not* be scheduled, although separate monuments in or under churchyards may be. And the Church of England is currently exploring how a more detailed inventory and assessment of all its heritage assets could be achieved.

Over recent years the Church has been spending well over £100 million per annum on the maintenance, repair, and running of its buildings. Following a recent survey, we have predicted that the expenditure required for listed parish church repairs alone, over the next quinquennium, is likely to run at around £90 million per annum. Towards the repair of its Grade I and II* historic buildings, the Church currently receives £12.8 million per annum from English Heritage, to which can be added occasional grants from the National Lottery funds and from various charities. However, the Church also pays the government more than £16 million a year in VAT, as a tax upon the repair of its buildings. Church people are hammering away at this particular inequity.

The bulk of the funds needed for repairs are therefore raised by voluntary effort at the local level. There is no central church authority responsible for repairs; it is essentially a community-based exercise.

Control over demolitions and alterations of parish churches has, since the thirteenth century, been exercised through the faculty jurisdiction of the Church courts — the first conservation legislation in this country by many centuries. Unlike secular control, this extends to the contents of buildings as well as to their fabric. Also, it extends to all buildings, and not just a selected sample deemed to be worthy of conservation.

Since 1913 the faculty jurisdiction has been progressively updated to take account of developments in public perceptions of conservation, and to respond to corresponding changes in the secular historic buildings and ancient monuments legislation. The relevant legislation currently in force for Church of England buildings is the Care of Cathedrals Measure (1990), the Care of Churches and Faculty Jurisdiction Measure (1991), and the Pastoral Measure (1983). We should also note that the Church of England pioneered the system of quinquennial inspection of its buildings, beginning with the Inspection of Churches Measure in 1955.

I would like to turn to the more specific issue of how Conservation Plans might work within this context. The study of church buildings, to understand their significance, has had a continuous history since the eighteenth century — from Walpole and Rickman, through Willis and Hope, to Pevsner, and to today's scholars, who try to combine architectural history and archaeology in a seamless discipline.

The Heritage Lottery Fund's current guidance note helpfully states that Conservation Plans should be 'primarily a tool for the owners or managers of heritage assets'. For the Church of England, therefore, the issue is this: if Conservation Plans are now to be regarded as integral to the proper management of heritage sites (and not merely as a hurdle for applicants to the HLF), how can or should the Church respond to make Conservation Plans part of its own agenda?

There are a number of inter-related steps that are necessary. First, those with the responsibility for forming the Church's policy on conservation matters need to attain a consensus view: both that Conservation Plans are desirable as a matter of principle, and that a format for them, relevant to the particular Church context, can be developed. Secondly, those with the potential responsibility for commissioning and funding Conservation Plans must be persuaded of their utility, relevance, and value for money.

These matters will require a dialogue within the Church and between the Church and other bodies such as English Heritage and the HLF, and I hope that that process is now beginning, following the publication of the guidelines.

From the general context and process I want to turn to a small number of particular issues that we, for our part, have identified so far. These will be drawn essentially from the cathedral context, where the discussion has been initiated, but will also be relevant in some cases to parish churches. I would ask you to remember that some parish churches are of cathedral-like scale, but without the administrative or financial resources of cathedrals.

Cathedrals and churches in use are very different from monuments such as castles, ruined abbeys, or prehistoric burial mounds, in that they continue to serve the purpose for which they were originally built — as centres of Christian worship and mission. This functional, community aspect is part of the significance of these sites, and one that has shown a remarkable continuity for up to 1400 years. It is summed up in the concept of the 'cathedral foundation' (analogous, for example, to collegiate foundations, which are an integrated entity, made up of scholars, of learning, and of buildings). Equally, we must take into account the heritage and importance of the Church's musical and choral tradition within the performing arts. Thus, a Church Conservation Plan may have a number of different aspects to a Conservation Plan for some other types of site.

But the very variety of the heritage significance of cathedrals raises a problem, since a Conservation Plan (in the HLF's guidance) 'should cover every aspect of heritage merit'. So, in addition to those human aspects I have already identified, a cathedral Conservation Plan would need to embrace:

Ely Cathedral: existing staff and professional advisers often have a great deal of knowledge about a site that is invaluable to the Conservation Planning process

- the architectural-historical significance of all phases of the buildings in all phases of their development;
- the archaeological significance of the site;
- the art-historical significance of all paintings, sculptures, glass, memorials, furnishings, treasures, textiles, etc;
- the significance of the library and archives;
- the significance of the churchyard;
- the natural-historical and landscape significance of the close;
- the geological significance of historic building materials, and so forth.

To identify this significance would be one thing if all the facts were well established. But they are not. A considerable volume of research in some cases would be required if the Conservation Plan were not merely to regurgitate accepted, but often erroneous, opinions.

It is my view that the achievement of a comprehensive and authoritative Conservation Plan for a cathedral should be a process taking perhaps several years of work. What would be achievable in the short term might be an outline Conservation Plan identifying the various areas of heritage significance, summarising what is reliably known on current evidence, and pointing to areas of necessary further research. Implementation would then be phased and would require appropriate time and resources. I should say that I do not see this research as being incorporated into the concise Conservation Plan itself, but as providing the 'appendix' element from which the Conservation Plan itself is drawn.

The required resources for this exercise are of both finance and availability of skills and I have to say that frankly I do not have confidence in more than a small number of people with the right expertise to advance the work.

In one area, that of archaeology, my Commission has been trying, over the past few years, to advance the preparation of strategic assessments of the archaeological significance of cathedral closes. One or two are under way or under discussion, with the considerable help of English Heritage, and these are complex and costly exercises. But it seems to me that such 'appendices' will be essential to the validity of Conservation Plans.

If Conservation Plans are to be widely accepted, there will need to be a process for validating draft plans to ensure their quality. In principle, this is something that could be put in hand within the Church system, through the existing structures of the Cathedrals Fabric Commission and local Fabric Advisory Committees in the case of cathedrals, and the Council for the Care of Churches and Diocesan Advisory Committees in the case of parish churches.

Finally, it is envisaged that Conservation Plans would be subject to continuing review. Within the Church's context, this would most advantageously take place as a five-yearly review, so that it kept in step with (while remaining distinct from) other aspects of planning on a quinquennial basis.

To conclude, some of those involved in the consideration of Conservation Plans from the Church's point of view believe that, whereas the HLF guidance provides a sound and helpful general statement of what Conservation Plans should be like, much more work needs to be done in partnership to produce a more detailed and shared understanding of the right profile of a church Conservation Plan. We look forward to continuing this dialogue over the coming months.

Chair

We have a number of issues to address, in particular, the question of how policies for sites should relate to statutory guidance.

On the question of designations, I would like to remind you that the environmental agencies have been collaborating since 1993 to try to get going some joined-up ideas for looking not just at the heritage, but at all the other aspects of the environment, and that includes the amenity considerations (led by the Countryside Commission) and the natural environment (led by English Nature). We have also now got the Environment Agency on board and are moving forward, as a powerful coalition, trying to characterise the environment in an integrated way.

We are, as usual, ahead of the game, as, indeed, Conservation Plans are perhaps ahead of the game. We have to allow the government time to catch up if we are going to capitalise on the ideas that we are producing.

Oran Campbell, Oran Campbell Architecture

Is this document going to be used as an advocacy document, or as a policy document, or as an objective document? Having worked on environmental impact assessments, I can see how easily they can be used simply to justify the new bridge or road scheme that you are working on. I have also worked on conservation area proposal statements, as they used to be called. I found these to be extremely useful documents. They involve public consultation and help the people living in the area to take pride and interest in their area. It seems to me that that is a more fruitful way to go forward. But I also stand in the field of fire, as an architect dealing with developers, who are risking millions of pounds and need to be reassured that we understand their problems.

James Semple Kerr, Conservation Consultant

It is, of course, a policy document, but you can do other documents for other purposes. I've done a document very recently for the Capitol Theatre in Sydney. This was done after all the decisions had been made, and it was designed to ameliorate the damage, and that's what I have said in the document. It is actually called a Conservation Plan because that's what the client wanted it to be called, but it's perfectly clear, once you read it, that it is actually something else. So, it is a matter for your integrity, as practitioners, to ensure that the funding agency, or English Heritage, or whoever it is, knows what it is getting. In general terms, the Conservation Plan has to be a policy document, it has to be reasonably impartial, and you have to be prepared, if necessary, to say things in it that are unpleasant.

Chair

Can I just ask whose policy document it is? Does it get adopted as a piece of supplementary plan guidance by the local planning authority, or is it simply an upfront undertaking by the owner as to what he will do for his site in the future? Or is it a combination of the two?

James Semple Kerr, Conservation Consultant

In Australia it varies from state to state, but in New South Wales, where I do most of my work, it is usually adopted formally by the New South Wales Heritage Council and local government, etc. So, yes, it does become a formal document.

Chair

The word 'policy' has certain resonances over here, and it relates to the plans and intentions of local authorities.

James Semple Kerr, Conservation Consultant

This is perhaps a different meaning of the word.

Ian Kelly, Heritage Council of New South Wales

I work for the Heritage Council of New South Wales that Jim has been talking about. To answer the earlier question about developers, they know that if a conservation document is endorsed by the Heritage Council, then that is the basis on which the Heritage Council will assess development applications. Any comment about whether a proposal to alter a historic building is good or bad is framed with reference to the policies in the Conservation Plan. Both parties are thus able to have a dialogue on common ground rather than on the basis of what I do or don't like, or what I think is good, bad, or ugly. So it provides an agreed degree of certainty for both the statutory authority and the private owner.

James Edgar, English Heritage

I work in the City of Westminster, where there are 1200 listed building consent applications a year. There are probably another 1000 conservation area applications, so there are in excess of 2000 applications to alter the historic environment in the City of Westminster every year. I'm convinced that Conservation Plans are an excellent idea for the curatorial side for the management of sites, but I am not certain that there is any role in the statutory development control process.

Delegate

English Heritage already has guidelines for the management of listed buildings, produced particularly for the Willis Corroon building [in Ipswich]. On a day-to-day basis I deal with Cambridge colleges, where the managers are taking many, many decisions, some greater in magnitude, some less so, that have an impact on the character and fabric of their important listed buildings. If we had in place some form of Conservation or Management Plan, agreed within the listed building consent system, it could set out what can be done and where you need to come back for further consultation. Above all, it could educate those responsible for commissioning the minor works for each of these buildings. That could be a great improvement, and for me that is probably the greatest single value to take away from this conference.

Richard Gem, Cathedrals Fabric Commission for England

There is a fundamental distinction between owners and developers, that is, between permanent owners of historic sites and a commercial developer who is only a temporary owner. I don't think that we should gear the production of a Conservation Plan to the development process.

Paul Monaghan, Court Service

I represent an owner, a department with a very large estate, quite a large proportion of which is listed. We already run very detailed Management Plans for some of our more important buildings — the Royal Courts of Justice, for instance. We have an ongoing dialogue with English Heritage and other authorities to ensure that we can maintain it in a sensible way. We have operational requirements that dictate that things have to be done quite rapidly. If the statutory process were allowed to take its normal course, it would not fulfil our requirements; we couldn't react quickly enough.

Earlier this week, I attended a meeting in North Yorkshire where a client was concerned about a Grade II* court building. He was worried that 'because it was listed you could do nothing to it'. I had to explain to him that this was not the case. The whole business of assessing significance is extremely relevant to most sensible buyers and building owners because it allows them to understand much more easily exactly what it is that English Heritage and the rest of the conservation lobby want to maintain. It allows them to understand what is relevant about those buildings, and it enables them to plan for the future and maybe keep these buildings in use.

Chair

It seems you are suggesting that there is a direct application for Conservation Plans for public owners who have a duty in stewardship to set an example for the rest of us.

Caroline Wilson, Julian Harrap Architects

Conservation Plans should encourage people to take control of the buildings, the sites, and the artefacts for which they are responsible. They can help to educate owners to take an intelligent and responsible attitude to them and carry out measures that are appropriate.

Chair

Do you think that there is a carry-over here between PPG 16's idea that there is a responsibility on the applicant to assess the impact of a proposal on the environmental resource before they alter it?

Caroline Wilson, Julian Harrap Architects

Levels of investigation and research must be appropriate to what you are planning to do with the place. And since you can never know everything, you must never close your mind and think that you have finished the research, that you have decided everything, and that there is no more to find out.

Delivering Conservation Plans
Chair: Simon Jervis, the National Trust

The Practicalities of Working Together
The Lord Hankey, Gilmore Hankey Kirke

In considering our topic 'The Practicalities of Working Together', my life's experience would suggest that our topic should be 'The Necessities of Working Together'. The work of my company — Gilmore Hankey Kirke (GHK) — is multi-disciplinary and includes architects, planners, conservation specialists, engineers, social scientists, and economists within the group. We take a holistic view of a problem and hope thereby to give a balanced response.

But I fail to see how professionals can get the appropriate answers if they do not work in teams. I challenge anyone to consider whether individually anyone can cope with the wide range of problems to be analysed and solved within historic buildings, which are essentially more complex than new construction. It is a problem of our age that, as professionals, we are all trained in a special area of knowledge; none of us has all the answers, and teamwork is essential.

But consider who are the players? Are they not the building owner, the investor, the professional team of advisers, the contractors, the lawyers, the local authority, the national government, and, of course, politicians? Depending on the scale of the problem, all these parties may need to understand the process of conservation of which Conservation Plans are a part.

There are also the investors, and their response to market pressures. For large conservation and conservation area projects, all of these parties might need to be considered and consulted.

But also very important is the fact that cultural identity itself is under threat as cross-cultural influences permeate every community in the process of globalisation. There is a great potential danger that we might, in defence of our own values, make cross-cultural judgements in our criticisms and observations of other cultural situations in past history and often of contemporary affairs. Such cross-cultural judgements can and do irritate and upset relationships between individuals, creeds, and the communities that support them. A Conservation Plan is essentially justified through its statement of the values and significance attached to the heritage as perceived by the interested sectors of contemporary society. But, as I said earlier today, we are still bad at understanding these human values, and the research and interpretation of these values should be better supported by the social sciences and by cultural anthropology. We do not have the language to express social values as clearly as we should, and much of the intangible social value is related to the spiritual and social value and impact of a place. It is only when we can interpret the heritage in terms of contemporary perceived spiritual values that the public will be more involved, and will itself associate with and 'own' the project. This local support and awareness of values and significance will contribute to the viability of the heritage, whether it is an urban area, an individual building, or even a simple artefact.

Cultural heritage is both tangible in terms of buildings (for example, design, artwork, architecture, structures, and services) and the remains of history, and intangible in terms of customs, moralities, beliefs, and the spirit of the age (for example, social and moral structures, political, legal, and institutional structures, and economic forces). The appropriate interpretation of these factors requires a diverse range of skills and the appropriate medium for the message must relate to the type of visitor and grows out of these values and significance contained within the Conservation Plan. The heritage is given meaning when such interpretation is built on the values of today and is related to the significance and meaning of the past. Values lie not just in those categories expressed in the Venice Charter and the Burra Charter; value also embraces direct and indirect economic and financial benefits, and those values that are built on local social and economic structures and market forces.

In conclusion, I would say that there are many special skills involved in the conservation process and in developing a viable Conservation Plan. It is understandable therefore that no one party can alone take on the complete task. Very large projects will involve a greater range of skills and institutions in the development of an agreed Plan. Very small projects, or artefacts in the hands of a curator, may need fewer people, but will often pass through the same considerations that I have outlined. Any of the necessary skills and persons involved can take the lead in my opinion, but perhaps it is better in projects of reuse and presentation for the creative designers, the architects, and the planners to take the lead.

Delivered to the Tower

Stephen Bond, Tower Environs Scheme

Our built heritage is a resource; a resource that is to be used and enjoyed, managed responsibly, and to be sustained. Conservation is an approach, an attitude of mind, a management strategy not only for the use and change of a historic asset but also for its sustenance.

It is all about the proper management of change in and around historic buildings, respecting the range of values involved. The Conservation Plan helps to define and record the parameters for that proper management. It seeks to determine the balance and full range of values that exist, although I don't mean by that that we should know absolutely everything about the buildings on a site.

At the Tower of London we have produced a Conservation Plan as part of a major scheme of work to transform the urban setting of the Tower. The Conservation Plan addresses the setting of the Tower just as much as the Tower of London itself. The Tower remains the popular jewel it always was, but outside there are no satisfactory facilities, no dignity, no style, no hope! No sense of place. No value management. The Conservation Plan, both for the heritage site itself and its wider environs, provides a platform to reintegrate the Tower with an appropriate urban setting. The Conservation Plan is an evaluation exercise, an assessment of the full range of values pertaining to the site and its true setting.

I do not believe that any one person can produce a Conservation Plan. Working in historic palaces as an intelligent client, I want nothing to do with anyone who says 'I could do all of your Conservation Plan for you': that person is either entirely unaware of what is actually required and involved or damagingly over-confident about their own capabilities.

To have any benefit at all, Conservation Plans need teamwork; we all have skills to bring to the party, but so do many other disciplines outside the conservation world. They may well be deterred by the notion of a Conservation Plan simply by its terminology.

I want to end by making one last point — 'ownership'. Without ownership, the manager of the asset is never going to use the Conservation Plan to manage change, and conservation is all about managing change. There is no point in producing a Plan without ownership, and managers do not ensure ownership merely by commissioning a Plan from a consultant and then detaching themselves. Managers who let others dictate policy for them probably don't care enough about the buildings or understand them properly.

Without ownership, we may end up with a vast number of wasted Plans, and much disillusionment with the process. I have already heard people saying 'oh, we've got to produce a Conservation Plan as another hoop to jump through to get funding or consent'. Every time that is said, that particular Plan is doomed not to be a platform for the satisfactory management of change. That is probably true of a greater percentage of the Plans being produced at the moment than we would care to think about.

Delegate

I think one needs to make the point that all our examples, both yesterday and today, have been of huge projects, where Plans are seen as an enormous burden. The fact that a Plan could be one A4 sheet must not be forgotten. I think that is important to the owner of a small building.

Robert Willis, Dean of Hereford and Legal Fabric Commissioner

As Dean of an old foundation, I would like to say that Hereford Cathedral's history is much older in human terms than any of the building's fabric. And my first responsibility is to the care of that human community. For me, the words 'significance' and 'vulnerability' have first and foremost to be applied to the human community. I need to protect the life of the cathedral organists and masons, singers and librarians, schoolteachers, archivists, and vergers, and to emphasise that heritage resides in the pattern of their lives, in their liturgies, in their scholarship, in their singing. All those things have to be understood by the person who is to come and help develop and manage the change of that heritage, both in stones and in living beings.

Anyone coming into a human foundation like mine is instantly recognised as someone who either does or doesn't understand this. The moment that a Conservation Officer or an architect who doesn't understand arrives and starts speaking, in however friendly a way, to the members of the foundation, you will notice a switch-off. And as they go, there is a sense of sadness that that person has not understood this historic foundation in human terms. The moment that someone comes who does understand, they can say what they like. They can be as brave as they like and they will be recognised as someone who understands the living atmosphere of the foundation. If someone comes to help or to write a Conservation Plan who doesn't understand, then let them write as cleverly as they like: the Plan will be seen as an irritating hurdle on the way to securing funding (which is how many of my colleagues see it now), never to be used again. Let them instead come and live in the human foundation, and hold themselves open to the living atmosphere, not the ghosts of nostalgia, so that the pictures of Wells Cathedral, instead of being empty of people, will have people standing in them! And then what they write will be a real tool for the management of change in a historic and present living community.

Marc Mallam, Blackburn Cathedral

What do I tell my client that the Plan is for, other than the cynical reason — to get a HLF grant?

James Semple Kerr, Conservation Consultant

A Conservation Plan is just to guide the way the site or building should be treated in the future. That's all.

Jane Stancliffe, Heritage Lottery Fund

May I say, on behalf of the Heritage Lottery Fund, that although we have produced these guidelines on Conservation Plans, we do recognise that we have got a long way to go yet. One particular problem is the relationship between the Private Finance Initiative and Conservation Plans. In the case of one recent Grade II* listed building which was a Private Finance Initiative project, the applicant produced an exemplary

Conservation Plan which I think the contractors simply put in the wastepaper basket. This is a problem with which both English Heritage and the Heritage Lottery Fund have had to battle, and we haven't yet found a solution.

John Goom, Architect in private practice

Can I address the potential worry of how the public sector should manage quality? I'm assuming that means the quality of the Conservation Plan. Are we suggesting that these Conservation Plans are going to be approved by somebody and that, having sent a Conservation Plan to the Heritage Lottery Fund and had the Plan approved, the Plan becomes fixed? If so, I think it is a very dangerous document. Conservation Plans must change, they must be able to adapt as we discover more about buildings.

Jack Warshaw, Conservation Architecture & Planning

It has been my experience that you are contacted by a client director, or agent — to say we would like you to agree with a certain proposition that we have in mind for the development of this site or even for its demolition. If I respond that I am very happy to do the appraisal but that you, the client, cannot dictate the answer, I will not get the job. Now there are plenty of people out there assembling teams composed of people who they know are going to give the answers that the client wants, before they start work. This is something we have to guard against.

Henry Owen-John, English Heritage

I would just like to come back to the point that was raised about how rigid the Plans might be during the process of implementation. I would like to draw an analogy with what English Heritage normally does in terms of grant-aid for, in my case, scheduled monuments. Whilst the offer of a grant is based on the statutory consent, it does allow flexibility as works proceed. There is no reason why agreement cannot be reached throughout the implementation so that account can be taken of new information that comes to light. In due course, this may lead to a comprehensive revision of the Conservation Plan or the Management Plan. I would like to think that the risk of inflexibility that was perceived might not be as great as was thought.

James Simpson, Simpson & Brown Architects

I'd like to say something about the question of which professions should take the lead. And I don't want to get into a slanging match between architects and archaeologists. I do want to address the assumption that all architects are necessarily in the development business. There is a long tradition of the family-doctor relationship in architectural practice. The cathedral architect and the church architect are good examples. In the case of a cathedral, there is everything to be said for the cathedral architect, working in close consultation with the cathedral archaeologist, to take the co-ordinating role in drawing up the Conservation Plan.

Marrianne Suhr, Ferguson Mann Architects

If you want a Conservation Plan to be as objective as possible, then surely it has to be carried out by someone who is totally independent of the future development of the site. If it is an advocacy document, on the other hand, then let's just be upfront about it, and not try and disguise it as something else.

Lindsay Cowle, Woodhall Planning and Conservation

We are about to start a Conservation Plan, and we have learnt a few lessons along the way. There is a great diversity within Conservation Plans — they range from Management Plans at one extreme to advocacy documents at the other. The way the Conservation Plan is being used in the Heritage Lottery Fund context tends to be more towards the advocacy end of the spectrum, using the document to justify or examine a scheme that is already on the table.

We're being encouraged to invite views from everyone on a project and then act. In effect, for a planning officer, there is a danger of this process bypassing the statutory procedures. The Conservation Plans that we have prepared recently have been quite prescriptive, with fairly tight proposals as to what physically should or should not be done to a building. When you get down to that level, you've got to be extremely careful that you're not treading on the toes of the people who would normally be involved. If we are the advocates acting in the interests of the promoter, we are not going to go out of our way to approach the Society for the Protection of Ancient Buildings (SPAB) or some amenity society; getting their views will only give ourselves another hurdle. We could end up with a project that has been agreed, but then find that the SPAB objects that the Plan has not gone through the statutory consultation process. Maybe Conservation Plans have got to be adopted by the local authority, as happens in Australia.

Chair

In trying to sum up this debate, I would say that balance is easy when you're stationary but more difficult when you're involved in a dynamic process. I think there are centrifugal and centripetal forces at work in this process. If you try and include too many people, it can act in a centrifugal way; it leads towards that which is ineffectual, depleted, and bland, but it can also be balanced and judicious. On the other hand, there are centripetal forces, such as the desire for picking out what is specific about a place — not all the details but the significant details — and that is obviously the key to understanding the spirit of the place. There can, though, be a downside to that in the form of parochialism, a partial approach, a lack of perspective.

As experienced professionals, even if we're not architects or archaeologists, we can try at least to guard against that and take the long perspective. We're trying to look at the interests of these places and buildings in a way that takes in the interests of the past, the future, and the present. It is obviously an impossible thing to do completely, since values change all the time, but it is our job to try and do that.

A final point about delivery is that James Semple Kerr placed great stress on brevity and lucidity of language. These are obviously very important if the Plan is to communicate at all. But they can be difficult to reconcile with flexibility. What is crisp often also tends to be rigid. I will leave you to ponder that thought.

The Use and Abuse of Conservation Plans

Chair: Gill Chitty, Conservation Consultant

Chair

The discussion has polarised over the last day and a half around the nature, value, and purpose of Conservation Plans. I've been collecting some descriptions over the last 24 hours. They include: 'a practical, sensible tool for owners and managers', 'a discipline', and 'a useful methodology'; more aspirationally, they have been described as: 'an attitude of mind' and 'a theology'; more cynically, they have been called: 'an advocacy document' and 'another hoop to jump through'. So, at one end of the spectrum we've got the Plan as a panacea, a continuous process of informed critical engagement for the management of change. At the other end, fears that it will become some kind of a formulaic, mechanical, and bureaucratic task bolted on to big projects. Either way, it is clearly still a concept that we are not yet comfortable with and that we cannot feel complacent about.

Perhaps this next session, which is very much about brass tacks, will bring the two views closer towards integration. It is called 'Use and Abuse', and the idea is to look at practical ways in which Conservation Plans are actually being adopted and implemented.

Conservation Plans and New Design

Ron German, Stanhope plc

I am going to address you today from the perspective of a Heritage Lottery Fund (HLF) assessor, rather than as the corporate property developer. I will take a quick canter through some of my observations of Conservation Plans in so far as they exist at present on HLF projects.

So, is a Plan required? My answer to that is 'always', which might seem strange in the light of the comments we have heard before. They are a real benefit to those who have to assess large-scale schemes, and they are also a real benefit to the client.

When should a Plan be prepared? Clearly, the best arrangement is for it to be prepared prior to any new work being considered. That is the ideal, although this has its drawbacks, and I will touch on those when we get to some real examples. If we have the Plan as part of the initial process, we can focus on what really is important about the application.

From my own perspective, I worry about two-stage assessment plans, with Conservation Plans being part of the second stage. I feel that it is unrealistic to expect funders and their advisers to devise a scheme, if only up to the concept stage, then switch off, do a Conservation Plan, and then switch back on again. This could be difficult, and certainly time-consuming.

Quite a few Plans have, in effect, been drawn up post-grant-award, especially where the HLF has persuaded the parties involved to draw one up ('insisted', if you prefer that phrase), basically as part of an attempt to start the policy of having them at all. Such post-grant Plans have their uses, particularly where massive schemes are involved, even if they are not as positive and as useful as those drawn up from the outset and available for guiding the initial application.

Who should prepare the Plan? Not the owner or the promoter, in my view, if only because they often do not have the expertise to do the work. Where people are employed who do have the expertise, they often have another job — they might be the director of the museum or opera house concerned, and they face competing demands on their time, so that it is often difficult to get the Plans finished. Sadly, they also come with a mindset that sees Conservation Plans as bringing unwanted complications in terms of time or money, or restrictions on what they want to do. They are often not aware of the kind of benefits that a Plan should provide in showing opportunities for the future and maybe making life easier as they go through the development process.

Maybe it should be an architect. I would say not *the* architect, in any event. We have talked already about the very real danger here of justifying a scheme that already exists. I think it is almost a 'mission impossible' for most architects to try and divorce themselves from the concept they are promoting and at the same time try to be dispassionate about a Conservation Plan.

Neither should it be the historian. Historians quite often put a very narrow focus on to preservation and reinstatement, perhaps tending to ignore the functionality. The reason people have brought these proposals forward is to try and get buildings into use, to make them sustainable in the future, and commercially successful to a degree, points that are not often part of the thinking of a historian.

So we need some wonderful independent person to bridge the gap. How do we find the right new person? That is something we could usefully discuss.

How do we prepare a Conservation Plan? Well, writing a brief is very important. It allows everyone to join in the process very early and gets people focused in on trying to deliver something that is appropriate and the right scale for the particular project. I think it is important to try and bring the widest collection of views into the process, even if it is done unofficially. Somehow or other you have got to bring in all those bodies that are going to be involved in the destiny of this Plan, and involved in the future of the building.

Beyond that, we need to find some mechanisms, based on good examples. I don't think we actually have a mechanism for doing so yet, at least officially. We need to develop examples of Plans that we think are acceptable and deliver the right sort of information. We need to make these available for new people to look at and appreciate.

You have also got to consider who will police the Plan. We would all like to think the client will use the Plan in the right manner. In reality, even if the Plan is adopted positively by a client, they are not always very diligent in spotting when they are diverting from it. The statutory bodies do not actually police the Plans on behalf of the HLF. Maybe it is unrealistic to expect them to do so. What about the funding bodies? They hold the purse strings and are in theory in a powerful position to monitor progress. In reality, they too have difficulty in making sure that things are happening in the right way. I don't think we've got the balance right yet, and I think that the HLF has a problem defining how much resource is spent giving people grants and how much in monitoring the way the grant is expended.

So, some problems, and here are a few more. Perhaps the one that everyone thinks of is cost, but there is more to this than just the cost of drawing up the Plan. Peter Inskip said yesterday that Plans can produce revelations. You will find things out about a building that you probably never thought about before. That is a risk both to your client and to the people who are going to fund it — not knowing what is going to fall out of the sky when this Plan is eventually produced. It might be good news, and it might be not-so-good news. But it is part of the issue that we need to consider from a funding perspective.

Another is functionality. I am talking about things that are actually contrary to the very spirit enshrined in the idea of Conservation Plans, and how you deal with some of the things that the applicants want to do with the buildings, and the ways in which they want to use them. These issues need to be considered, and I am not sure that they are resolved yet in terms of the Conservation Plan.

Perhaps we also need to be explicit about the purpose of the Plan. Are we trying to maintain the status quo? Are we trying to recover something? If we are trying to recover something, let's all be clear about it, so that we all embark on the project with a single mind. I think we sometimes dodge this issue.

My final word is on the issue of whether a Conservation Plan should attempt to define net benefit. In other words, is there a trade-off between what you might want to do to one part of the building and the benefit to the building as a whole and, if so, how do you measure those things?

One Plan Too Many? Conservation in the Planning Framework

Paul Simons, Bath Spa Project and Head of Economic Development and Tourism, Bath

I work for an elected authority. We have 67 politicians who tell us what to do. They represent 172,000 people who have aspirations. We also have thousands of historic buildings. The entire city of Bath is a World Heritage Site and everything is a conservation area, so we have lots of supplementary planning guidance. We produce many other documents about the quality of our urban spaces, and how to design shopfronts in Bath.

We have five major directorates in a unitary authority. I am in one of them, with the planners, the strategic policy, and the built heritage teams. The directorate has a triangle of sustainability. Imagine an equilateral triangle with the word 'Sustainability' in the middle; the top point of the triangle is labelled 'Community', and the bottom two points have 'Environment' and 'Economy'. You cannot divorce any of those issues — and I don't think a Conservation Plan can either.

Some 90% of the projects in our district on historic buildings are funded through private investment. Most of these are small, individual buildings. They do not need a Conservation Plan in my view. With these smaller buildings, what we should have is a simple statement of significance, or whatever you want to call it.

So, there's a reality there. The reality of who is funding buildings and the politicians who want investment in their area. And therefore a Conservation Plan will not be developed for a lot of the projects we are involved in prior to that process starting. Once it does start, I think everybody involved in the process, and I hope the intelligent client as well, will believe in consultation.

We are talking about starting a process that leads from initial research and context seeking to establishing a Conservation Plan; but then that process must clearly continue straight into a more detailed feasibility study and business plan and then going on beyond that into a Management Plan. I see the whole thing as a continuous process and I think we might again be in danger of creating some artificial boundaries.

I was very pleased to hear Simon Cane mentioning user guides or plans yesterday, because I think the other thing we need at the end of the Conservation Planning process, as well as translation into a Management Plan, is to create a practical user plan. After all, who is the Plan intended for? Who are the users, at the end of the day?

Bath is unique because it has the only hot thermal waters in the whole of the British Isles. There are three springs in Bath. One feeds the great public bath, the second spring was a sacred site, and the third spring fed private Roman villas.

In order to bring forward the Spa project we studied a whole quarter of the town producing a conservation area character appraisal order under English Heritage guidelines. This prepared the context within which we wanted to take the project forward.

We proposed to demolish one building while preserving the other listed buildings in the area. The building we plan to demolish is the 1920s swimming-pool. All previous schemes have tried to refurbish that building and that is partly why they have all failed: there is not enough space in it, for an economically viable scheme.

Nicholas Grimshaw's architects are working with Donald Insall on this project. We have a computer model of a stone cube inside and we have wrapped it around with a lot of glazing, which will have heat exchangers, because we want to use the energy in our water.

As water is such a useful part of the architecture of our building, there will be fountains and the sound of water; there will be water textures and water finishes. We might not quite make it go uphill, but we will see what we can do.

Chair

Thank you. The first question that we have been given to focus our discussion is how do we prevent Conservation Plans becoming no more than a *post-hoc* justification for a particular scheme? We have heard fears expressed that such Plans might become no more than an advocacy document for a preconceived scheme. Marc Mallam similarly voiced his concern that, in a very competitive marketplace, the Conservation Plan might become no more than a means of adjudication between the relative merits of projects, to be either publicly or privately funded.

June Taboroff, World Bank

I work for the World Bank, though the word 'bank' is a bit of a misnomer. It is not a real bank so much as a large international development agency. We work in many different sectors and what has been very interesting is to see how we situate cultural heritage work within a larger developmental framework. For at least 10 years it has really been quite marginal, but what we are coming to see, in grappling with this issue, is that it is much more central to development work than we would have originally thought. We are coming to see that it is really central and we have a very articulate president, James Wolfensen, who is a tremendous advocate of cultural heritage.

So how do Conservation Plans sit within this context? I see our role as trying to encourage good practice, remembering that we are dealing with the disadvantaged countries of the world. Many of them do not have the kind of planning framework we have in either the United Kingdom or the United States, and they do not have a cadre of conservation specialists, although in many countries you do have very, very talented people.

Typically, we deal with the ministry of finance, with the department of antiquities or culture, and various other ministries. Many of these countries are so starved of investment and resources that they do not see what the options are or even that there is a chance to set priorities, in terms of both policies and individual projects. Many of our projects begin in odd ways and we often have artificial deadlines and all kinds of targets and hurdles to jump, so things often happen in a reverse way — though we do try (at least in the projects with which I am involved) to encourage Conservation Planning, specifically to have a better understanding of the significance of a place.

I work a lot in the countries of North Africa, which have inherited the French colonial system and where the only buildings that are on any kind of protected list are the ones that were determined by the French. Local people, entrusted with the responsibility of conserving these buildings, may not feel that much connection to the structures on that list. Moreover, the list is often biased towards those built before 1800 or 1850.

There is no acknowledgement of twentieth-century buildings, which in these countries can be very important. In almost no country that I know is there any acknowledgement of cultural landscapes.

At the same time there is often the beginning of an awareness of such issues, so the Conservation Planning process is extremely important in extending the range of cultural heritage and the whole process of the consultation and participation of the community. When you are working in places that are starved of resources, the contribution that a local community can make to any kind of viable planning or maintenance is absolutely critical. Without it, there is no point because World Bank projects typically have a life of five or six years; after that, funding, in theory, ends.

Jean-Marie Teutonico, English Heritage

I have been asked to say a few words about the Getty grant programme, which is funded by the J Paul Getty Foundation, based in California. I have been advising this organisation for a couple of years on grant assessments, especially architectural conservation grants.

The Getty grant programme has always had two categories of grants. One is called Project Preparation Grants, which is what we call the Conservation Plan, and the other is known as Project Implementation. The distinction is important and failure to make it accounts for some of the confusion we have encountered in discussion with applicants.

The first thing you have to do is understand what the object is that you are dealing with, be that a building, a site or whatever, before you can make decisions about the actual intervention — or, indeed, if any intervention is called for. So, in the Getty experience, there are two stages — although sometimes it will fund the preparation process but not the implementation, and sometimes it will fund an implementation process, but only if the proper preparation has already occurred on the project.

As a funding agency, the Getty has been very progressive in saying that if you are going to ask for proper practice, you have to fund it.

Even so, the process is not without its problems: in recent years we have seen preparation proposals costing more and more, and engaging more and more consultants. In a way, there is the danger that they can become an end in themselves instead of a means to an end, and it has started to become something of an industry in the United States. I think the challenge for funding agencies is to promote the practice but at the same time to try to make sure that the pre-project preparation stages are appropriate to the scale of the project's complexities and values.

Nic Durston, Heritage Lottery Fund

I'd like to speak in more detail about two-stage application processes. As an example, one project that I looked at involved a major museum situated in a Grade II* building, set in a park. The application involved the demolition of a Victorian extension to provide better housing and collection care and exhibition space. The museum did not undertake any Conservation Plan thinking. It did not look at the significance of the Grade II* building and, more critically, it did not really consider the significance of the Victorian extension. The sum of £100,000 was spent developing an application to the HLF and, on assessment of that project, our expert advisers agreed that the proposal would lead to significant damage to the building. It is in such contexts that we decided that it would be useful to introduce the two-stage application process.

The two-stage application process is set out in more detail in our application pack. It has been introduced in response to the very considerable amount of time and money that applicants are putting into projects, developing them up to RIBA stage D or E with no surety of what the HLF's position on them will be. Linked to that is an understanding of the various assets involved in projects and of the significance of those assets. The two-stage process will be mandatory for all projects with total costs of over £500,000.

This has to be seen in the context of our new powers to fund a much wider range of projects, such as access and education, the new emphasis on the lottery distributors to focus on people-based, community-based projects, rather than major capital programmes. We will have to reject a higher proportion of applications to the Fund. The two-stage process is therefore a way of trying to help applicants put forward schemes to the HLF and get a much speedier response as to whether we think they are a priority.

We want applicants to look at the issues that a Conservation Plan sets out and demonstrate that they have gone through the thinking that lies behind the key stages articulated in the Conservation Plan document. We recognise that applicants should, ideally, have full Conservation Plans in place. But as this may not always be practicable, projects over £500,000 in value can use the two-stage process. Stage One will be accompanied by a conservation statement, which essentially addresses in an outline form those key elements contained in the Conservation Plan document.

Projects under £500,000 will not be subject to a two-stage process, but we do need to get people to address the key stages contained in the document. The application form has been structured so that people have to demonstrate that they have an understanding of the site and its importance, and that they have made an assessment of its significance and have a conservation policy in place.

Critically, for both the one-stage applications and the first stage of two-stage projects, we will be measuring projects against the Conservation Statement and the key stages that are set out in this document. So it is wrong to look at a scheme in isolation from the thinking that should underpin all good Conservation Planning philosophy.

David Heath, English Heritage

I am head of the cathedrals team and a specific issue for us is that cathedrals were informed last May that they could not apply to the HLF unless they already had a Conservation Plan. We were the only group of applicants to the HLF to be singled out in this way

Who should prepare a Conservation Plan? We, English Heritage, and the Heritage Lottery Fund, have formed no view as to who is the most appropriate person or persons to carry out this. It is for the applicants to demonstrate that they have appropriate consultants on board. We say that because we recognise that there are actually very few people nationally who can do these things. There are a lot of people who have the potential to do them, and we would like to see many more people come forward and try and put Conservation Plan methodology into practice.

Following on from that, our negotiations place considerable emphasis on establishing the brief for the Conservation Plan. Establishing at the outset what the Conservation Plan is going to be about is the most important thing that you can do as an applicant or as an adviser to an applicant. One benefit is that you can use the brief as a consultation document, so that you can tell other people, including English Heritage, the Heritage Lottery Fund, the local planning authority, and the community what it is that you are planning to do before you do it. That way, you get people on board, so that they understand the process before it starts and you can get feedback on that.

The second benefit is that you can't actually start talking about how much the process is going to cost and how long it's going to take until you've decided what it is. And that is why the brief is so important — it addresses those issues to do with how much and how long that are very closely involved in the process.

I would also like to try and clarify, if I may, my understanding of where the HLF stands in regard to grant-aid in Conservation Plans. At the first stage of the HLF process, the idea is to submit a statement of significance and enough information about your project for the HLF Trustees to decide whether they can give you an amber light to move to the next stage. You can also submit, as part of your first-stage application, an outline of project development costs. Preparing a Conservation Plan — a full Conservation Plan in accordance with the meaning in the document that has now been published — can be part of those project development costs.

The opportunity is therefore open for the HLF, after a first-stage application, if it likes the idea of where the project is leading, to offer a grant towards the production of the full Conservation Plan, and other development costs that it may consider to be eligible. Thus, by the time you come back, at the second stage, you should have been through the iterative process that we have been discussing over the last few days. In addition to a Conservation Plan, you should already have the scheme fully worked out, with statutory consents in place after full-scale consultation. In effect, what you get offered after the second stage, if you do get an offer, is something with minimal risk — in other words, it should be quite clear what the project is and how much it is going to cost. That being the case, the monitor role, about which English Heritage and Stanhope clearly share a concern, is going to be minimised, because the big sums of money will be clear, or clearer than is the case now.

Nic Durston, Heritage Lottery Fund

I apologise if this hasn't been made clear in any of the presentations that the HLF has given. The position is exactly as you have described it. Where projects are seen as a priority in the mind of our Trustees, we will consider funding the costs of developing the projects. And that, if applicable, will include the preparation of a full Conservation Plan. But I would like to emphasise that not all of those projects will need the very big leap to the Conservation Statement. Our guidance on where we feel Conservation Plans are needed is set out on the first page of the guidance note [*Conservation Plans for Historic Places*, page 3].

Chair

I think we ought to spend a few minutes discussing the situation in Bath, where 90% of conservation projects are funded by the private sector.

Philip Whitbourn, Secretary, ICOMOS UK

World Heritage Sites have been mentioned several times today. My organisation, ICOMOS, is the official adviser to Unesco on cultural World Heritage Sites and one of our main activities in ICOMOS UK is to help and advise on Management Plans for World Heritage Sites, as mentioned in PPG 15 and encouraged by the government. There isn't one for Bath as far as I know, is there?

Paul Simons, Bath Spa Project

No. People say, 'The place is well protected'. But it's not. We need a wider plan.

Philip Whitbourn, Secretary, ICOMOS UK

We do indeed. I have a good one here for Greenwich and I look forward to the day when there is one for Bath. Pam Alexander, when she opened this conference, expressed a hope that I share, that Conservation Plans will fit in within the context of World Heritage Site Management Plans, so that there is a seamless web.

I am very keen that Management Plans for World Heritage Sites do not go out of date and gather dust on a shelf. They need to be something that the key parties have signed up to and they need to be in a loose-leaf format that can be regularly updated, especially in somewhere like Greenwich, where a lot is happening. It may be that Conservation Plans ought also to be in a loose-leaf format that is kept up to date.

Christopher Young, English Heritage

A statement of significance for a World Heritage Site must be an integral part of the Management Plan. The Management Plan for a World Heritage Site has to be broad — it has to set the statement of significance against the other pressures and opportunities of the site to achieve a balance, which the managers can use to manage the site. The Management Plan for Hadrian's Wall is very different from the one that you would prepare for Blenheim Palace or Fountains Abbey, because it is so much bigger. The key point here is that there is a need for flexibility. The Plan must fit the purpose that it will serve, and the site for which you are doing it, rather than being tied to a particular formula that has to be applied time and again.

Chair

It is rather fitting that this session ends with Christopher Young's reminder that 'the Plan must be fit for the purpose' and indeed this theme has run through the session. We seem to have consensus on the value of the 'statement of significance' as the basic foundation block for building any plan for conservation action or management. Beyond this there has been helpful clarification from Nic Durston on behalf of the HLF and David Heath on behalf of English Heritage, and in Ron German's admirably clear presentation, that the Conservation Plan approach is of greatest value when it is integrated (though not necessarily fully developed) from the inception of a project. There are useful insights to be gained from Paul Simons' case study of Bath, too, with recognition that the full-blown Conservation Plan has its place at a particular stage, in a particular type and scale of conservation project; and, above all, in articulation with all the other tools for conservation management that are appropriate to a continuous, complex, and dynamic process of change.

SESSION FOUR

PLANNING FOR A SUSTAINABLE FUTURE

Chair: Richard Morris, Council for British Archaeology

The 'S' word — or Sustaining Conservation

Graham Fairclough, English Heritage

How do we sustain the idea of conservation; why is keeping old buildings sustainable; is conservation a minority interest, or has it become a social process (will historians look back on the late twentieth century and identify conservation as a historical process like capitalism or Christianity?)?

In relation to nature conservation, and the global environment, sustainable development is about finding ways to design developments that allow essential or desirable resources to be renewed faster than they are destroyed, or, at the very least, to be sustained in equilibrium.

For the historic environment (see *Sustaining the Historic Environment*, published by English Heritage in 1997), the aim is somewhat different — the resource itself cannot be renewed, merely kept (whether altered or not) or lost. What *is* renewable, however, is the contribution (often non-place-specific) that the past can make to present and future environments. This contribution will continually change: it can be expanded or altered. It is therefore renewable, even though its general form may change.

This way of looking at sustainability — of sustaining character and use rather than intrinsic, physical remains — brings to the fore the concepts of perception and valuation, and therefore people. Perception and valuation, as we have heard, are relative, and thus they slightly push into the background the intrinsic value and qualities of heritage resources. As an example, here is the list of values identified in *Sustaining the Historic Environment* (English Heritage 1997b). It is not exhaustive, but it makes the point about use and value — which could also be called 'affordances' — not being the same as significance defined by conservation professionals:

- **cultural values**: the historic environment helps to define a sense of place and provides a context for everyday life. Its appreciation and conservation fosters distinctiveness at local, regional, and national level. It reflects the roots of our society and records its evolution;
- **educational and academic values**: the historic environment is a major source of information about our ancestors, the evolution of their society, and the characteristics of past environments. It provides a means for new generations to understand the past and their own culture. We can also use archaeology to learn about the long-term impact (and sustainability or otherwise) of past human activity and development, and to use this knowledge when planning our future;
- **economic values**: the historic environment can make a significant contribution to economic development by encouraging tourism, but, more generally, it also supports viable communities by creating good environments where people will prefer to live and work;
- **resource values**: longer-life buildings usually make better use of the energy and resources that were used during their construction, and re-use is usually more economic than demolition and redevelopment. Conservation is inherently sustainable;

- **recreational values**: the historic environment plays a highly significant role in providing for people's recreation and enjoyment. Increasingly, the past, and its remains in the present, are becoming a vibrant part of people's everyday life and experiences;
- **aesthetic values**: archaeology and historic buildings make a major contribution to the aesthetic quality of townscapes and landscapes, enhancing the familiar scene of our historic towns and villages and giving historic depth and interest to our countryside.

Conservation Plans must not focus exclusively, therefore, on the inherent significance of buildings and monuments. If they do, they might not contribute as much to sustainability as we would hope. They might even prove unsustainable in certain circumstances. They should look at society's values: as James Semple Kerr has said, making a Conservation Plan is essentially a process of debate and consensus building, which presupposes the bringing together of different viewpoints and perspectives.

The other characteristic of the way that *Sustaining the Historic Environment* looks at the sustainable development debate is therefore in putting people, and their needs and understanding, at least on an equal, and probably a superior, footing to the resource itself. The remains of the past are significant if they are valued or used (not necessarily economically) in some way. All the ways that seem most useful for promoting sustainability revolve around ideas like participation, involvement, community awareness of roots and of historic character, and the relationship of the local environment to the people who live there. If we really want conservation to be part of a sustainable economy, to be a partner in regeneration, for example, it is essential for it to arise from local and popular initiatives, and not to be purely profession-led.

This is the most important message: the over-riding need for us to find ways to sustain conservation by rooting it in popular understanding and awareness. This is not just a question of persuading others to our viewpoint; it is also about noticing what people want in their surroundings (which you will find is usually a familiar and recognisably old landscape as a setting for their lives) and helping them to achieve it. It may not always be what the conservation professions want — 'ordinary', unlisted buildings may be valued more than the occasional Grade I set-piece — but it will represent sustainable conservation in the sense outlined earlier: ie, the conservation of an ever-changing, both physically and in perception, historic dimension to the future landscape. An important task for conservation professionals, therefore, is to help people engage with the historic environment — at home, on their doorstep as it were, with part of their daily life. Not the big Grade I houses — they are valued differently — but the small details of their place.

Kate's original title for me was 'The "S" word'. She meant the 'S' to stand for 'Sustainability', but in putting these thoughts together I settled instead on the word 'stakeholders'. Stakeholder is an inelegant word, but at least it summarises the idea that we need the general public to buy into conservation. For this to happen we have to give them access to some of the decision-making, which in turn implies a 'letting-go' to some extent by professional conservationists. Once or twice today, comments in discussion brought into my mind the words 'You're all a bunch of control freaks'. Don't be. Let go a little, and listen to your constituencies.

We have been discussing a fairly old idea at this conference — that in conservation, as in other spheres of life, a period of thoughtful planning and reflection, and perhaps study and research, should precede action. Interference with the historic environment needs to be planned with the significance of the site and the impact of the changes fully known in advance. This is just as true of the beneficial conversion or reuse of a building (see PPG 15) or of archaeological work (see PPG 16) as it is for the planning of a development of new housing in the countryside, or for the management of the whole landscape, and has been true for a long time.

What is different about the emerging new generation of Conservation Plans (apart from the optimistic climate of Lottery funding, which creates the opportunity to think big) is their determination to cover all issues. That is, to be holistic in their approach to the environment, whether natural or cultural, physical or spiritual. And this is greatly to be welcomed.

Does this holism go far enough? It must bring in the social and the economic as well as the historic and environmental. It must find a way to engage with community-based ideas of significance as opposed only to those of experts. There must be room for the commonplace as well as the special.

In other words, the Conservation Plan is, inarguably, a necessary, useful, and desirable tool. But it is a tactical instrument, and to be most effective it should be set in its wider context. This can be summed up under two headings: significance and place.

'Significance', no matter how widely defined in terms of the different conservation professions (archaeology, architecture, ecology, etc), is rarely an absolute, as we have heard all day. In most cases it has to be measured alongside use and social value, particularly when (as is usually the case) the impact of future proposals is being assessed and decisions are being made about future use. This is the first context — *social value*. Conservation, to be sustainable, must take account of social preferences and requirements, just as much as we need to look at economic feasibility in many cases.

'Place' is also a concept of which we should be wary. Everyone recognises the idea of place, but scale varies widely from individual to individual, and is dependent on circumstance. An individual street might rank as a place for some; elsewhere, a whole city or territory. But place need not be only the big monumental places that are typically the subject of Conservation Plans, and it is important that the everyday, the commonplace, is not somehow devalued by focusing on special places. This is where the widest sense of place is likely to reside, where conservation needs to be rooted. The aim of conservation, and therefore of Conservation Plans, should be to promote and sustain a historic component of all places, as part of a community's sense of place and socio-economic viability. This, therefore, is the second context — *community relevance*. Again, this amounts to making conservation sustainable.

Many of these ideas are, of course, implicit in *Sustaining the Historic Environment*. This emphasises that a major reason for preserving the past is to create, and pass on, a good environment, in which origins and evolution can be read, and which allow future generations to understand and appreciate their past.

A number of key principles have been identified:

- taking a long-term view of our actions;
- looking at the environment as a whole;
- achieving greater public involvement — participation — in making decisions about society's needs of the environment;
- deciding which elements of the environment are important at various levels;
- keeping our activities to levels which do not permanently damage the historic environment and do not prevent future generations from learning about their past from surviving physical evidence;
- ensuring that decisions about the historic environment are made on the basis of the best possible information, invoking the precautionary principle where there is insufficient information.

Above all, though, it is essential to take account of who it is that makes the many value judgements — whether on significance or future use. Is it experts or local residents, business or politicians? Or can we find a way to involve everyone, through, for example, focus groups, visioning conferences, real-planning techniques, and capacity-building and awareness-creating projects such as Village Design Statements? All these techniques have in common an attempt to move away from consultation towards participation. Consultation is healthy enough in its way, but it can be partial, elite-led, and imperfectly involving. It always carries the underlying message of 'this is what we have decided — please agree'.

The debate needs to move closer to first principles. Trying to draw in community and local views ought to be the first step in drawing up a Conservation Plan, as we heard in some talks yesterday. One of the main issues flagged up at the end of *Sustaining the Historic Environment* was: 'How to create stronger public participation in conservation debates'.

Conservation Plans, purely by virtue of the processes of their production, ought to take this on as a major aim, irrespective of whether a HLF grant or a regeneration project results. Indeed, there is a case for carrying out Conservation Plans before any specific proposals for repair and development have been defined: the process of bringing a community together to produce a Plan will build up that community's capacity to define its own sense of place, its own awareness of the historic environment that always, everywhere, sits within the modern world, and this is perhaps the best starting point.

This is what my title of 'Sustaining conservation' really means: that conservation now needs to become more of a grass-roots social activity. It is already a social process — the *conscious* reuse of historic buildings for their own sake (and in some cases — for example, English Heritage monuments in care — without economic use) is already likely to be seen by future generations as a recognisable aspect of late twentieth-century social processes. We can look back to earlier periods for similar examples of using the past. I think, for example (as obvious instances), of conscious medieval and Renaissance adaptations of Roman buildings by Church and State to symbolise continuity (and thus permanence) of power and status, or the early Christian reuse of pagan sites and symbols (such as fonts carved from Roman inscriptions) to underline the triumph of a new religion. The rise of proto-conservation in the more modern sense in the last half of the nineteenth century could be seen as the appropriation by a newly empowered middle class of hitherto aristocratic claims to symbols of the past. This was achieved,

An English Heritage discussion document addressing issues to do with sustainability

as in other spheres, by the creation of 'ring-fenced' professions, claiming special and original knowledge, and this is to a large extent where we risk standing today with the many conservation professions.

In other words, conservation has always been a part of society, and will continue to be so, but the mantle of promoting it has been passed on several times. It has always been a *part* of society, however. We tend now, as survivors of the 1980s, to look for economic justification when arguing for conservation — the financial value of listed buildings, the contribution that good conservation area schemes make to regeneration and thus to the economy — but an equal truth is that there can be no sustainable conservation without social support. This is why the question of values is so central: a site or monument valued socially is likely to be preserved even without economic use; the converse is only true in extreme cases where the evidence of value is so crudely obvious that even the marketplace can recognise it without too much assistance.

Values have to be socially based, however, which brings us again to the need for:

There can be no sustainable conservation without social support

- holistic assessment, so that everyone, whatever their interest, has a *stake*;
- the widest possible participation in the process, so that everyone has a *stake*;
- an embrace of the commonplace, or rather acceptance that the commonplace is special, again, so that everyone has a *stake*.

To put it another way, social viability is as important as economic viability, sustainability is about people, 'use' isn't just economic.

I will end with six of the most significant points that I have taken from talks at this conference:

- it does not matter who writes Conservation Plans as long as that person involves the right people; the principal skills required are interpersonal/facilitative rather than knowledge-based;
- Conservation Plans sum up our understanding of what we understand or perceive (they are not complete, not objective, not definitive, etc);
- they are most valuable as a summary of consensus (growing out of James Semple Kerr's concepts of 'conciliation and arbitration' — a process of debate);
- they are not about the past, but about the present and the future;
- nor are they about monuments and buildings, but about people;
- they should not be confused with advocacy documents or business cases, even if this means stopping the process after significance.

A Radical View from the Countryside

David Russell, the National Trust

Between 1992 and 1995 I was responsible for a review of the National Trust's role in conservation in the countryside. That review resulted in a conference and in the publication of a consultation document, both entitled *Linking People and Place* (Russell 1995). During the review we considered the guidelines for Conservation Plans put forward by James Semple Kerr and concluded that, particularly in their promotion of 'Statements of Significance', they offered an important extra dimension to the processes of planning already adopted by the Trust. Since then, I have had the job of drafting guidelines for the development of Statements of Significance within the National Trust.

It is impossible for me to take a dissenting or radical view in respect of the need for the type of planning process that James Semple Kerr advocates, especially the development of Statements of Significance. Rather, I would amplify what has already been said at this conference in their support.

Let us be clear that it is not merely yet another chore to accommodate in the burgeoning bureaucracy of conservation. It is not something to do mechanically or expeditiously, and it is not a once-and-for-all account of everything that planners need to take into account. A genuine enquiry into significance is not just the start of a programme of conservation; it is at the very heart of conservation, and the enquiry never stops.

The search for significance is not new, but the elevation of this part of the planning process to generate a statement is a means to make the search more comprehensive and the process more transparent. Views on significance must be actively gathered. The search should be conducted with an open mind and a willingness to reconsider established ideas. The result is the best possible summary of those features and attributes of a place that, at the time of writing, are believed to be most significant.

There are problems, of course, but they are not new either. They relate to the fact that different groups within the conservation world are culturally distinct; there are, for example, radically different discourses of conservation between people whose predominant concern is the built heritage and those preoccupied with ideas of environmental sustainability. There is also a question about how 'expert' judgements can be balanced or reconciled with the views of people who might be regarded as 'uninformed'.

Let me explain what I mean. There is more than a passing congruence between the soaring arches and fan vaulting of a cathedral such as Peterborough and the lofty, sun-dappled stems of the mature beech wood. Trees were understood by the ancients to harbour deities, and architecture has continued to replicate the sacred grove in the fabric of religious buildings. The difference is that while the cathedral has a recognisable state of perfection, which allows conservationists to detect deterioration or subversion, the forest does not. The essential nature of nature is change. Ecosystems are always becoming something else. The temptation, for most of us who are imbued with the notion that nature is as perfect as a cathedral, is to believe that any unplanned change in structure or loss of species is a failure of conservation. The storms that assailed southern England in 1987, however, reinforced our appreciation of the essentially dynamic quality of nature. The initial reaction that the woods had been destroyed was replaced by the recognition that they had merely changed.

We are locked into a largely scenic aesthetic. A researcher for the United States Department of Agriculture Forest Service has commented that we have inherited 'a narrowly defined and largely visual scenic aesthetic', and goes on to suggest that what is needed is an ecological aesthetic which would require 'a learned experience of the multi-modal, dynamic qualities of forest environments' and appreciates 'both subtle and dramatic changes exhibited in the cycle of life and death'.

The other side of this coin is the tendency for environmentalists to describe the forest as a habitat. That diminishes the rich experience of 'place', which is self-evidently culturally and spiritually enriching as well. If we are to understand what a place is, we must be concerned with both the biological and the cultural dimensions.

Here is something that our enquiry into significance will highlight and help to resolve, if we do it with an open and enquiring mind. Differences of culture or perception are resolved only through the sort of dialogue that the process will generate.

Specialists can resolve their problems of culture and discourse through dialogue. They can conclude that some things are more significant than others on a regional, national, or international scale of values. They might even conclude that the lifestyles of local people are highly significant. Now, who is going to tell the local people?

Perhaps with good reason, people have become more sceptical as they have become more aware of the sometimes insensitive imposition of expert opinion, and doubtful about the rhetoric of 'authority' and vested interest. A place may have an international importance as a habitat or as a monument but it is brought alive by people working the land or developing businesses as well as by the memories and associations attributed by individuals and communities.

Specialists cannot claim a monopoly on deciding what is significant. People will no longer allow conservation 'to be done to them'. Conservation has become a participative and engaging business. In our report *Linking People and Place* we made the following recommendation to the National Trust:

> The best way for the Trust to understand perceptions is through a process of listening to others and sharing through dialogue … by sharing perceptions the Trust can enter productive dialogues, learning how to communicate what is important to the Trust and learning what is significant to others … by telling people with humility what the Trust feels is significant and why, a productive dialogue can commence. This will give others the confidence to support what must ultimately be the Trust's own determination of significance.

There must be dialogue here too. Dialogue, interpretation, and education, which used to be considered as bolt-on activities to the real business of conservation, now assume centre stage.

In conclusion, then, I would say that the Statement of Significance is the provisional record of an ongoing dialogue, between specialists of all types and amongst the many communities of interest. It is not the conclusion of a brief episode of research. It is a working document, never monolithic and never complete. It lies at the heart of conservation.

From Conservation Plan to Management Plan

Jeff West, English Heritage

I want to start by asking the question, what is the point of a Conservation Plan? It is not (in that unfair and pejorative sense of the word) an 'academic' exercise. It is part of a practical, decision-making process. It is *applied* history or archaeology, not pure research. Conservation Plans are needed when we have to decide what to do with something — a site, a building, an object or a landscape. They are needed because unavoidable practical decisions have to be made, decisions that deserve to be made on the best available evidence and with the best informed judgement, decisions that should not be made by default, or in ignorance, or on the basis of prejudice.

What, then, is the difference between a Conservation Plan and a Management Plan? Conservation Plans lead to policies for the retention of significance, policies that tell us what has to be done in managing a heritage object, what must not be done, and — by implication — what may be done but need not be. Management Plans take us further than that. They are what results when, as James Simpson put it yesterday, we consider 'commodity and firmness' as well as 'delight'. He defined commodity and firmness in this context as, by implication, the practical circumstances, including the economic and political context, in which we work. Given, for example, the state of the property market, or the existence of a regeneration initiative, we need to know what opportunities there are to make use of a historic building in ways that will sustain whatever is important or interesting or significant about it, not diminish it or put it at risk. In the same way, we need to know the condition of a building before we can draw up a prioritised schedule of repairs, and we need to know what skills or resources are likely to be available before we draw up a maintenance programme.

We have been reprimanded for forgetting about tourists and visitors. One possible function of a building or a monument is display to the public. When this is the case, any Management Plan needs to consider the needs and interests of visitors and the level of knowledge that can be assumed. When I joined the Inspectorate in the early 1970s, I remember a senior colleague of mine saying that we should not litter our ruined abbeys with little labels saying 'nave' and 'cloister' and 'chapter house' because (he argued) if visitors could not work that out for themselves, they shouldn't be visiting a monastic site. Our attitude today is rather different. We welcome visitors who have limited knowledge, and try to send them away understanding a little bit more and keen to return. We are in the education business. This means that in drawing up a Management Plan we need to think about our visitors, who they are, and who they are likely to be in the future. When deciding how best to conserve and restore a building or a site, we need to think how best to present and display it to the public.

So what should a Conservation or Management Plan look like? Drawing up a plan is not simply a bureaucratic process or a job-creation exercise for consultants. I am not sure that we can or should be prescriptive about the format; I can certainly see a place for something much shorter, which might perhaps be called a 'conservation statement' rather than a 'Conservation Plan'.

Education is an important consideration in the management of heritage sites

The value of Conservation Plans lies not in their format, or even in their content, but in the process they oblige us to go through, a process with value for everyone involved in the practical management of the historic environment. The discipline of thinking hard about significance, of consulting widely, is not a way of avoiding decisions. The whole point about practical involvement with the management of the historic environment, particularly when the environment is in continuing everyday use, is that one cannot avoid difficult decisions.

Anyone with practical curatorial responsibility has to make value judgements: evaluation, the exercise of judgement, is unavoidable. And all value judgements are subjective. Paul Drury suggested that there are no right or wrong answers. Jane Grenville said this morning that value is not inherent in an object in itself, but lies in the relationship between that object and an observer. When investigators were first appointed to draw up lists of historic buildings in 1947, they were all on short-term contracts because the government thought that it would be a once-and-for-all job. The country was to be listed, the list would exist, and no further investigation would be needed. If you think that this is an outmoded approach, remember that even the relisting programme of the 1970s and early 1980s was originally conceived as a one-off exercise. I am sure that some people still imagine that once a Conservation Plan has been produced, it won't need revision. So we mustn't get too complacent.

The Conservation Planning process forces us to be aware of what it is we are dealing with, why it is significant, and — most importantly — to whom. Local communities need to participate in the process and give their views. But remember that it is not simply the people living in the immediate locality who may care about something, and that there are places where the people who care most about them are *not* the people who live locally. This can pose serious political problems.

The Conservation Planning process forces us to make our assumptions explicit, and therefore testable. There has been quite a lot of complacency about the Conservation Planning process over the last two days. Several people have said that they've been doing it for years — that the idea has been part of conservation theory and practice for decades. Yes, of course good conservation practitioners, good managers of the historic environment, have been doing something very like Conservation Planning for years, and there are plenty of good examples that can be quoted. But then, archaeologists have been acknowledging the importance of publication for years as well, and that didn't stop a large post-excavation backlog building up, which only began to be tackled when funding was made available and a responsible attitude towards publication became a necessary part of professional respectability. Almost everyone here has said, yes, of course we must do Conservation Planning, but there are plenty of skeletons in the cupboards of all managers of the historic environment.

In summary, the process of writing Conservation Plans, in whatever format and whatever they are called, is useful for one main reason. They make managers be explicit, transparent, and open about their assumptions. They make those assumptions available to be tested. They are not a way of avoiding or fudging or delaying decisions, but rather the best way we have of avoiding decisions based on over-confidence or ignorance, or ones taken by default.

Christopher Young, English Heritage

Having now written two Management Plans, one in this country and one not, I want to make the point that the process goes on after the Plan is written. Implementation is important and that involves dealing with people in the community, getting them involved, and keeping them going. You have to keep it going once you've done it.

Involvement isn't always terribly easy, particularly if you're dealing with a large area of countryside, because people don't necessarily perceive that it affects them until it is too late. You can hold public meetings, but people won't come. In my experience the best way to get public input is to get a headline, as we once did in a press article headlined: 'English Heritage accused of ethnic cleansing'. Something controversial like that arouses public interest. It gives you a very rough ride, but it also gives you the public involvement that you can then carry forward and go on with. It is the process of carrying it through that is important, as much as the document itself.

Jack Warshaw, Conservation Architecture & Planning

I would just like to make a quick planning point — it is simply that we should remember that everything that we produce, under this or any other regime, will automatically become a material consideration when the work leads to any form of proposal regarding the use or development of land. And those proposals will normally be judged by the local authority. The fundamental reason for the creation of the planning system in this country, and of any form of heritage control, has been to do so in the public interest, irrespective of who happens to own the object, the building, the land or anything else. We should not forget that as we go away from here.

CLOSING REMARKS

James Semple Kerr, Conservation Consultant

Roger Wools has reminded me of the strange and varied concepts of the rhinoceros held by late medieval and Renaissance artists. The Conservation Plan took a similarly uncertain form in this morning's discussion and seems to have inspired both fear and dread about what it might and can't do.

I have two suggestions: first, get hold of some well-put-together Conservation Plans and see what they actually do; second, remember that you are in control of the Conservation Plan and can make it do whatever you want. Nothing need go into a Conservation Plan that is not necessary to the determination of policies to guide the future development of the place. For example, this means no recording (an expensive and time-consuming exercise, which belongs in another context) and no excavation or intervention in the fabric (except for sampling purposes). Nor should it be confused with development or master plans, which should respond to the Conservation Plan and set out actual proposals.

Conservation Plans can become the front end of a Management Plan just as Management Plans can be attached to the tail of a Conservation Plan. What you call it is not important. What is important is setting down the argument in an appropriate sequence so it can be transparent, tested, adjusted (where necessary), and adopted.

Finally, remember flexibility — the Conservation Plan must be tailored to the place and its problems. It is the old cliché of horses for courses: you wouldn't take a mud runner to Alice Springs.

Speakers' Bibliography

Ambrose, T M, and Runyard, S, 1991 *Forward Planning: a basic guide for museums, galleries and heritage organisations*, Routledge, London

Carver, M O H, 1996 On archaeological value, *Antiquity*, **70** (no. 267, March), 45–56

CLRAE, 1998 *The Draft European Landscape Convention*, Congress of Local and Regional Authorities of Europe, Recommendation 40, Strasbourg

Connaughton, J C, and Green, S D, 1996 *Value Management in Construction: a client's guide*, Construction Industry Research and Information Association, London

Cossons, N, 1977 *Ironbridge: landscape of industry*, Cassell, London

Countryside Commission, 1998 *Site Management Planning: a guide*, Countryside Commission CCP 527, Cheltenham

Countryside Commission, English Heritage, and English Nature, 1993 *Conservation Issues in Strategic Plans*, Countryside Commission CCP 420, Cheltenham

DoE, 1990 *Planning Policy Guidance Note 16 (PPG 16): archaeology and planning*, HMSO for Department of the Environment, London

——, 1994 *Planning Policy Guidance Note 15 (PPG 15): planning and the historic environment*, HMSO for Department of the Environment/Department of National Heritage, London

English Heritage, 1995a *Conservation Area Practice: guidance on the management of Conservation Areas*, London

——, 1995b *Developing Guidelines for the Management of Listed Buildings*, London

——, 1997a *Conservation Plans: a brief introduction*, London

——, 1997b *Sustaining the Historic Environment: new perspectives on the future*, London

Forestry Authority, 1998 *The UK Forestry Standard: the government's approach to sustainable forestry*, London

Grenville, J C, 1993 Curation overview, in *Archaeological Resource Management in the UK: an introduction* (eds J Hunter and I Ralston), 125–33, Alan Sutton/Institute of Field Archaeologists, Stroud

Guillery, P, 1993 *The Buildings of London Zoo*, RCHME, London

Harrison, R (ed), 1996 *Manual of Heritage Management*, Butterworths, London

Heritage Lottery Fund, 1998 *Conservation Plans for Historic Places*, London

Holland, A, and Rawles, K, 1993 Values in conservation, *Ecos*, **14** (1), 14–19

Kerr, J S, 1987 *Admiralty House: a Conservation Plan prepared for the Department of Housing and Construction*, The National Trust of Australia (NSW), Sydney

——, 1992 *The Haymarket and the Capitol: a Conservation Plan for the area bounded by George, Campbell, Pitt and Hay Streets, Sydney*, 2nd impression, for Ipoh Garden (Australia) Limited, The National Trust of Australia (NSW), Sydney

——, 1993 *Yungaba Immigration Depôt: a plan for its conservation*, Q-Build Project Services, Brisbane

——, 1995 *Parramatta Correctional Centre: its past development and future care*, commissioned by New South Wales Public Works for the Department of Corrective Services, Sydney

——, 1996a *The Conservation Plan: a guide to the preparation of Conservation Plans for places of European cultural significance*, 4th edn, The National Trust of Australia (NSW), Sydney

——, 1996b *The Sydney Opera House: an interim plan for the conservation of the Sydney Opera House and its site*, 2nd impression, commissioned by New South Wales Public Works for The Sydney Opera House Trust

——, 1998 *Fremantle Prison: a policy for its conservation*, 2nd edn, Department of Contract and Management Services for the Fremantle Prison Trust Advisory Committee, Perth

Lipe, W D, 1984 Value and meaning in cultural resources, in *Approaches to the Archaeological Heritage* (ed H F Cleere), 1–10, Cambridge University Press, Cambridge

Lord, B, and Lord, D G, 1996 *The Manual of Museum Management*, HMSO, London

Marquis-Kyle, P, and Walker, M, 1996 *The Illustrated Burra Charter*, ICOMOS Australia

Museums and Galleries Commission, 1995 *Registration Guidelines*, MGC, London

National Trust, 1996a Management Plans: review of property Management Plan guidelines, *Estate Management Manual*, Cirencester

——, 1996b Biddulph Grange Garden, Mercia Region, garden Conservation Plan, unpublished report (third draft, February 1996)

——, 1996c Llanerchaeron nr Aberaeron, Ceredigion, a rural conservation and regeneration project, unpublished report (South Wales Region) in support of an application for Heritage Lottery Fund grant assistance

——, 1997 Guidelines for long-term Conservation Plans for historic parks and gardens, unpublished report (updated August 1997), Cirencester

——, 1998a *National Strategic Plan March 1998 – February 2001*, London

——, 1998b Guidelines on the preparation of a Statement of Significance, unpublished document, Cirencester

Plenderleith, H, 1956 *The Conservation of Antiquities and Works of Art*, Oxford University Press, London (2nd edn, 1971)

Russell, D, 1995 *Linking People and Place*, The National Trust, Cirencester

Smith, J T, 1989 The archaeological investigation of standing buildings: a comment, *Vernacular Architect*, **20**, 20

EPILOGUE
Conservation Plans since Oxford

Kate Clark, English Heritage

A year has elapsed since the conference, and in that time many Conservation Plans have been prepared — some good, some bad — but almost everyone has recognised that a good Conservation Plan is not an easy thing to write.

The extraordinary explosion of interest in Conservation Planning was already well underway before the Oxford conference, particularly within the National Trust. Since then, the Trust has continued to explore the idea of statements of significance through a series of seminars. Although much of the continued interest outside the National Trust has come from the requirements of the Heritage Lottery Fund (HLF), there is a growing interest from bodies responsible for government buildings, from local authorities, and from the owners of complex sites. Plans have been prepared for sites as diverse as ships, canals, workhouses, major public buildings, art galleries, museums, parks, and gardens. Some Plans run to many volumes, others are much shorter. They have been written by architects, archaeologists, landscape historians, canal enthusiasts, historians, surveyors, and facilitators. Some involve complex teams of professionals, others informed individuals. Some Plans have been well-presented models of clarity with incisive policies, others volumes of ill-digested history disguising little more than an application for funding. Some have been put on the shelf and ignored, others are grubby from use.

It is useful to look back at what has happened since the conference, to examine some of the most common misconceptions which have emerged, and to explore some useful techniques which make the process easier.

The importance of the process

The central message of Conservation Planning must be that the Conservation Plan is not a recipe, with a fixed list of quantities, which, if followed precisely, will guarantee success. It is, instead, an intellectual process, a way of structuring thinking about a site. As long as the basic building blocks of the process are there, in roughly the right order, the process can be as long or as short as necessary, and can be adapted to any kind of site.

One of the most common mistakes in Conservation Planning is to confuse a Conservation Plan with a document that justifies a particular proposal, such as a new visitor centre. The Conservation Plan is not primarily about where to put visitor facilities, or about to which period a garden should be restored, or how wide plough margins should be, or how the aspirations of the owner of a historic building can be accommodated — although it can help inform any of these decisions. A Conservation Plan involves stepping back from the immediate requirements of management, development or finding appropriate uses for historic sites. The central focus of the Conservation Plan is *significance* — how and why a site is significant and how that significance can be retained in any future use, alteration, management or development.

Once a Conservation Plan is in place, it is much easier to make decisions about maintenance regimes. It is possible to prioritise repair strategies or to begin to think about where new development can be accommodated. Conflicts between different types of significance — ecology and the historic landscape, archaeology and visitor requirements, the viability of a farm and the conservation of its ecology — can be recognised and balances made. Interpretation strategies are greatly helped by a new understanding of the site, and, finally, it is possible to work cumulatively.

Understanding the site — issues and problems

How much information is needed?

A particular area of difficulty has been how to specify the amount of information that should be included in a Plan. Those involved with complex sites, such as cathedrals, have been genuinely struggling to create a balance between the need for an overview of the site, which might cover spiritual values, historic buildings, and musical, social, ecological, and collections issues, with sufficient depth of understanding of any one of these areas to ensure that key decisions can be made about scarce resources. A Conservation Plan must be based on understanding a site, but for most sites, that understanding might range from a quick photograph to enough material for several PhDs. Too little understanding will generate a Plan which is no more than a restatement of existing views or prejudices; too much information can swamp a Plan, and create delay and expense.

The key seems to be to match the level of information with the expectations of the Plan. A Plan which will be used by a site manager to inform day-to-day decisions needs to be based on an understanding whose degree of resolution includes those things to be managed — if decisions have to be taken about floor surfaces, fixtures, and fittings, for example, or individual areas of planting, then the information should be there in the Plan to inform those decisions, and the analysis of fabric will have to be undertaken at that level of detail.

What about gaps in our existing knowledge?

It is important that the information-gathering exercise should also identify what is *not* known about the site. Gaps in existing knowledge are often the reason for inadvertent damage. The survival of buried remains may not be predicted; an earlier garden design may be obscured by later changes. The most common problem when dealing with built and landscape sites is our lack of knowledge about changes to the site over the past century. The twentieth century is often poorly documented, yet it is changes of this period which are most likely to be scraped away in any restoration scheme. It is rarely possible in a Conservation Plan to fill all the gaps in one's knowledge, but it is essential to identify where those gaps are likely to be and how or in what circumstances they should be filled.

Paint analysis is a useful example of a gap that may exist but may not need to be filled. Paint analysis involves the microscopic analysis of layers of paint in order to establish past decorative schemes. It is usually too specific a technique to be used in a Conservation Plan (although the results of past paint analysis should be drawn into the Plan). However, a Conservation Plan could recognise the value of the technique and might include a policy setting out in what circumstances (for example, prior to any redecoration) paint analysis might be used. A similar approach could

Scarborough Castle, North Yorkshire: the purpose of a gazetteer is to organise large amounts of information about complex sites

- *What do we know about a site?*
- *What don't we know about a site?*
- *What do we need to know now in order to make decisions?*
- *What will we need to know in the future?*

be taken to other specialist investigation, such as detailed ecological species surveys or building analysis. Nevertheless, it is essential that the *lack* of such information is recognised so that decisions are not made without it.

Gazetteers and room data sheets

It is very easy for a Conservation Plan to become overwhelmed with information. Most heritage sites have already had a great deal of research carried out on them. Experience shows that such research usually focuses on the main area for which the site is significant, at the expense of other aspects such as its recent history, the wider context or landscape, less 'mainstream' features of the heritage or even the unexpected.

A very useful tool in any Conservation Plan is the gazetteer — a systematic survey of the site, identifying almost anything that needs to be managed, and setting out, in effect, a mini-Conservation Plan for it. This approach will ensure that the Conservation Plan is based on a broad understanding of the site and balances the well-known aspects of the site with lesser known ones. It also provides a degree of rigour in the information-collecting process as history must be tied to fabric. A gazetteer will normally include the following information as a minimum for each entry: documentary information, description of the feature, significance, any management issues (for example, condition), and sources.

For a building, room data sheets can provide the same systematic information collection exercise. One of the keys to dating historic interiors may be the forms of mouldings, joinery, windows, fittings or doors. To make things simpler, a typology of such features can be drawn up; the data sheets can then simply note the type each time, rather than describe the feature. A room data sheet should identify existing and past uses, and describe and date floors, doors, windows, decorative detail, fixtures, and any historic decorative schemes. The information should be keyed to sources such as historic photographs or building plans.

An ecological survey or a survey of historic planting should be included within the framework of the gazetteer unless the data is too difficult to integrate. It is important, however, to avoid the experience of one HLF applicant who had three different surveys for the same landscape (ecological, archaeological, and historic landscape), each with different criteria and different numbering systems, and no way of relating any one to the others.

Phasing

Most sites go through a coherent sequence of changes. Phasing is a technique that involves grouping these changes into coherent 'phases', which makes it much easier to understand a site. A phase will usually be a group of major changes. For example, the first phase in a monastic site might be construction of the abbey, a second phase rebuilding of the church, a third phase the destruction at the Dissolution, the fourth phase the creation of a new seventeenth-century house and garden, and the fifth phase nineteenth-century alterations. Phasing is simply a way of modelling change.

An understanding of the broad phases of change — which could include previous land-management regimes — is very useful for the Conservation Plan. Policies about restoration or the significance attributed to Victorian changes to the site, for example, all depend upon understanding these phases.

Phasing is based on gathering together all kinds of information. For a landscape, a map regression exercise will help with at least the last two or three hundred years. For a building, an analysis of the patterns of change in the fabric can be used. Documents and illustrations will help with the phasing of any site.

It is useful for the information-gathering stage of the Conservation Plan to include an understanding of the basic phases, preferably supported by plans or reconstruction drawings, to help others understand what can be a quite complex matter. Phasing is not a method restricted to the built heritage — it can be carried out for landscapes or for any site where there is map, field or documentary evidence for past land-management regimes.

Scheme-specific investigation

A Conservation Plan should normally provide a broad 'helicopter view' of a whole site. In practice, there are circumstances where the Conservation Planning process may require more information about one part of a site. An example might be where there are proposals to reuse an individual building or to create a new car park, where the proposals are broadly acceptable and where it is not practical to delay work until a Conservation Plan has been prepared. In these cases it is useful to bring forward some more detailed work into the Conservation Plan. For example, a topographical survey might be needed to identify any historic earthworks in an area proposed for car parking, or a good-quality base metric survey of a building may be needed as a basis for developing new proposals. This work will be relevant to the new scheme (and would be needed in any case) and also inform the Conservation Plan. Another common class of work that could be brought forward is the condition survey. In this case, a Conservation Plan will be a far more useful document if it draws on an up-to-date condition survey in writing policies, rather than setting out a policy that will almost certainly say that a condition survey is necessary.

How much does a Conservation Plan cost?

The biggest single factor in determining the cost of a Conservation Plan is how much information is to be included. Some Plans cost more because they include information-gathering exercises such as condition surveys or measured survey (see above). Whilst that information will be useful for many other purposes, and will almost certainly save money if done well, it will make a Plan look expensive. For this reason it is impossible to state what the cost of a Conservation Plan should be.

Another factor affecting costs is the experience of the consultant or person producing the Plan. Because Conservation Plans in this format are relatively new in the United Kingdom, many consultants are learning as they go. Those who have now prepared several Plans confirm that the process becomes easier and quicker with experience, so the cost of some early Plans may not be representative.

It can be difficult to persuade a site manager or owner of the value of a Conservation Plan, especially when the document appears to involve up-front expenditure for no apparent immediate gain. If, however, a Conservation Plan can be seen as part of the risk assessment exercise and can contribute directly to minimising uncertainty on historic sites, then there are likely to be benefits in the long run in terms of saving time and money. Certainly a Conservation Plan produced before outline designs are prepared for a new building, or before money is spent on feasibility studies or business plans, can help to reduce the likelihood of such schemes being abortive. A good Conservation Plan can also help a site manager to have more flexibility — it is easier to adapt a building or a site whose limits are clearly understood.

It is impossible to estimate the cost of a Conservation Plan unless the body commissioning the Plan has some idea of how it wants the Plan to be used and of the range of issues to be addressed by the Plan. The best way of anticipating the requirements of a Plan is through the preparation of a brief.

The importance of a brief

> A model brief is set out in the Appendix to this volume.

Every Conservation Plan should be tailored to the needs of an individual site and the site owner or manager. Because of this, and because of the need to manage the collection of information quite carefully, a standard brief has been developed, and is set out at the end of this volume, in the Appendix. The brief is just a starting point, and must be adapted to individual circumstances, but the aim is to help those thinking about preparing or commissioning a Plan to decide how much information is needed, and what areas the Plan should cover.

Appointing a consultant

Over the past year there has been much discussion about who is best qualified to write a Conservation Plan.

One area of disagreement is whether the person should be 'in house' or external. An in-house person, such as a cathedral architect or site manager, will have the advantage of a large amount of existing knowledge about the site and familiarity with the issues facing the site. This should be balanced against the fact that it is almost impossible to write a Conservation Plan on top of holding down a full-time job, and that an in-house person will often have a very personal and fixed view of the site, which the Conservation Plan may simply reiterate. If possible, it is better to employ an outside consultant. However, the 'in-house' adviser *must* play a leading role in setting up the Plan, in writing the brief, commissioning the document, and project managing the work. They must be prepared to participate in the preparation of the Plan, to guide the consultant towards the right information, and to ensure that work is not duplicated.

Which is the best profession to write a Conservation Plan? James Semple Kerr stresses the value of the 'single mind' and has shown how documents in Australia become unwieldy through being written by a committee. Against that, how can one person possess all the skills needed to balance competing heritage interests?

The most important skills required to draft a Conservation Plan seem to be:

- the ability to assimilate a large amount of information, to summarise it, and to present it clearly;
- knowledge of basic techniques for analysing fabric, whether buildings, landscapes, collections or archaeology;
- the ability to use pictures, graphics, and layout to create a document which is inviting to read;
- a broad understanding of professional heritage issues, including the statutory framework;

- a knowledge of conservation principles and philosophy, and their application;
- the ability to facilitate dialogue with stakeholders and to manage consultation effectively.

These might be found in one person, or alternatively in a team. So far, a number of different ways of writing a Plan have emerged:

- one practice — led by a conservation architect and including archaeologists, a historian, junior staff, and someone with graphic-design skills — is commissioned to carry out the entire job;
- a lead practice (architects) joins up with firms of engineers, leisure consultants, and/or planners to undertake the whole job;
- the gazetteer, background research, and phasing are undertaken by in-house staff; the Conservation Plan is written by a single non-specialist external facilitator in consultation with others;
- the gazetteer, background research, and data sheets are commissioned from an archaeologist; the first draft of the Conservation Plan is written by a specialist; 'ownership' and stakeholder dialogue is undertaken by the facilitator; the Plan is completed by in-house staff;
- one individual (a historian, archaeologist or landscape specialist) is commissioned to write the whole Plan;
- relevant in-house staff write separate sections of the Plan.

Not all of these methods have proved successful, and there has also been a wide variation in costs. As a general rule, information collection is best done by a dedicated specialist/s with the right skills, and one person, who has consulted widely, should write the Plan: skills in mediation and facilitation are essential.

Assessing significance

The assessment of significance lies at the heart of a Conservation Plan, but the HLF guidance does not provide nearly enough information on how this should be done.

The assessment should contain two sections:

1 A broad overview of the values embodied in the site

This overview is not just a clinical analysis of significance. It should try to express in words the atmosphere of the site, the range of values it has, and what makes it special. Ideally, it should be written on one side of A4 paper. The assessment can include traditional and non-traditional values — heritage values — but also social, aesthetic, atmospheric, community, and associational values, for example.

2 A more detailed breakdown of the significance of the fabric

If the Conservation Plan is going to be used to inform decisions about the fabric of the site, or to help balance competing types of significance, it is useful to provide a more technical analysis of significance. This is akin to an analysis of sensitivity, and should address significance at the level of the individual gazetteer entry. It could also include such elements as the significance of different materials, different phases of change to the site, individual species, spaces or views. The aim is not to match one site against another but to establish a basis for managing individual parts within the site.

The latter exercise can be carried out in different ways. Kerr stresses the need for flexibility and common sense in assessing significance, and suggests that the approach will vary with different sites. It is strongly recommended that his discussion of the assessment process (1996a, 11–21) is read before this part of the Plan is prepared. The exercise involves two processes: the first establishes the criteria to be used, and the second defines levels.

No one set of criteria is likely to be appropriate for every site, and places are usually significant for more than one reason. The legislative values — 'national importance' in the case of archaeology, 'architectural or historic interest' for buildings, and 'character' for conservation areas — were designed to inform decisions about designation, and are not really useful for balancing significance within a site that is probably already designated. Broad heritage criteria — ecological/historical/archaeological/ aesthetic — could be used to create multiple values. Alternatively, it is possible to look at what is important for each phase or area of a site. Kerr uses 'ability to demonstrate', 'associational links without surviving evidence' and 'formal or aesthetic qualities', which equate broadly with archaeological value, historical value, and architectural or aesthetic interest, but do not deal with landscape qualities, ecological or wildlife issues or collections values. Other criteria might be technical or social significance, and educational or community values.

The other decision to be taken is whether or not significance should be graded, and if so, how. Values such as high/medium/low can be used, although it is important to be aware of the risk of identifying something as being of low significance without enough information. Other degrees of assessment might be representativeness/rarity or intactness/seminal/ climactic. As an alternative, exercises in characterisation for sustainability make use of the concepts of 'critical' and 'tradable' assets — those whose preservation is essential, and those which could potentially be 'traded' for something else. The advantage of this approach is that it stresses that the loss of a feature should be associated with a benefit, and it means that levels of significance are not seen in isolation.

Finally, there is the matter of who defines significance. The person writing the Conservation Plan should aim to establish a view that is consistent with legislation, justified in terms of our understanding of the site, and a fair representation of views. The assessment of significance should be accepted by those responsible for the site and agreed with statutory bodies.

This is a debate that will continue to develop as our experience grows. The important point is that the person writing the Conservation Plan should do their best to articulate significance and to make clear the basis on which it has been done. If the assessment of significance is vague or too general, policy writing becomes impossible.

Vulnerability

A frequent criticism of the Conservation Plan methodology is that by focusing on how significance is vulnerable, there is no chance to consider the more positive opportunities for enhancing the significance of the site. It is useful to think about opportunities and this will greatly help future planning, but some care is needed not to confuse thinking about general opportunities with using the Plan as a disguise for a very specific scheme. An analysis of opportunities should be broad-ranging and creative, resulting in policies for enhancement rather than presenting a single, fixed scheme.

The concept of vulnerability is emerging as a very useful stage in the preparation of Conservation Plans, but many people seem nervous that admitting to problems or issues is a sign of failure and can be reluctant to let Plan writers address this. *All* heritage sites are vulnerable — this is why their careful management is so vital. The analysis of vulnerability has direct parallels in sustainability practice and is now a generally accepted concept. If there are particular sensitivities, the writer of the Plan can overcome this through the tactful use of language, mentioning broad issues rather than pointing the finger at individuals or events.

Writing policies

Policies in Conservation Plans veer between the highly general ('motherhood and apple-pie policies'), which are little more than restatements of the legislation, and the highly specific, which at times are simply recommendations from, for example, a condition survey.

Again, Kerr (1996a, 24–8) provides a very useful guide to writing policies and covers the issues set out below in more detail. Although largely buildings-based, his approach can easily be adapted to landscapes, collections or vessels. He does not use the term 'vision' — but the first policies in the Plan, which effectively set out the philosophical approach to the site, equate with the management-planning concept of vision. *Conservation Issues in Strategic Plans* (Countryside Commission *et al* 1993) also provides useful examples of integrated policies, albeit at a strategic rather than site level. Finally, it is useful to read other Plans as a guide to developing policies.

Policies need to be based on an understanding of the significance of the site, and of how that significance is vulnerable. The client's requirements and resources need to be taken into account if the policies are to be practical. Physical condition is important (although policies should not be restricted to repair recommendations). It is particularly important that policies are drafted in the light of the existing statutory and non-statutory policies — legislation, planning policy guidelines, local plans, and appropriate advisory notes. Conservation (heritage, countryside, and wildlife), access, and health and safety guidance and/or legislation are all important, as well as local authority guidance or supplementary planning advice in these areas.

Broadly, policies should do the following:

- explain the philosophical approach to the site;
- address relevant management issues which impinge upon the care of the site;
- identify appropriate uses;
- guide change by enabling adaptations to be made;
- explain how services can be provided;
- guide the care of fabric and the setting of the site;
- address specific areas of the site.

This staircase rail at the Bank of England is an example of how sensitive new design can help facilitate access to historic buildings by visitors with disabilities

These broad principles may vary across the site, so it is useful to balance 'issue' policies with 'area' policies which tackle the treatment of specific areas or elements of the site, such as the exterior of the building, individual spaces, parts of the landscape, collections, and so on.

'Issue' and 'area' policies will, inevitably, cut across each other, and editing may be required to keep the text concise.

Policies should be numbered for ease of reference. Sometimes it is useful to include a short reason or justification for a policy (usually drawn from the understanding of vulnerability), as many readers will only read the policy section of a Plan.

A policy may set out a broad principle, but can be accompanied by specific pointers for implementation to make the policy more useful. For example, a broad policy indicating the potential of a building for reuse could be accompanied by 'policyettes' highlighting specific areas of sensitivity (such as the treatment of openings) and what might need to be done to resolve this.

It is very tempting to include, as a policy in a Plan, a specific proposal such as an immediate programme of restoration. This confuses the Plan, which should seek to set guidelines to inform decision-making. Developing specific options and, finally, choosing a scheme should follow the preparation of a Conservation Plan (see below).

Ultimately, the test of good policies lies in their usefulness. If the policies genuinely help the decision-making process and ensure that the significance of the site is retained, if they help to resolve conflict or to keep a site in use without damaging it, then they can be judged a success.

Conservation Statements

Something that has emerged very strongly over the past year is the need for shorter 'Conservation Statements'. These are akin to initial site assessments, the early stages of information gathering. A Conservation Statement is, in effect, a mini-Conservation Plan. It might cover:

1 An outline history of the site
2 A description of what survives today
3 A short statement of significance
4 An overview of the main conservation issues on the site
5 A short statement of conservation principles, which explains how the site will be cared for and noting any constraints on new work
6 Next steps — a discussion of what might need to be done next, for example, filling gaps in existing knowledge, undertaking site survey or preparing a full Conservation Plan
7 List of existing reports or sources

If there are already outline proposals for new work, the Conservation Statement should also include an impact assessment or mitigation table.

A Conservation Statement will not normally require any new research but, because of that, is likely to reinforce existing ideas. In some cases it will be sufficient, particularly if the site is very straightforward, but in most the exercise will raise more questions than it answers, and will not provide sufficient detail either to manage a site or to take forward a new scheme of work. A Conservation Statement could be prepared in-house before a full Plan is commissioned, and this will go a long way towards defining the scope of a Plan.

'Heritage impact' assessment

A Conservation Plan simply sets out guidelines, which will help to retain significance, identify compatible uses, meet statutory requirements, and work within resources. A Conservation Plan is not a feasibility study or a set of proposals.

However, in many cases the site owner or manager will be in the process of making an application for funding for new work or will be actively considering changes. Many people see the Conservation Plan as a potential brake on such development, which will cause delay and stop progress. How can the Conservation Plan help move things forward?

The first point is that time and money can be wasted on developing inappropriate schemes if the right information is not available in advance. The Conservation Plan should therefore be as well advanced as possible before any other work such as business plans, feasibility studies or option appraisals is undertaken.

In practice, this is rarely the case, and thinking about new work is often well advanced before the Conservation Plan is commissioned. The key is to keep the scheme and Plan separate. Once the scheme begins to emerge, it can be assessed against the Conservation Plan to establish whether or not it will retain the significance of the site.

The process of impact assessment involves assessing the consequences of specific proposals to establish whether they will retain the significance of the site. In some cases a proposal may be acceptable or even beneficial, but could have minor impact on the site. Often this impact can be mitigated through minor changes in design, through the gathering of further information. When a minor loss is an unavoidable consequence of an otherwise beneficial scheme, it might be appropriate to make a record of the lost fabric, although this should always be done as a last resort.

For example, refurbishment of an interior could be beneficial, but earlier paint schemes might be damaged by the work. The mitigation strategy would be to undertake detailed paint analysis before finalising a decorative scheme. Equally, restoration of a garden may be beneficial but could damage buried archaeological deposits. A small amount of further investigation would need to be undertaken before the restoration scheme was put in place.

Guidance on undertaking impact assessment is set out in the HLF guidance note (page 15 and reproduced below). It is very useful to set out the assessment as a table, with columns for the proposed work, the significance of the fabric affected, the possible impact of the work, and any suggested mitigation. As the Conservation Plan develops, specific policies can be set out in the table. The table can be adapted as needed — columns setting out benefits can be added, for example. The impact assessment table can then be used to decide on options, to brief an architect or works team or otherwise to take a scheme forward.

Heritage impact assessment table

Proposed work	Relevant Conservation Policy	Significance of element affected by work	Possible impact of work	Mitigation
Specific works envisaged	Refer to policies in Conservation Plan	Refer to significance section of Plan	Assess impact in light of Plan	Suggest design alternatives, or archaeological mitigation

Thus, 'impact assessment' is the essential final stage of the Conservation Planning process. It is a simple tool, which ensures that a scheme or set of management proposals is measured against the benchmark of the guidelines in the Plan. It is a pragmatic tool, as it shows how a scheme can be developed or modified in minor ways to make it less damaging.

The table also helps to identify future information requirements. For a complex site, the Conservation Plan is often the beginning of the information-gathering process. As work continues, more information about a site will come to light. The impact assessment can target information-gathering strategies to the needs of a scheme.

Although it sounds complex, impact assessment is a simple and pragmatic tool which, like the Conservation Plan, orders one's thinking, anticipates problems, and negotiates the transition from the past to the future.

A nine-day wonder?

There has been much concern that the value of Conservation Planning is potentially devalued by being tied to funding requirements. It is possible that those who prepare Plans but who nevertheless are unsuccessful in their funding bids will see the process as having been a waste of time. Others are concerned that Conservation Plans are not specifically mentioned in the relevant government guidance on conservation and therefore have no future.

Conservation Planning is not new. The approach has direct parallels in all areas of heritage management, whether wildlife, countryside, World Heritage Sites, built heritage or archaeology. Even the idea of integration is not new, as shown by the work done by the Countryside Commission, English Heritage, and English Nature. There will always be a need to understand sites, and our ambitions for heritage sites will always outstrip the amount of time we are prepared to put into understanding them. That this is not new is illustrated by Neil Cossons, who, in 1977, wrote:

> The reconciliation of the voices of the past and future with the obvious necessities of everyday life today demands much more than considerable sums of money which in themselves can be a recipe for disaster. It requires understanding depth as well as breadth, a detailed archaeological, historical and ecological appreciation of why what is there is there, a conscious ability to exercise restraint and a dedication to doing nothing when nothing might be the right answer, but above all, a sense of humility (1977, 20).

APPENDIX: MODEL BRIEF FOR A CONSERVATION PLAN

Notes on the brief

The Heritage Lottery Fund guidance note, *Conservation Plans for Historic Places*, provides a general introduction to Conservation Plans for site owners and others.

However, all sites and all proposals for them are different. A Conservation Plan needs to be tailored to the requirements of a particular site and its circumstances. It can be very difficult to establish how detailed a Conservation Plan should be, and therefore how much it might cost. For this reason, the Model Brief has been produced to help site managers or their professional advisers commission a Conservation Plan that fits the needs of their site.

Another factor that can affect the scope and amount of detail in a Conservation Plan is the existence of a set of proposals for new work. Normally, a Conservation Plan is a general document that should provide an overview of the whole site and is done before a new scheme is developed. In practice, many Conservation Plans are prepared in the context of a proposal for new work, and may need more detail about some areas of the site to help progress the scheme. Suggestions for the type of additional work that you may need to commission are set out in the brief.

Please note: no single brief will be appropriate to every type of site. This model brief provides initial ideas only — adapt it to your own particular requirements.

Finally, a set of sector-specific requirements are included to help you tailor the content of your Plan to the different requirements of buildings, collections, landscapes, buried archaeology, and ecology. They provide ideas for the sorts of questions that the Conservation Plan should answer for each area, and could also be used by anyone reading a Plan, such as a conservation officer or curator, to evaluate the document.

This brief is an evolving document. I have tried to incorporate the experiences of many of the people currently undertaking Conservation Plans in the United Kingdom and to range across the requirements of different professions, but would be grateful for any comments, suggestions or alterations. An e-mail copy of the brief can also be provided.

Kate Clark
English Heritage
23 Savile Row
London W1X 1AB

0171 973 3724
Kate.Clark@English-Heritage.org.uk

Model Brief for a Conservation Plan

1 Background information

1.0 Introduction

Provide a brief introduction to your site and the circumstances of the brief.

This brief sets out the requirements for the production of a Conservation Plan for [ ]. The brief has been prepared by [ ] in consultation with [ ].

1.1 Purpose of commissioning the Plan

Explain why the Conservation Plan is being commissioned and how you intend to use the Plan.

The purpose of the Conservation Plan is to:

❑ inform day-to-day management;
❑ inform a programme of repair/restoration;
❑ provide a basis for developing proposals for a new scheme;
❑ support an application for statutory consent;
❑ support a Stage Two application to the Heritage Lottery Fund for [ ];
❑ inform the preparation of a full Management Plan.

Please note that a Conservation Plan should not be used to justify a particular scheme and it is inappropriate to ask a consultant to do so.

1.2 Background to the site

Provide a brief description of the site and the reason for its significance.

The site has the following statutory designation/s:

❑ scheduled ancient monument;
❑ listed building;
❑ lies within a conservation area/Area of Outstanding Natural Beauty;
❑ Site of Special Scientific Interest;
❑ registered park or garden;
❑ other heritage/natural/geological/countryside designation;
❑ registered museum.

1.3 Context for the Plan

Most Plans prepared in the context of funding bids will have to complement other reports that have been prepared or are underway. Complex sites will already have a huge amount of existing information that will be relevant to the Conservation Plan and this should not be duplicated (although it can be summarised).

The consultant should take into account the following documents that are available/in preparation:

❑ business plan;
❑ condition survey or quinquennial inspection;
❑ visitor survey/traffic study/other;
❑ conservation area appraisal;
❑ feasibility study/options appraisal;
❑ measured survey;
❑ ecological survey;
❑ collections policy;
❑ other.

Identify these and explain where copies may be obtained.

2   Objectives

2.1   Primary objectives

This section should briefly summarise the objectives of the Plan. More detail on how they will be achieved is set out later. These objectives should be broadly common to any Conservation Plan.

The objectives of the Conservation Plan are to:

Understand the site by drawing together information about the site, including documents and physical evidence in order to present an overall description of the site through time, as well as a description of each of the components which make up the site.

Assess the significance of the site both generally and in detail for each of the main components, making specific value judgements about the historical, biological, wildlife, geological, cultural, archaeological, technological, social (recreational, public), and other types of significance.

Define those issues which are affecting the significance of the site or have the potential to do so in the future, including physical condition, ownership objectives, uses, areas and boundaries, siting, available resources, external factors, existing information and gaps in our knowledge, past damage, public and community expectations, access, statutory controls, and potential conflicts.

Develop conservation policies that will ensure that the significance of the site is retained in any future management, use or alteration. These policies should be in accordance with all relevant legislation, government guidance, local/structure plan policies, European Community directives, and other forms of policy, and should make use of guidance from non-statutory organisations.

The approach will be consistent with that set out in *Conservation Plans for Historic Places* (published by the HLF).

2.2   Additional objectives/strategy

A Conservation Plan should normally provide a broad overview of a site, and specific proposals should follow. In practice, many Plans are prepared in the context of a set of new proposals for a site. Any new scheme — however carefully conceived — can potentially damage a site. You or your advisers may already have identified areas of concern that will need to be resolved for the scheme to progress successfully. The consultant should be asked to develop policies that will help solve these problems. The policies should not simply justify the proposals but should be an independent review.

The Conservation Plan is being prepared within the context of outline proposals for [ ]. In addition to the broad policies set out above, the consultant is also asked to address the following policy areas:

❏ treatment of a specific area;
❏ identification of specific opportunities.

Where a Conservation Plan is being prepared as part of the development of a scheme, it may also be sensible to ask the team which prepares the Conservation Plan to use the knowledge gained in writing the Plan to go on to develop strategies for the site. This is particularly important for parks and gardens or natural landscapes where the person who has prepared the Conservation Plan may also be the person who works up detailed proposals for management or restoration. NB: these requirements are over and above the preparation of the Conservation Plan and may require additional skills.

Once the policies in the Conservation Plan have been agreed, the consultant will then be asked to:

❏ undertake an impact assessment for an existing scheme and identify any mitigation action (eg, design changes, archaeological recording, etc);
❏ put forward an immediate programme of management action/complete a Management Plan;
❏ put forward a specific scheme of restoration or enhancement for the site;
❏ identify options, for example, for new facilities, interpretation centre, cover building, etc, and assess the suitability of those options against the policies in the Conservation Plan;
❏ prepare outline/sketch design for [ ] and show how the proposals reflect the policies in the Conservation Plan.

3   Content of the Plan

3.1   Understanding the site

This is the most important and most difficult part of writing a brief for a Conservation Plan. In it you have to explain what information you will need and how much detail is appropriate. This can make a significant difference to the cost of a Plan so it is important to get the balance right. Too little information will result in a bland Plan that tells us nothing new; too much information can be overwhelming. The more care you put into drafting this section of the brief, the more likely it is that the Conservation Plan you commission will meet your particular requirements.

Different heritage sectors have slightly different approaches. Specific requirements for buildings, archaeology, landscapes, collections, and ships are set out in the section on sector-specific requirements. Draw on these requirements to complete the following sections of the brief. The overall aim of understanding the site is to tie the historical understanding of the site to an understanding of the physical fabric in a way that is concise and easy to read.

The following is a guide to the information that will be required to understand the site. You may wish to place much of this information in a supporting document, and summarise the results in the main part of the Plan.

3.1.1 Background research (chronology and context)

The sector-specific requirements provide further guidance on background research for landscapes, buildings, wildlife, collections, and archaeology.

The consultant is expected to draw together the readily available documentary evidence relating to the site, including copies (subject to copyright restrictions) of maps, illustrations, and photographs, as well as any other correspondence, leases, rate books accounts, oral history or other sources. Copies of existing reports, surveys or other information should be used where available.

The research should aim to understand:

❏ the history of the construction, use, and pattern of alteration of the [building/site/landscape/vessel];
❏ the history of the collections; and
❏ the historical evidence for previous land management regimes

through time up to the present day.

Further background research should be undertaken in order to place the site in its wider [historical/archaeological/technical/ecological/museological/landscape/townscape/other] context, at a local/regional or national level.

This research will be used as a basis for the assessment of significance.

3.1.2 Site gazetteer/room data sheets

The consultant is asked to prepare a [gazetteer/set of data sheets/table] for the site, for each element/area identifying its:

A large amount of disparate information often already exists for complex sites with different types of heritage. There are likely to be gaps in that information, however, and the history may not be 'tied' to the fabric. The landscape survey/ gazetteer or set of room data sheets provides a systematic method for organising this material. The choice of 'element' depends on the nature of the site — for a building it may be rooms or spaces, in a landscape it may be areas, paths, spaces or features; in a vessel it may be structural elements. The level of detail is a pragmatic decision: it is always possible to add further information to the data sheets or entries. Information should be intelligent and judgmental rather than rigid.

❑ documentary history;
❑ description of fabric, including dating of features;
❑ significance;
❑ designation (if relevant);
❑ management issues, including condition if relevant;
❑ sources (refer to any more detailed reports).

Elements should be numbered for ease of reference and a key plan showing numbers provided. It should be illustrated with photographs.

Adapt this approach as appropriate to a landscape, building, site, buried archaeology or collections. This information should help with the management of the site in its own right, and can provide in effect a mini-Conservation Plan for parts of the site.

3.1.3 Phasing

One of the most contentious aspects of a Conservation Plan is the treatment of recent changes to the site, which are often removed. Restoration decisions can also involve deciding between the importance of different phases of the site — for example, Victorian changes to a seventeenth-century formal garden. In order to resolve these issues it is necessary first to understand the importance of any changes. Remember that this should set out changes to the fabric of the site and not simply reiterate historical information.

The consultant should use the information in 3.1.1 and 3.1.2 to set out the major phases for the evolution of the fabric of the site, drawing on archaeology, history, architectural and landscape history, past management regimes, and the history of repair or alteration. Where relevant, it should include an overview of previous philosophies of land management, repair or alteration. If possible, the chronology should be illustrated by sketch reconstructions or plans. Each phase should be placed in its wider historical context.

This exercise should also include an understanding of the impact of change on the overall significance of the site, and the importance of any phases of change in their own right.

3.1.4 Other values

One of the most important aspects of understanding the site is to establish significance. Before making judgements about significance, it may be necessary to ensure that sufficient background research has been carried out to place the site and its elements into a wider context. This will vary according to the type of heritage.

Before assessing the significance of the site, the consultant is asked to make sure that they have sufficient understanding of:

❑ the social, spiritual, community, and other values placed on the site;
❑ any other way in which the site/collection is currently used or valued;
❑ the wider art historical, landscape or architectural context of the site;
❑ the archaeology of the site; and
❑ the importance of the technology or machinery on the site

as a basis for making judgements about significance.

3.1.5 Gaps

Part of the process of understanding the site is to identify what is and is not known, and, from there, what information may be needed in order to progress a scheme, and what information may be of interest in the future.

The consultant should identify any gaps in our knowledge and state which of those may need to be filled through further investigation or recording in either the short or the long term.

3.1.6 Drawings and specialist investigation

In order to progress or develop a particular scheme, it may be useful to have additional information about the site. In most cases this will initially involve drawings, although other types of investigation may also be useful. You should seek specialist advice on what is needed, on the appropriate specialists, and on commissioning procedures.

Advice on drawings is set out in section 9 (page 168) and on specialist investigation in the sector-specific requirements (page 169).

3.2 Assessing significance

The assessment of significance is the heart of the Conservation Plan. It should arise directly from understanding the site, and there should be a direct link with the assessment of vulnerability and the policies. Further guidance on assessing significance is given in Conservation Plans for Historic Places. *You should also read Kerr 1996, who provides more detailed guidance on assessing built sites, but the approach can be adapted to natural sites and landscapes.*

The aim of the exercise is first, to set out the overall significance of the site; secondly, to show how the different elements of the fabric of a site contribute to its overall importance. The assessment involves defining two sets of criteria: the values to be used, and the way in which 'degrees' of significance are to be established. These will depend upon the individual nature of the site. The exercise needs some care, and there is always a danger that rigid tables of significance or scoring systems can be misinterpreted later. If done well, it should enable the site manager to make informed decisions about how to balance competing types of significance.

The consultant is asked to produce:

You may wish to highlight specific areas to be taken into account by the consultant. The elements in the gazetteer could be used as a basis for the detailed assessment of significance or you might use the major phases of the site to structure the assessment. The consultant might also consider drawing on the ideas relating to 'critical' and 'tradable' assets defined in debates on sustainability.

- ❑ a general statement of significance, no more than one page of A4 setting out the key values for the place;
- ❑ an assessment of the significance of the elements of the site in such a way as to reflect historical, architectural, archaeological, visual, landscape or social significance. This assessment should include the significance of each phase of alteration. It may also be useful to identify features that at present significantly detract from the site.

This section requires the consultant to take an independent view of factors affecting the significance of the site. Some people are reluctant to do this as they feel it may jeopardise their chances of funding or obtaining a successful consent. In fact, the process derives from ideas about sustainability — ie, it is important to understand what is happening to a site in order to manage it — and simply helps focus the policies. Guidance on writing this section of the Plan is set out in Conservation Plans for Historic Places. *This section can also take into account any other issues you may have already identified — for example, problems in balancing competing types of significance. A gallery in a historic building, for example, may have to balance the needs of the collections against the fabric of the building.*

3.3 Assessing issues/vulnerability

The consultant should identify all issues relevant to the Conservation Plan. These will include any factors affecting the significance of the site now, in the past, and in the future, and may include cumulative losses or changes to the site, management issues, possible conflicts created by different types of significance, requirements for access, external requirements or the requirements of the owner and any issues this might raise. This section of the Plan can also address any opportunities for enhancing the significance of the site.

As well as general issues, the consultant is specifically asked to address:

❏ [identify any areas of concern you may have].

Again, guidance on writing policies is set out in Conservation Plans for Historic Places *and examples of policies can be found in Plans published by James Semple Kerr or others (see 'Further reading' below for examples). If there are specific policy areas that would help in planning the future of the site or specific areas of the site where a policy framework would be useful, identify those in this part of the brief.*

3.4 Writing policies

The consultant is asked to use his/her understanding of the site, the assessment of significance, and the analysis of issues — as well as consultations with others — as a basis for drafting policies which will guide the future care, use, development, restoration, and alteration of the site. These policies should, at a minimum, aim to:

❏ define an overall philosophy or vision for the site;
❏ retain the significance of the site;
❏ identify appropriate uses;
❏ define an effective approach to repair;
❏ satisfy statutory requirements;
❏ work within available resources;
❏ enhance public appreciation of the site;
❏ prevent future damage or deterioration;
❏ control future intervention.

These policies should not simply be a justification for a single scheme, but should provide an independent review of all relevant issues.

These policies should include:

❏ general policies relating to the care and operation of the site, including philosophy, appropriate uses, alteration, maintenance, access, land management, restoration, setting, services, control of intervention;
❏ specific policies for individual parts of the site (eg, areas, rooms, spaces, exterior, interior, fabric, landscape, cathedral close, below ground archaeology, collections, setting, etc);
❏ [other (eg, opportunities for enhancement)].

4   Further work

If you have identified areas of additional work (*see* '2.2 Additional objectives/strategy' *above*), you should use this section of the brief to explain clearly what is required and how it fits into the programme. Identify any additional skills that the consultant may need.

5   Management and consultation

Ideally, a Plan should be prepared as early as possible, and certainly before a scheme reaches the detailed design stage. In practice this may not be possible, but the emerging results of the Plan can still be fed into the scheme as it develops.

5.1   Timing

Use this section of the brief to explain how the Conservation Plan fits into the overall project, and identify deadlines for producing the Plan.

5.2   Project management and monitoring

The project will be managed by [steering group/individual body].

The client for the work is [   ].

The day-to-day contact for the project will be [   ].

Access to the site can be arranged by [   ].

The site manager/owner and their professional advisers will need to play an active part in managing the Conservation Plan to ensure that it is relevant to their needs. It is worth setting up a formal management and monitoring structure to ensure that deadlines are met, and that there is a chance to read text and discuss findings as the Plan develops.

A small steering group of key players should come together to review the Plan at regular points.

The [following people/steering group] shall be consulted at the following stages in the Plan process:

- ❏ on appointment, to agree work programme and dates for review points;
- ❏ on production of gazetteer and text on understanding the site;
- ❏ on production of the statement of significance;
- ❏ on completion of the text on conservation policy;
- ❏ on completion of the first full draft of the Plan.

Payments will be made at the following stages/performance indicators/dates.

5.3   Consultation process

The following organisations/individuals will need to be consulted during the preparation of the Plan:

The strength of a Plan depends upon the amount of consultation. Involving partners, statutory bodies, and others in the Plan process provides them with an opportunity to comment and avoids unexpected matters arising at a late date. Identify the most important bodies and ensure that the consultant allows time for consultation.

- ❏ local planning authority/conservation officer;
- ❏ neighbouring landowners or stakeholders;
- ❏ statutory bodies (English Heritage, English Nature, Countryside Commission);
- ❏ advisory bodies (amenity societies, Council for Protection of Rural England, etc);
- ❏ community groups, parish councils, conservation area advisory committees, local societies, etc;
- ❏ specialist groups or individuals;
- ❏ [others].

The consultant should allow time for the issuing of draft documents, and to incorporate any resulting comments.

Identify the need for any exhibitions or public meetings, and ensure that reasonable time for consultation is built into the project.

5.4 Adoption

The consultant will be responsible for the process of adoption of the Plan by [date], including the attendance at meetings and reworking needed to achieve this.

6 Procurement

6.1 Commissioning the Plan

The lead consultant will provide a project design in response to this brief, setting out how the Conservation Plan will be approached, the method of working, and any matters not covered by the brief. The project design for the Conservation Plan should include:

- ❑ how the consultants will respond to the brief, including a method statement, timetable, and how the consultation process will be managed;
- ❑ the range of professional skills which will be brought to bear on the project, including the names and cvs of proposed team members;
- ❑ a resource plan showing the breakdown of chargeable hours between professions and stages;
- ❑ a separate cost for publication and printing of the final document;
- ❑ previous experience of the organisations involved and personnel proposed, including the project leader;
- ❑ the extent of professional indemnity cover.

It is essential that a Plan be adopted by all the major stakeholders in the property, in particular by any trustees. It can take time and negotiation for this to happen, and it is important that the consultant allows enough time to achieve this.

In most cases, the site owner, manager or professional adviser should take the lead in specifying, commissioning, managing, and monitoring the Conservation Plan. They should also ensure that the consultant has access to existing knowledge and information. It is important to ensure that the person writing the Plan is able to take an overview of the site, and has the specialist skills needed to produce a Plan.

It may be helpful to evaluate tenders in two stages. First, ensure that the consultants have the right mix of skills and experience, understand the site, and are able to prepare a good Plan. Secondly, ensure that you get the best value for money. The project design for a Conservation Plan provided by the consultant should satisfy the first evaluation, and consultants who do not fulfil the needs of the brief should be eliminated before considering price. Alternatively, you may set a fee for the work and evaluate the quality of the tenders on the basis of which offers best value for money, taking into account the quality of the response to the brief, the scope of the work proposed, and the skills and experience of the team. Given the difficulty of setting boundaries to the amount of information to be collected in a Conservation Plan, the latter approach is often the fairest way of establishing value for money.

There is some debate over who is best qualified to write a Conservation Plan. The choice of person will depend upon the nature of the site. In most cases an external person is needed to provide an independent overview of issues, although they may draw on information gathered by an internal team (to a clear brief) or another party (eg, specialist ecologist, archaeologist). The person who writes the Plan will need a broad knowledge of conservation issues as well as skills in writing and facilitating stakeholder dialogue.

It is unlikely that all of these skills will be found within a single practice. In some cases this expertise will already be available within the team managing the site. The person drafting the Conservation Plan should ensure that the skills and knowledge of the local team have been drawn upon.

6.2 Consultant skills

The project team should be headed by a lead consultant with expertise in architecture/archaeology/nature conservation/project management/other discipline, and will require team members with expertise in:

- ❏ archaeology (landscape, building or below ground);
- ❏ architectural history;
- ❏ conservation architecture and new design;
- ❏ collections management;
- ❏ conservation engineering;
- ❏ ecology;
- ❏ garden or landscape history;
- ❏ historical research;
- ❏ heritage management or interpretation;
- ❏ metric survey and recording;
- ❏ museum curation;
- ❏ object conservation;
- ❏ conservation planning;
- ❏ technological history (eg, maritime history, mill machinery, industrial archaeology);
- ❏ wildlife conservation.

7 Other matters

7.1 Format and number of copies

Identify any requirements relating to your own house style. A good Conservation Plan should be widely available, and preferably formally published, especially if the site is publicly accessible. Allow for more copies than you think you will need. This means ensuring that the Plan is in a format which is easy to copy. You may want fewer copies of bulky appendices but many more copies of the main text.

The Conservation Plan will comprise an A4/spiral-bound document/loose-leaf folder with photographs and illustrations set within the text.

Reduced copies of maps and plans should be provided in the text; full-size copies of maps/plans/drawings should be provided on a stable medium.

The report should be in colour/black and white.

Supporting information should be provided in bound appendices.

Copies of the final Plan should be provided for:

- ❏ site owner/occupier;
- ❏ scheme architect or professional adviser;
- ❏ other consultants;
- ❏ local authority (county record office/Sites and Monument Record);
- ❏ Heritage Lottery Fund/other funding body;
- ❏ other interested parties;
- ❏ National Monuments Record.

Again, a Conservation Plan should become a publicly available document, and this should be made clear to the consultant at the outset. Copyright issues should anticipate this.

The preparation of a Conservation Plan involves the drawing together of archival material, not all of which may be reproduced in the final Plan. The archive will nevertheless be useful in the future to the site manager, and if possible should be kept on the site or easily accessible to the site manager. If storage on site is not adequate, a local record office may be willing to hold the archive although it should be consulted first.

Any scheme of work — however carefully considered — has the potential to have an adverse effect on the historical significance of a site. A Conservation Plan can help to resolve conflicts or identify ways of avoiding damage.

7.2 Copyright and confidentiality

Copyright for a Conservation Plan lies with the author, who should be prepared to grant the funding body and site owner a licence to make use of the Plan for the purposes of conservation of the site.

Copyright for any illustrations or other material used should be cleared by the lead consultant.

Sections of the Conservation Plan relating to [specified areas] will remain confidential, but the remainder of the Plan should be made available for public consultation.

7.3 Archiving

New archival material gathered during the preparation of the Plan will be passed to [specify].

7.4 Other issues

Use this section to identify any other issues that are relevant to the preparation of the Conservation Plan.

8   Appendices to the brief

Assist the potential consultant to draw up a project design, and avoid any duplication by including information directly relevant to the preparation of the Conservation Plan in appendices to the brief.

The appendices might include the following.

8.1 Areas of concern

It is useful at an early stage to identify any areas of concern raised either by your own professional advisers, by HLF advisers or by others. Include a note of any areas of concern, and copies of relevant correspondence in an appendix to the brief.

8.2 History and sources

Use this section of the brief to avoid any duplication by identifying key sources to be consulted in writing the Conservation Plan. Include any surveys or historical research you have already commissioned, or if you have access to an archivist, identify the most relevant material to be consulted.

8.3 Development proposals

If the Conservation Plan is being prepared to inform some or all of a set of development proposals, it is useful for potential tenderers to be aware of the nature and scope of these. A short summary of development proposals is useful.

Use this section where you are asking the consultant to undertake drawings or specialist investigation as part of the Conservation Plan. Be aware that such information will certainly be useful in the long run, and if carefully targeted will undoubtedly reduce risk and benefit a project, but can increase considerably the cost of a Conservation Plan.

9 Drawings and specialist investigation

The consultant will be responsible for commissioning or providing the following work.

9.1 All sites

A topographic survey of the site and/or record drawings of the building (elevations, sections as needed) at a suitable scale/level of detail to be used as a basis for interpretation and analysis.

9.2 Buildings

- ❏ photogrammetry/good-quality bromide prints of a photomosaic/drawn outline overlay, suitable for use as a base for archaeological fabric analysis (use this for ruins or complex masonry structures);
- ❏ overlays to the base survey/s/photomosaic identifying [joinery/mouldings/interior or exterior details/evidence for construction/alteration/use/phasing];
- ❏ a typology of mouldings/joinery/bricks/other features illustrated by more detailed drawings at an appropriate scale;
- ❏ other investigation (eg, dendrochronology, mortar analysis, paint analysis) in order to clarify the sequence of construction or to inform decisions. All such work must be tied to the understanding of the evolution of the fabric.

9.3 Archaeology

- ❏ overlay/s to the base survey/s, analysing [historic features/map regression/previous excavations/known depth of significant archaeology/building or landscape archaeology/changes or alterations/landscape elements];
- ❏ an archaeological evaluation of [selected area] of the site [a more detailed brief may be needed] in order to establish whether or not significant archaeology survives;
- ❏ a geophysical survey.

9.4 Landscapes/ecology

- ❏ a map regression exercise in order to identify the likely location of historically documented features or changes to the landscape. Plot this information on an overlay to the metric survey;
- ❏ undertake or commission a Phase II ecological survey, and establish the need for other specialist surveys (eg, birds);
- ❏ archaeological evaluation;
- ❏ geophysical survey;
- ❏ specialist surveys (eg, fauna).

Sector-specific requirements

1 Historic buildings

Historic buildings subject to proposals for new work are likely to require some form of base survey and analysis before the detailed design stage. The client and local authority/funding body should agree whether these will be needed for the Conservation Plan, or may be required later on in the project. More detailed fabric analysis may also be required, but not necessarily at the stage of preparing the Conservation Plan. The Plan should identify when and why further information will be needed should a scheme go ahead.

The following notes and questions are designed to help you to begin to focus on the specific needs of a historic building in the Conservation Plan. The aim is to provide some ideas that may help with commissioning a Plan or in preparing a method statement. They are not intended to be comprehensive. The 'Further reading' section includes guidance and reading on the assessment of historic buildings.

1.1 Background research

Use documentary evidence to explore such questions as:

- ❑ When and how was the building constructed?
- ❑ What was the original intention of the architect or builder?
- ❑ Did it change during construction?
- ❑ What documentary evidence is there for alterations?
- ❑ To what uses has it been put? Are there likely to be earlier buildings or features on the site?

1.2 Gazetteer

For a building or complex, the gazetteer should initially identify each room, space or small structure, and include the following types of information:

- ❑ documentary history — what documentary evidence is there for this room or space?
- ❑ description of fabric — what survives today? What evidence for change can be seen?
- ❑ Can you date any features/decorative finishes/floor/walls/ceiling/joinery/functional features/historic and modern services?
- ❑ significance — what is important about the space? What detracts from it?
- ❑ collections — note or include a cross reference to any collections or important fixtures;
- ❑ issues — what issues are faced in managing this space: visitors/lighting/decoration/condition (refer to any condition survey if need be)? Have past alterations adversely affected it?
- ❑ sources — is any further information available?

1.3 Phasing

Draw documents and physical fabric evidence together to establish:

❑ What were the main phases of change? What is old? What is new? How has the building been adapted?
❑ How was each phase significant? Were the changes piecemeal or part of a coherent scheme?
❑ How have previous phases of repair or alteration affected the significance of the site?

1.4 Gaps

❑ Are there likely to be hidden features/historic paint finishes/buried remains?
❑ Would further investigation (recording, paint analysis or dendrochronology) help resolve important questions?
❑ How well do we understand the recent history of the site? Do we understand all aspects of the building or, for example, do historic services or domestic offices need further investigation?
❑ Do any of these questions have a bearing on how the building will be used or on future plans for it? What areas of the building will be affected by future plans, and how much is known about those areas?
❑ How good are the record drawings of the building?

1.5 Other values

❑ What is the social role of the building? The spiritual role? How else do people use the building or how have they used it in the past?
❑ How does this building sit with the architect's other work?
❑ How does it relate to its physical context — landscape or town?
❑ What about ecology? Old buildings are often important for bats, mosses or lichen-rich walls. Is further information needed here? (*See* '6 Wildlife and ecology on historic sites' *below*.)

1.6 Significance

General statement of significance:

❑ What is the quality of the original building or design?
❑ What impact have later changes had on the significance of the site?
❑ What is the architectural, historical or social importance of the building?
❑ What visual significance does it have?
❑ Why does it matter today?
❑ What does this building demonstrate?
❑ How important is its present use?

Significance of different elements of the fabric:

❑ How do the different parts or elements of the building contribute to the whole?
❑ Are there elements that detract from it?
❑ What is important about the spaces, architectural elements, elevations, interiors, plan form or materials? Which is the most important view?
❑ How important are previous changes to the building?

Other values:

❏ What other types of significance are attached to the building? Ecological, social, commemorational?
❏ Are these associated with all or just part of the building?

1.7 Issues/vulnerability

❏ Are there conflicts between the current or future uses of the building and the historic fabric? What other conflicts exist? Are past and present rates of change sustainable?
❏ What impact does or could the needs of collections or contents have on the building?
❏ What opportunities are there for new uses or the better use of space?
❏ What are public expectations of the site?
❏ Is disabled access possible and what impact would better provision have on the fabric?
❏ Does our lack of knowledge of some aspects of the building put any of the fabric at risk?
❏ Does multiple ownership create problems?
❏ Which elements of the site are the most sensitive?

1.8 Policies

Activities:

❏ What is the most appropriate maintenance regime? How should management of the site be co-ordinated?
❏ What uses are appropriate for the building? Which ones are not? How can conflicts between use and fabric be avoided?
❏ How should the setting be protected? Views of and from the building?
❏ What principles should govern disabled access?
❏ What is the best approach to lighting? Renewal of services?
❏ What opportunities are there for new uses, work, access, etc?
❏ How should future interventions be controlled? Is recording needed — where and why?

Areas or elements:

❏ How should individual rooms or areas be treated? What management issues arise?
❏ Which elements should not be changed and which might be?
❏ Which areas are priorities for repair or new work?

2 Checklist for collections in historic buildings

Use the following checklist to decide what specific information you will need for the Conservation Plan and how much detail is required. Select items that are relevant to your site and your requirements.

Please note that this is only a checklist.

The requirements for a Conservation Plan are not identical to a Forward Plan for the museum/library/historic house or to a collection Management Plan. However, if you have either or both of these documents, it would be helpful to include them as appendices to the Conservation Plan.

2.1 Understanding the site: general requirements

In order to understand fully the site you need to understand the relationship between the site and the collections. To achieve this you need to:

Understand the history of the site (see the checklist below)

❑ When was the building erected? By whom? For whom? For what purpose?
❑ What different uses has it undergone since first built and now?
❑ When and under what circumstances did it become a public building/accessible to the public?
❑ How important is the building — historically and architecturally?

Understand the history of the collections

❑ How did the existing collections come to be here? Are they essentially one core/foundation collection with additions, or have the collections been built up over many years?
❑ What is the provenance of the collections? Where did they come from? How were they acquired? What do we know about the history of each item or collection of items?
❑ How much of the collection — if anything — is firmly associated with the building it is now in?
❑ Are items associated with the building prior to its 'public' use?
❑ Have the collections been in the building since it originally came into the public domain?

Understand the nature of the collection

❑ Assess the range of items in the collections: is this a varied collection or very focused?
❑ Assess the size of the collection: how many items does it contain?
❑ What appears to be the overall condition of the items in the collection? (If you have any concerns, seek the advice of your Area Museums Council immediately.)

2.2 Significance

Understand the significance of the collections:

❏ Are the collections designated by the Museums and Galleries Commission as being of pre-eminent importance?
❏ Are you aware of any publications (including catalogues) specifically about them?
❏ Consult standard reference works about the subject matter of the collections — are any of your items cited?
❏ Have the collections been assessed in the context of a wider evaluation — either by region or by collection discipline?

(Contact your Area Museums Council for further advice or assistance.)

What is the nature of the association between the buildings and the collections?

❏ Are the collections (or part of them) historically associated with the building?
❏ Does this association pre-date the building's current public accessibility?
❏ Are there special features of the buildings which relate to the collections and are of interest in their own right (eg, historic services such as ventilation systems in art galleries, historic decorative schemes, picture rails, natural lighting)?
❏ Were the collections mainly associated with the building at the time it became publicly accessible, or have they largely been added since?

How do the collections relate to the building in terms of interpretation?

❏ Do the collections harmonise with the building? Are they of the same period or associated with owners/occupiers of the building?
❏ Are all or part of the collections displayed/presented/interpreted to the same period as the building itself?
❏ Are any of the collections an integral part of the building?

Are there any outdoor collections associated with the site?

❏ Do the gardens or associated park/land include any sculptures or outdoor works of art?
❏ Do they include any other moveable collections including, eg, redundant farm implements?
❏ Are they important/relevant to the history or understanding of the site?

An Elizabethan manor house displayed to a late-seventeenth-century date (to harmonise with internal period features) using appropriate collections acquired for the purpose will be less *significant than a Regency terrace house, retaining all the period furniture from its owners throughout the nineteenth century, but* more *significant than a Palladian country house used by a local authority museum service to display its randomly acquired fine and decorative arts collections, none of which is associated with the house.*

2.3 Assessment of significance

❑ How long have the collections been associated with the building, its owners and occupiers?
❑ How well harmonised are the collections with the historic importance/historically important periods of the building?
❑ How intrinsically important are the collections?
❑ To what extent are the items in the building a discreet collection (as opposed to a random gathering of items)?

2.4 Issues

❑ Are there any conflicts of use between the building and the collections?
❑ Do the collections require particular types of settings that may be incompatible with the historic importance of the building (eg, white painted walls for display of paintings)?
❑ Do security requirements lead to disfigurement of the building?
❑ Do environmental requirements potentially conflict with the historic fabric of the building (eg, air conditioning)?
❑ Are there fundamental conflicts between the nature of the collection and the fabric of the building (eg, timber in libraries)?

3 Buried archaeology

The following questions are designed to help you focus on the specific needs of buried archaeology on a site in the Conservation Plan. They can be used in commissioning a Plan or in preparing a method statement. The section 'Further reading' includes guidance and reading on archaeology.

It may not be logical or practical to separate buried archaeology from the archaeology of landscapes and buildings. In this case, simply use the appropriate brief.

3.1 Background research

A desk-top study should address the following questions:

- ❑ What is the likelihood of buried remains on the site?
- ❑ Where are the areas of greatest archaeological potential? How significant could they be?
- ❑ Has there been any previous archaeology on the site? Or other work that might cast light on potential archaeological remains?
- ❑ Is there a single plan showing the location of previous excavations?
- ❑ Is it possible to predict the likely depth and state of preservation of any archaeology?

3.2 Gazetteer

Any gazetteer for a site should include the sites of former structures or areas of archaeological potential. Include any information on the likely depth, potential, and management issues in the gazetteer.

3.3 Phasing

Is it possible to provide a series of phase maps of the known archaeology of the site?

3.4 Gaps

- ❑ What are the main gaps in our knowledge?
- ❑ What are the main research questions?
- ❑ What work would be most useful in answering these questions?

3.5 Other values

- ❑ How does archaeology relate to other aspects of the site?
- ❑ Are there other values placed on the archaeology of the site — eg, spiritual, social or community?
- ❑ What role does this site play in our wider understanding of the period/site type?

3.6 Significance

Specific criteria for assessing the importance of archaeological remains are set out in PPG 16. Use these to assess the importance of the archaeology generally and for specific areas.

3.7 Issues

❑ How do present or potential uses for the site impact on archaeology? What impact has previous work such as ploughing or construction had on archaeological remains?
❑ Are there opportunities to improve the display of archaeological remains?
❑ What are the conservation and maintenance requirements created by archaeology?
❑ How easy is it to get information about previous archaeological work?

3.8 Policies

❑ Are archaeological controls on future site interventions needed?
❑ Are policies needed on archiving or access to data?
❑ What policies would help to avoid any future archaeological damage?

4   Historic and designed landscapes

The following questions are designed to help you focus on the specific needs of historic and designed landscapes in the Conservation Plan. They can be used in commissioning a Plan or in preparing a method statement.

You will need to read *Site Management Planning: a guide* (Countryside Commission, 1998) for further guidance on the assessment of sites. Other suggested publications are listed under 'Further reading'.

Note: landscapes combine natural and cultural features that the Conservation Plan should aim to bring together. You may also need to draw on the archaeological and wildlife checklists.

4.1   Background research

Use documents such as burial plans, descriptions, correspondence, archaeological records, ecological surveys, and published articles to try to answer the following questions:

❏ What evidence is there for previous management regimes?
❏ What changes have there been to the landscape through time?
❏ Is it possible to map the likely sites of historically documented features?
❏ Was this a designed landscape? What was the intention of the designer? How much of this was actually achieved?

Pay particular attention to collecting together copies of estate and Ordnance Survey maps, plans, illustrations or views, aerial photographs, and historic photographs. Obtain copies of Phase I and any subsequent ecological or planting surveys, and any other sources that cast light on the site.

4.2   Gazetteer

Use this to identify surviving historic features, including designed and natural features, terraces, earthworks, planting, the pattern of alterations in the landscape, and historic garden features such as walks, planting, and views. For cemeteries, identify important tombs or monuments, the pattern and sequence of burial, and the interest of the monumental sculpture. Include built and landscape features.

4.3   Phasing

❏ Is it possible to reconstruct the original design of the park?
❏ How much of today's planting is original?
❏ Can the major changes to the landscape be grouped into phases?
❏ How are these important? Did they add to or detract from the qualities of the landscape?

4.4   Other values

❏ What are the other ways in which we value the landscape? What are its scenic qualities? What feelings does it evoke?
❏ What contribution does landform and relief make to the landscape? Assess the scenic qualities of the landscape.

4.5 Gaps

❑ How well do we understand the landscape?
❑ What questions might tree survey, archaeological evaluation or geophysical survey answer?

4.6 Significance

General statement of significance:

❑ How important is this landscape to the history of designed landscapes?
❑ What does the landscape contribute to the importance of the site as a whole?
❑ What is the quality of the surviving walks, planting, views, and features?

The significance of elements:

❑ What have been the positive and negative impacts of past changes on the landscape?
❑ What are the areas of archaeological, ecological, and landscape importance or sensitivity?
❑ Which aspects of the landscape are crucial to the area's character and cannot be compromised?
❑ What significance have past alterations had in their own right?

4.7 Issues

What impact have current and past management regimes (eg, grazing, ploughing) had on the significance of the site?

4.8 Policies

❑ What approach should there be to restoring lost features?
❑ What guidelines should govern new planting?
❑ Which elements of the landscape should be protected?
❑ What opportunities or areas are there for new features?
❑ What principles govern traffic or access?
❑ What approach should be taken to maintenance and day-to-day management?
❑ What lighting, if any, is appropriate? What materials?

5 Historic vessels

Use the following checklist to decide what specific information you will need for the Conservation Plan and how much detail is required. Select items that are relevant to your site and your requirements.

The Conservation Plan process is as applicable to historic vessels as it is to any other item of significance. It is particularly important to assess the significance of an item and the pattern of past alterations if you need to make decisions about whether or not it is appropriate to restore machinery to working order or whether it should be 'mothballed'.

5.1 Background research

❏ Draw together readily available documentary evidence relating to the history of the vessel, including copies where possible of builders' drawings showing hull arrangements, rigging, and sail plans, log books, accounts, manifests, historic photographs, any Lloyds Register of Shipping reports or surveys, any paintings, drawings, and engravings, and any other sources which cast light on the construction, use, and repair or alterations to the vessel. Consult published material, including the National Register of Historic Vessels, and any material relating to the more recent history of the vessel, including reports of preservation groups or others associated with it.

❏ Produce a metric survey/the lines of the vessel at a suitable scale/level of detail to be used as a basis for analysis.

❏ Produce overlay/s to the base survey/s, analysing and identifying historic features/changes or alterations/repairs/replaced elements.

❏ Establish the chronology of the vessel, drawing together archaeology, history, technical information, phases of repair or alteration, and other information to establish major historical phases, including recent repair or restoration.

❏ Prepare a gazetteer or inventory of the historic components of the vessel (including equipment, machinery, rigging, sails, interiors, and fabric), identifying for each the history/description/significance/condition/ management issues/sources. This should be supported by maps or drawings.

❏ Draw together information about any collections or archives associated with the vessel, their nature, provenance, date range, and coverage.

❏ Identify any other ways in which the site may be significant (eg, importance to the community).

5.2 Assessment of significance

As part of the general assessment of significance, the consultant should:

❏ undertake sufficient research to place the vessel in its historical, technical, and social context, as well as its national and international context;

❏ identify other surviving vessels of a similar age or nature in order to establish the rarity of the vessel, and of the elements or equipment on it;

❏ assess the pattern of past changes, replacements, alterations, and repairs to the vessel, and their impact on the significance of the vessel and its degree of authenticity or intactness.

5.3 Issues

As part of the general analysis of issues affecting the significance of the site, the consultant should also:

❏ assess the impact of past work to the vessel, including the choice of materials and any problems this may have created. Note the performance of past materials or treatments;
❏ consider the ecological implications of any anti-fouling or other conservation techniques.

5.4 Policy

The conservation policies for the site should include policies for:

❏ the repair and replacement of items, including the extent of acceptable replacement;
❏ use — whether or not the vessel should sail or whether machinery should be repaired to an operable state; what requirements may arise if the vessel is to comply with modern regulations, and what impact this may have on the historic authenticity of the vessel;
❏ a philosophy of restoration — whether or not it is appropriate to restore the vessel to a particular phase or point in time, and, if so, what justification there is for this;
❏ siting — whether or not the vessel is sited in an appropriate place (ie, in dry dock or on the water) and what short or long-term issues arise from the siting of the vessel;
❏ the appropriate materials to be used in repair and conservation.

6   Wildlife and ecology on historic sites

Use the following checklist to decide what specific information you will need for the Conservation Plan and how much detail is required. Select items that are relevant to your site and your requirements.

Archaeological sites, historic and designed landscapes, and even buildings are often significant in terms of living heritage. Rare mosses and lichens may grow on the walls of historic buildings; bats frequently roost in them; archaeological sites are found in species-rich grassland, and ancient trees are abundant in landscape parks.

6.1   Understanding the site: general requirements

Where any site, including an archaeological site, cemetery or historic building, is likely to have ecological significance, the following steps should be taken.

❑   The consultant should draw together readily available information about past land use, including tithe maps, Ordnance Survey maps, and reports on ecology or wildlife. Discussions with current and previous landowners and farmers will assist with establishing past forestry or farming practice.

❑   Obtain a copy of the Phase I habitat survey from the local authority or nature conservation agency. This is an initial ecological summary for the vegetation in the United Kingdom that is near completion. Areas on the map coloured red, orange, yellow or green (rather than white or grey) have some ecological interest.

❑   If the Phase I survey shows that the site has ecological importance, the next step is to discover whether a more detailed Phase II habitat survey has been carried out. This provides a detailed analysis of the habitats at a site using the National Vegetation Classification (NVC). If this is available, the site map and account will provide the necessary information on vegetation for the Conservation Plan.

❑   If no Phase II survey exists you may need to commission one from a professional ecologist. Even if the Phase I survey indicates that the site is of little importance, it may be useful to ask an ecologist to visit the area to determine whether it is likely to be of interest for fauna.

❑   The Conservation Plan must take account of legally protected or rare species. Professional advice should be sought concerning the desirability of carrying out bat, bird, insect, animal, and lower plant surveys. They will not always be required.

All British bats are protected by the Wildlife and Countryside Act (as amended) 1991. Whenever dealing with historic buildings, particularly redundant structures, a bat survey should be carried out.

Further reading

Essential documents

Countryside Commission, 1998 *Site Management Planning: a guide*, CCP 527, Cheltenham

Countryside Council for Wales, 1996 *Guide to the Production of Management Plans for Nature Reserves and Protected Areas*, Bangor

English Heritage, 1997 *Development in the Historic Environment*, London

Feilden, B, and Jokilehto, J, 1993 *Management Guidelines for World Heritage Sites*, Rome

Kerr, J S, 1996 *The Conservation Plan: a guide to the preparation of Conservation Plans for places of European cultural significance*, 4th edn, The National Trust of Australia (NSW), Sydney

Examples of Conservation Plans

Kerr, J S, 1996 *The Sydney Opera House*, New South Wales Public Works for The Sydney Opera House Trust (2nd impression)

There are many Conservation Plans currently in preparation in the UK, but most of these are not yet in the public domain. Your HLF case officer may be able to assist by identifying appropriate Plans that you can look at.

Understanding and assessing sites

ARUP, BDP, and Breheny, M, 1995 *Environmental Capacity: a methodology for historic cities*, London

Countryside Commission, 1987 *Landscape Assessment: a countryside approach*, CCP 18, Cheltenham

——, 1993 *Landscape Assessment Guidance*, CCP 423, Cheltenham

DoE/Welsh Office, 1989 *Environmental Assessment — a guide to the procedures*, London

ICOMOS, 1990 *Guide to Recording Historic Buildings*, London

Landscape Institute, Institute for Environmental Assessment, 1995 *Guidelines for Landscape and Visual Impact Assessment*, London

Ralston, I, and Thomas, R, 1993 *Environmental Assessment and Archaeology*, Institute of Field Archaeologists Occasional Paper no. 5

Countryside management

Andrews, J, and Rebane, M, 1994 *Farming and Wildlife: a practical handbook for the management, restoration and recreation of wildlife habitats on farmland*, RSPB, Sandy

Countryside Commission, Countryside Council for Wales, 1997 *National Park Management Plans Guidance*, CCP 525, Cheltenham

Countryside Council for Wales, 1996 *A Guide to the Production of Management Plans for Nature Reserves and Protected Areas*, Bangor

Nature Conservancy Council, 1990 *Earth Science Conservation in Great Britain: a strategy*

Sutherland, W J, and Hill, D A, 1995 *Managing Habitats for Conservation*, Cambridge

Site management

Hunter, J, and Ralston, I (eds), 1993 *Archaeological Resource Management in the UK: an introduction*, Stroud

Integrated approaches to conservation

Berry, A Q, and Brown, I W, 1995 *Managing Ancient Monuments: an integrated approach*, Mold

English Heritage, Countryside Commission, English Nature, 1993 *Conservation Issues in Strategic Plans*, London

——, 1995 *Ideas into Action for Local Agenda 21*, London

——, 1996 *Conservation Issues in Local Plans*, London

English Heritage guidance:

——, 1992 *Register of Parks and Gardens*

——, 1993 *Principles of Repair*

——, 1994 *Investigative Work on Historic Buildings*

——, 1995 *Conservation Area Practice*

——, 1995 *Developing Guidelines for the Management of Listed Buildings*

——, 1996 *Guidelines for Historic Parks and Gardens Surveys*

——, 1997 *Sustaining the Historic Environment: new perspectives on the future*

Government legislation and guidance

Ancient Monuments and Archaeological Areas Act 1979

National Heritage Act 1983

Planning (Listed Buildings and Conservation Areas) Act 1990

Town and Country Planning Act 1990

Wildlife and Countryside Act 1991

Civil Rights (Disabled Person) Act 1994

Planning (Listed Buildings and Conservation Areas) Scotland Act 1997

Town and Country Planning (Scotland) Act 1997

DoE, 1990 *Planning Policy Guidance 16: archaeology and planning*, London

——, 1993 *Planning Policy Guidance 7: the countryside and the rural economy*, London

——, 1994 *Sustainable development — the UK strategy*, Cmd 2426, London

DoE, DNH, 1994 *Planning Policy Guidance 15: planning and the historic environment*, London

Historic Scotland, 1993 *Memorandum of Guidance on Listed Buildings and Conservation Areas*, Edinburgh

Scottish Office, 1994 *National Planning Policy Guideline 5: archaeology and planning*, Edinburgh

——, 1994 *Planning Advice Note 42: archaeology — the planning process and scheduled monument procedures*, Edinburgh

Welsh Office Circular 61/96 *Planning and the Historic Environment: historic buildings and conservation areas*

Conservation charters

Venice Charter 1964 *The International Charter for the Conservation and Restoration of Monuments and Sites*

Burra Charter 1988 *Australia ICOMOS Charter for the Conservation of Places of Cultural Significance*

Council of Europe 1996 *Helsinki Declaration on the Political Dimension of Cultural Heritage Conservation in Europe*

Publications on related issues

Allison, G, Balls, S, Cheshire, P, Evans, A, and Stabler, M, 1996 *The Value of Conservation? A literature review of the economic and social value of the cultural built heritage*, London

Fladmark, J M (ed), 1993 *Heritage, Conservation, Interpretation and Enterprise*, London

Holland, A, and Rawles K, 1993 Values in conservation, *Ecos*, **14** (1), 14–19

Liniado, M, 1995 *The National Trust Centenary Countryside Conference Proceedings*, The National Trust, Cirencester

Russell, D, 1995 *Linking People and Place*, The National Trust, Cirencester